TOWARD EQUAL OPPORTUNITY IN EMPLOYMENT

The Role of State and Local Government

SYMPOSIA ON LAW AND SOCIETY

GENERAL EDITOR: LEONARD W. LEVY

Claremont Graduate School

TOWARD EQUAL OPPORTUNITY IN EMPLOYMENT

The Role of State and Local Government

Proceedings of a Conference in Memory of
Honorable Philip Halpern Held April 24 and 25, 1964,
at the School of Law, State University
of New York at Buffalo

Co-Chairmen: Jacob D. Hyman and Herman Schwartz

DA CAPO PRESS · NEW YORK · 1971

The papers contained in this volume appeared originally in the *Buffalo Law Review,* Volume 14, Number 1 (Fall 1964). They are reprinted by permission of William S. Hein & Co., Inc., and of the Editors of the *Buffalo Law Review.*

Library of Congress Catalog Card Number 74-152228

SBN 306-70120-0

Published by Da Capo Press, Inc.
A Subsidiary of Plenum Publishing Corporation
227 West 17th Street, New York, N.Y. 10011
All Rights Reserved

Manufactured in the United States of America

๛ Preface ๛

The papers which follow will speak for themselves. We believe that they will speak helpfully to the thousands of dedicated public officials and lawyers throughout the United States who are struggling to make real in the near future the American dream of equality of opportunity for all of its citizens. This conference, which was held in the hope of being able to afford some assistance in that difficult struggle, honors the memory of the late Justice Philip Halpern,[1] who contributed so much to the development of human rights.

As these papers make clear, the American Negro community is undergoing an economic depression of major proportions, a depression in which the rate of Negro unemployment is more than twice that of whites; in which the median Negro annual wage in 1962 was $3,023, about $2,400 less than the average white man's. There are indications that this wage gap is increasing.[2] Such a depression in the midst of our longest post-war prosperity intensifies a despair created by centuries of discrimination. It debilitates egos already subjected to ubiquitous humiliation and further weakens a social structure assaulted and distorted by centuries of repression.

In a society still desperately short of schools, teachers, housing, hospitals and the numerous other necessities of a decent life, such unemployment—which encompasses whites as well as Negroes—represents a waste of human resources which neither our needs nor our sense of justice can long permit. Yet, discrimination, poor education, an apparent shrinkage of jobs in precisely those areas for which Negroes are presently able to qualify, all conspire to keep a disproportionate share of the strains of unemployment on the Negro.

The magnitude of our present crisis stems not only from the harsh, tangible consequences of centuries of social injustice and deprivation, but also from the above-mentioned emotional factors which are too frequently disregarded. Many of our leading citizens of goodwill still fail to see this aspect of the problem. They point to the progress that has been made in the past 35 years in expanding the range of opportunity for Negro citizens, to what seems to be the recent acceleration in the rate of that progress, and they see the Negro now as simply going through the stage of winning a place in the American community which successive waves of immigrants of varying ethnic, national, and religious backgrounds have in their turn gone through. What they fail to recognize is the staggering extra burdens which the Negroes have faced and do face. *An American Dilemma*[3] and the reports of the United States Commission on Civil Rights[4]

---

1. Buffalo Law Review, Vol. 13, No. 2 (1964) was dedicated to Justice Halpern, and contains comments on aspects of his work, pp. 303-338.
2. See testimony of Undersecretary of Labor John F. Henning, in *Hearings on Equal Employment Opportunity Before the Subcommittee on Employment and Manpower of the United States Senate Committee on Labor and Public Welfare*, 88th Cong., 1st Sess. 97 (1963); Testimony of Herman Miller, *id*. at 321; see also, generally, Hill, *infra*.
3. Myrdal, An American Dilemma (1944).
4. See 1963 Report of the U.S. Commission on Civil Rights, 265-68, Appendix II, List of Publications as of Sept. 30, 1963.

document beyond reasonable dispute the basic elements of the difference. No other group started in this country as slaves. The prejudice against no other group has been worked so deeply into the fabric of American *mores*. Despite the overwhelming consensus of scientific opinion,[5] the notion still persists in some quarters that there is a racial discrepancy in human capabilities. Finally no other group has been so readily identifiable as to preclude an individual's opportunity to present himself as an individual before the prejudices directed against his group have been aroused.

Furthermore as the pace of corrective effort has begun to increase since World War II, the movement toward social justice has been almost buried under the two nationwide problems of urbanization and technological change. The explosive growth of the cities has brought to them thousands of people totally inexperienced in urban living just at a time when job opportunities for the untrained and uneducated have begun to shrink rapidly. Wholly apart from any question of group prejudice, the major domestic problems of our day are the problems of urban education and employment for the unskilled.

Under these conditions, a total change in the situation of American Negroes in a year or even a decade is beyond the range of possibility. Yet the *Brown* case,[6] by its uncompromising reaffirmation of the American ideal, illuminated the enormous gap which remains between what has been achieved and what remains to be done. Inevitably it created a dramatic rise in the level of expectation. In this new perspective two things are demanded of American society. The first is intangible:—an assurance that the American community as a whole has decisively and for all time rid itself of any idea of racial superiority and inferiority. The second is the immediate adoption of decisive measures to remedy the present consequences of past injustice. The passage of the Civil Rights Act is dramatic evidence of the fact that the preponderant opinion of the country has followed the Supreme Court's affirmation of equality and has moved to effectuate it. But every local failure to break down an existing barrier to advancement or recognition not only brings its immediate disappointment, but also carries jar-

---

5. See the quotations in the *Advice to the Reader*, prefacing the 1962 (Meridian) edition of Kardiner and Ovesey, The Mark of Oppression, which the authors accept as a statement of their scientific position:

> The prospect of continuing inferior status is essentially unacceptable to any group of people. For this and other reasons, neither colonial exploitation nor oppression of minorities within a nation is in the long run compatible with peace. As social scientists we know of no evidence that any ethnic group is inherently inferior. (Signed by eight social scientists including Gordon W. Allport, Georges Gurvitch, Harry S. Sullivan).

> 16. Lastly, biological studies lend support to the ethic of universal brotherhood; for man is born with drives toward cooperation, and unless these drives are satisfied man and nations alike fall ill. Man is born a social being who can reach his fullest development only through interaction with his fellows. The denial at any point of this social bond between man and man brings with it disintegration. In this sense, every man is his brother's keeper. For every man is a piece of the continent, a part of the main, because he is involved in mankind.

(Concluding point of UNESCO "Statement on Race," July 18, 1950).

6. 347 U.S. 483 (1954); 349 U.S. 294 (1955).

ring overtones which stir anew the fear that the commitment has not been made, that the idea of full acceptance has not been sincerely embraced.

In such a context the only possible check on steadily growing frustration and tension is the formulation, community by community, of a comprehensive program for the total solution of the problem, the spelling out of detailed plans for the achievement of the program, and the steady fulfillment of the plans.

The purpose of the Conference was to provide some assistance to those who are developing this approach in the field of employment. There were three sessions, addressed first to general problems, then to the operation of the fair employment practice commissions, and lastly to supplements and alternatives to the commission approach. The papers presented and the comments on them make available in compact form the results of much experimentation and thoughtful consideration by the participants, all of whom have had significant experience as administrators, lawyers and students, about the methods of achieving equality of opportunity and employment. Some points not mentioned or fully developed in the formal presentations were brought out during the course of the discussion. Brief summaries of the highlights of those discussions appear after the papers of each session.

It is never easy to reshape a society, but our commitment to do so is based upon reason, justice, and history. We hope that this type of conference, bringing together scholars and administrators, will be followed by many similar meetings in order that our collective experience may be studied, evaluated and disseminated.

J. D. Hyman
Herman Schwartz
Co-chairman

CONTENTS

CONTENTS

III.

2484

PART I: BASIC QUESTIONS

THE FEDERAL INTEREST IN EMPLOYMENT DISCRIMINATION: HEREIN THE CONSTITUTIONAL SCOPE OF EXECUTIVE POWER TO WITHHOLD APPROPRIATED FUNDS

CLARENCE CLYDE FERGUSON, JR.*

The proper allocation of governmental power between the states and the central government has, since the birth of the Republic, been the subject of continuing commentary. The topic to which these remarks are addressed continues in the tradition of that commentary. That this symposium is within the mainstream of that tradition is made clear by the very subject matter of this conference. One of the more striking characteristics of non-academic discussions of American federalism problems is the frequency with which race provides both the context and the subject matter of analysis. One need only recall the historical dialogue regarding slavery and the nature of the federal union transpiring from the Constitutional Convention to the Civil War—and its final doctrinal benediction delivered in *Texas v. White*.[1] Even now, public discussion of federalism tends to be provoked by and centered upon considerations which relate predominately to issues of civil rights. Thus, in the grand tradition of American federalism analysis, we are gathered together again to explore the appropriate extent and roles of federal state and local regulation regarding discrimination, based on race, in employment.

Perhaps it might be well to expose at the beginning—expressly—the central theme of these remarks: that is, there is an overriding federal responsibility for both policy declaration and policy implementation in employment discrimination which has been overlooked on the one hand, and, on the other hand, where power has been perceived it has remained for the most part unexercised.

It might be well also to point out that in this context of our present social revolution, there are two major dynamic forces at work. Firstly, there is the continuing drive to eradicate racial discrimination in employment through utilization of the processes of the legal system. Surprisingly, this now dynamic force in the United States has only lately come to be a major factor in the civil rights movement.[2] There is another dimension to the struggle against discrimination in employment which is only slowly coming to be recognized. It now seems clear to most perceptive observers that what is truly involved in the civil rights revolution is a fundamental remaking of the entire American society.[3] The removal of race as a relevant factor in the employment relation

---

* Dean and Professor of Law, Howard University Law School, Washington, D.C.
1. 74 U.S. (7 Wall.) 700 (1868).
2. See 1961 Report of the U.S. Commission on Civil Rights, *Employment*; Pasley, *The Nondiscrimination Clause in Government Contracts*, 43 Va. L. Rev. 837 (1957).
3. See, *e.g.*, Ferguson, *Civil Rights Legislation 1964: A Study of Constitutional Resources*, 24 Fed. B. J. 102 (1964).

1

must inevitably drastically alter the structure and dynamics of our economic order. And, just as inevitably, fundamental reordering of traditional concepts of federalism will follow. Thus, as has been true in so much of our social history, the necessity for resolving a crisis in racial adjustment in our society generates not only the occasion, but the very mechanisms through which our federal system is reordered.

I. The Dimension of the Employment Problem

The total effect of discrimination in the employment relation is almost impossible to calculate. The statistical profile of the problem tells a dire tale indeed. For the last four years the unemployment rate among adult Negro males has consistently averaged almost twice that of the white adult male.[4] Median money income for nonwhite families and individuals is slightly over half that for whites.[5] In some of the major industrial cities more than one-third of the Negro work force is unemployed.[6] Similar disparities can be projected for almost any statistical criteria.[7]

It is clear, of course, that the mere statement of disparity between white and nonwhite averages and medians is not necessarily the description of the results of discrimination in the employment relation. Certainly, lack of educational opportunity is a contributing cause. Over half the Negro, adult males have less than a grade school education;[8] school dropout rates continue to increase at a time when more and more educational background is demanded.[9] And, increasingly we are reminded that frustration breeds in a social environment based on discriminatory patterns of life and attitudes. Frustration in turn destroys motivation and lowers horizons of aspiration. Yet, few will assert that provision of economic opportunities without regard to racial considerations has perhaps the highest potential for dramatically alleviating the most pressing problems of the current crisis.[10]

What is being lost to our economic system now is indeed impossible to assay. Most reliable estimates are that the dollar cost is of the order of $17 to $20 billion in gross national product every year.[11] We know, however, that the cost of discrimination is much higher. While the impact upon the individual of cyclical and structural unemployment may be no different for members of one minority group than for others—the environment of the nonwhite in the

---

4. U.S. Dep't of Labor, Manpower Report of the President and A Report on Manpower Requirements, Resources, Utilization, and Training 43, 145 (1963).
5. U.S. Bureau of the Census, Statistical Abstract of the United States 331 (83rd ed. 1962).
6. 1963 Report of the U.S. Commission on Civil Rights, *Employment* 83-87.
7. See, *e.g.*, Ferguson, *A Brief Commentary on Urban Redevelopment and Civil Rights*, 9 How. L.J. 101 (1963).
8. Notes 4, 5 *supra*; National Urban League, Survey of Unemployment in Selected Urban League Cities (1963).
9. *Ibid.*
10. See Hays, A Southern Moderate Speaks (1959).
11. Council of Economic Advisers Report quoted in Critical Issues Paper (No. 4) 4 (Critical Issues Council 1964).

United States is such that unemployment and underemployment have a special dimension. Thus, the role of the nonwhite in the economic system in large part may be attributed to discriminatory factors in areas other than in the employment relation. We need not document the proposition, however, that at least one of the major causes of the statistical disparity between the white and nonwhite economic profiles is that of racial discrimination in the employment relation itself.

II. The Federal Role in the Employment Relation

The federal government is a major force in the totality of employment relations in the United States. It is itself by far the largest employer in the country.[12] It creates and supports millions of employment opportunities through its direct contracting activities and direct grants-in-aid programs.[13] The federal government subsidizes a system of public employment offices and is engaged extensively in financing an array of job training programs.[14] It supervises and regulates certain activities of labor unions.[15] Finally, it has a constitutional concern with the flow of interstate commerce—which means substantially any commerce which is more than of a *de minimus* level.[16]

Attention has been focused on the role of the Court, both in its role as constitutional adjudicator and on its function of policy making in the general area of racial discrimination. Now, attention is focused on Congress and the legislative role in elimination of discrimination in job opportunities.[17] On this occasion I should like to address the problem of the federal executive—the Office of the President—in eradicating discrimination in federally connected employment. It is recognized that there are two dimensions to the problem of discrimination in such employment. The first is that of removing discriminatory practices and patterns. The second dimension is that of affirmatively taking steps to remove the disabilities created by past deprivation of opportunity. In treating of the proper role of the federal executive our concern is with the first of these dimensions: removing discrimination from federally connected job opportunities.

The nature of the federal employment problem can be best grasped by considering the findings of a survey conducted by the Civil Rights Commission for its *1961 Report*. Federal agencies in the five metropolitan areas were asked to count the number of Negro employees in each of three categories of federal employment; to break down their figures to reflect grade levels and job descriptions of Classification Act employees; and to indicate the number of Negroes who held supervisory jobs. The major findings reported by the Commission were as follows:

---

12. 1961 Report of the U.S. Commission on Civil Rights. *Employment* 19.
13. *Id.* at 55.
14. *Id.* at 95.
15. *Id.* at 127.
16. Ferguson, *supra* note 3, at 115.
17. Civil Rights Act of 1964, Title VII.

(1) In the five cities as a whole, 23.4 percent of federal employees were Negroes; 24.4 percent in Washington, D.C.; 28.5 percent in Chicago; 17.9 percent in Los Angeles; 18.2 percent in St. Louis; and 15.5 percent in Mobile.

(2) 42.7 percent of all Negro employees in the five cities were in Classification Act positions; 31.1 percent were in Wage Board positions; and 26.2 percent were in "Other" positions, primarily in the Post Office Department.

(3) Of Negro employees in Classification Act positions, 85.4 percent were in grades 1 through 4; 14.3 percent in grades 5 through 11; and 0.3 percent in grades 12 through 15.

(4) 5.2 percent of the total Negro employees were in supervisory positions.[18]

This finding speaks for itself. It tends to confirm the allegations that in the most accessible employment opportunity (*i.e.* most free from discrimination), there is a general confinement of Negroes to the lower paying positions and a general non-presence in supervisory positions.

It should be pointed out that there has been an improvement in this matter since that Commission report.

What then can be the response of the executive based on administrative power?

On March 6, 1961, Executive Order 10925,[19] continuing the policy of the Truman and Eisenhower administrations, established the President's Committee on Equal Employment Opportunity with jurisdiction ". . . to promote and ensure equal opportunity for all qualified persons, without regard to race, creed, color, or national origin, employed or seeking employment with the Federal Government and on government contracts. . . ." Part II of the Order, relating to government employment, provides, in part:

SECTION 201. The President's Committee on Equal Employment Opportunity established by this order is directed immediately to scrutinize and study employment practices of the Government of the United States, and to consider and recommend additional affirmative steps which should be taken by executive departments and agencies to realize more fully the national policy of nondiscrimination within the executive branch of the Government.

SECTION 202. All executive departments and agencies are directed to initiate forthwith studies of current government employment practices within their responsibility. The studies shall be in such form as the Committee may prescribe and shall include statistics on current employment patterns, a review of current procedures, and the recommendation of positive measures for the elimination of any discrimination, direct or indirect, which now exists. Reports and recommendations shall be submitted to the Executive Vice Chairman of the Committee no later than sixty days from the effective date of this order, and the Committee, after considering such reports and recom-

---

18. 1961 Report of the U.S. Commission on Civil Rights, *Employment* 27.
19. 26 Fed. Reg. 1977 (1961).

mendations, shall report to the President on the current situation and recommend positive measures to accomplish the objectives of this order.

The Office of President as Chief Administrator.

Among the functional roles of the President is that of chief administrator of the federal establishment.[20] This function of chief administrator derives directly from article II, section 1 of the Constitution providing that "The executive Power shall be vested in a President of the United States. . . ." There is some question, however, of the extent of the executive power in regard to employees of the so-called independent agencies. In our context the question is whether the Office of the President may take steps to secure compliance with the unquestioned federal policy of nondiscrimination as regards employees of the independent agencies and offices.

Independent agencies have been defined as those "entirely outside any regular executive department" of the federal government.[21] In this, the more usual sense of "independence," the characterization is in contradistinction to the agency within the executive branch of the government.[22] Upon the authorities it is clear that characterization of an agency as independent, as distinct from executive, has proved viable in resolving certain issues in regard to control by the President.[23] It does appear, however, that analysis of the status of an agency as "independent" or otherwise in regard to its function, would be very useful in regard to the power of the President to administer a constitutionally based policy. (The basis of this conclusion is set forth in the following section: *The Office of the President as Chief Executive.*)

Moreover, although the growth of the independent regulatory agency has created what Mr. Justice Jackson called the "fourth branch of government," Congress in establishing such agencies still recognizes three branches only. It consistently creates agencies and commissions within "the executive branch."[24] To give to the words "in the executive branch" their plain meaning would lead to the conclusion that the agencies are subject to executive direction in at least their housekeeping functions (administration) even though they are independent of direct presidential supervision in formulation and implementation of regulatory policy. Recent history of the administration of President Kennedy indicates quite clearly that a willingness to remove discriminatory patterns can be vigorously exercised within the context of employment throughout the executive branch.

Few legal problems have arisen in regard to appointments to so-called

---

20. See Corwin, The President: Office and Powers 114-21 (4th rev. ed. 1957).
21. Cushman, The Independent Regulatory Commissions 3 (1941).
22. Landis, The Administrative Process 111 (1938).
23. See, *e.g.*, Humphrey's Executor v. U.S., 295 U.S. 602 (1935) (removal of a Commissioner of the Federal Trade Commission by the President without cause before expiration of statutory term); *cf.* Myers v. U.S., 272 U.S. 52 (1926).
24. *E.g.*, Public Law 85-315, 71 Stat. 634 (1957).

exempt positions directly within the administrative establishment. Actually, considerable political advantage has been taken of nonwhite appointments to high positions available to the President.

More difficulty has arisen in regard to federal positions covered either by Civil Service[25] or Postal Service regulations.[26] Two incidents of recent time summarize the kinds of problems involved.

It has been reported that the Corps of Engineers office in Louisiana, had required that if on any appointment under Civil Service a Negro was one of three eligible candidates for the position and, if for any reason the Negro was not appointed, administrative explanation would be required on the appointment of the non-Negro. The second involves the promotion of a Negro supervisor in the Dallas post office, allegedly over the heads of several white eligibles who ranked higher on the list of eligibles.

The problem is, of course, whether in both or either of these instances the result of administrative action was to discriminate in reverse.

In my judgment neither of such cases raises the problem of discrimination in reverse. First, it should be made clear that neither case lies within the main theme of the present analysis: they do not involve removing discriminatory bars. They are in fact examples of administrative techniques designed to assure equal opportunity in situations where prior discriminatory practices would result in continued deprivation. In the first case the issue is the creation of an administrative technique to "police" the administrators. It might be suggested that the reporting device has at least the utility of building into the direct administrative process an awareness and consciousness of the problem of discrimination. As such, it is responsive to one of the basic and fundamental problems of administering norms based on nondiscrimination—how to build into normal work-a-day administration a concern for implementing policy. In this sense, this technique is the same as the reporting requirement in many state administrations imposed after a finding of past discriminatory practices. In our case, it is arguable that past discriminatory practices in the federal establishment are so notorious that official notice might well be taken of them—and reporting obligations established immediately. In the second case, a much different problem is raised. Whites seem to be deprived of a legitimate expectation. But, that expectation is in fact based upon prior discrimination. And, to employ equitable doctrine, it is not inequitable to destroy an expectation based upon wrongful treatment of Negro competitors in the past.

In sum, it might be safe to predict that the employment of vigorous, and in some cases imaginative administrative techniques, ultimately resting upon presidential power, will show dramatic changes in direct federal employment. On the other hand, it is clear that many problems surround the "agency" of

---

25. The Pendleton Act (Civil Service Act), 22 Stat. 403 (1883) 5 U.S.C. §§ 631-58 (1958).

26. 39 U.S.C. §§ 31-219 (1958).

the President's Committee as an effective specialized organ within the executive branch.

Executive Power as Chief Executive

Second only in importance to federal contracts as a mechanism for creating job opportunities is the federal grant-in-aid.[27] These grants are made to state and local governmental units and public agencies, to public institutions and to private nonprofit organizations.[28] It is in regard to these programs of some 155 kinds[29] that the greatest inroads have been made in traditional concepts of federalism. And, it is as to these programs and their secondarily generated job opportunities that executive power is at its maximum. Ultimately, the power to assure equal opportunity in these programs rests upon the executive power to see to the faithful execution of the Constitution. And, experience here indicates that the most effective administrative technique is the threat to withhold previously appropriated funds. It is to the constitutional basis of this power that the following analysis is directed.

The power to appropriate federal funds is vested in Congress.[30] Congress not only has such constitutional power of appropriation but can attach limiting conditions to the expenditure. But it is clear that Congress cannot attach an unconstitutional condition to an appropriation.[31] In *U.S. v. Lovett*,[32] the Supreme Court held that a condition attached to an appropriation prohibiting expenditure of funds to pay salaries of certain individuals was an unconstitutional bill of attainder. The principle is well settled that exercises of congressional power are limited by the Constitution.[33]

Section 8 of article I of the United States Constitution grants to Congress the ". . . Power To lay and collect Taxes . . . and provide for the . . . general Welfare . . ." The federal government, like state governments, must exercise its powers to distribute funds, as well as its other powers, ". . . so as not to discriminate between [its citizens] except upon some reasonable differentiation fairly related to the object of regulation."[34]

It has been squarely held that governmentally required or permitted racial segregation ". . . is not reasonably related to any proper governmental objective. . . ."[35] To the same extent that the equal protection clause of the fourteenth amendment has been held to prohibit discrimination based upon race where a state is involved, the due process clause of the fifth amendment

---

27. U.S. Bureau of the Budget, Special Analysis of Federal Aid to State and Local Governments in 1962 Budget 3-4 (1962).
28. 1961 Report of the U.S. Commission on Civil Rights, *Employment* 81-93.
29. *Ibid.*
30. U.S. Const. art. I, § 8.
31. U.S. v. Lovett, 328 U.S. 303 (1946).
32. *Id.* at 315.
33. Marbury v. Madison, 5 U.S. (1 Cranch) 137 (1803).
34. Railway Express Agency, Inc. v. New York, 336 U.S. 106, 112 (1949) (Jackson, J., concurring opinion.)
35. Bolling v. Sharpe, 347 U.S. 497, 500 (1954).

prohibits discrimination where the federal government is so involved.[36] Thus, the federal government is prohibited from expending its funds in the support of racial segregation in its own projects, activities and programs under the due process clause of the fifth amendment.

The adherence by the federal government to the policy of nondiscrimination in its own activities, while at the same time financing racial discrimination by supporting state conducted projects and activities where such practices are maintained is an obvious inconsistency. The issue raised by this inconsistency is whether the congressional appropriation and subsequent executive expenditure of federal funds are federal activities exempt from the limitations implicit within the due process clause of the fifth amendment merely because the government is one step removed from the forbidden activity. The applicable principle of law has been succinctly stated by Justice Frankfurter:

> Congress may withhold all sorts of facilities for a better life but if it affords them it cannot make them available in an obviously arbitrary way . . ."[37]

Examination of cases in which this principle has been applied as a limitation on expenditure of state funds under the equal protection clause of the fourteenth amendment demonstrates that the due process clause of the fifth amendment necessarily prohibits *support* by the federal government to racially segregated state conducted projects, activities and programs.

In a series of cases it has been held that where state funds have been used to purchase, build, operate, or lease for operation public facilities, the equal protection clause of the fourteenth amendment requires that those facilities be available on a nondiscriminatory basis.[38] Clearly for the federal government to furnish funds to the states to underwrite the cost of similar activities in a racially segregated manner would result in that Government's sanctioning discriminatory practices which, under the Bolling formulation, the federal government could not itself conduct without contravening the prohibitions of the fifth amendment's due process clause. That the federal government cannot escape its constitutional limitations by furnishing the ways and means for a private individual, corporation or state to discriminate against its own citizens is clearly indicated by the Supreme Court's denouncement of such practice by a state under the fourteenth amendment. In *Burton*, the state leased a public restaurant facility to a corporation which excluded Negroes solely because of their race. In holding that the restaurant was subject to the

---

36. *Id.* at 499.
37. American Communications Ass'n v. Douds, 339 U.S. 382, 417 (1950) (separate opinion.)
38. For cases relating to state owned facilities, see, *e.g.*, Muir v. Louisville Park Theatrical Ass'n, 347 U.S. 971 (1954) (per curiam) (city park facilities); Gayle v. Browder, 352 U.S. 903 (1956) (per curiam) (buses operated on city streets.) For cases relating to facilities leased from the state, see, *e.g.*, Burton v. Wilmington Parking Authority, 365 U.S. 715 (1961) (restaurant); Turner v. City of Memphis, 369 U.S. 350 (1962) (restaurant in airport.)

strictures of the fourteenth amendment, the Court noted that in its lease the state could have expressly forbidden racial discrimination, and then went on to say:

> But no State may effectively abdicate its responsibilities by either ignoring them or by merely failing to discharge them whatever the motive may be. It is of no consolation to an individual denied the equal protection of the laws that it was done in good faith. . . . By its inaction, the Authority, and through it the State, has not only made itself a party to the refusal of service, but has elected to place its power, property and prestige behind the admitted discrimination.[39]

Surely the due process clause of the fifth amendment does not require less where the federal government plays a vital role in the support of racial segregation. Thus, the proscriptions of the fifth amendment are as binding on the federal government itself as on the grantees of federal funds.

The scope of due process limitation upon the power of the federal government is clearly laid down in *Cooper v. Aaron.*

> State support of segregated schools through any arrangement, management, funds, or property cannot be squared with the Amendment's command that no State shall deny to any person within its jurisdiction the equal protection of the laws. The right of a student not to be segregated on racial grounds in schools so maintained is indeed so fundamental and pervasive that it is embraced in the concept of due process of law. *Bolling v. Sharpe,* 347 U.S. 497.[40]

The President's duty to faithfully execute the laws is not limited solely to acts of Congress or treaties made pursuant to the Constitution, but includes "the rights, duties and obligations growing out of the Constitution itself, . . . and all the protection implied by the nature of the Government under the Constitution."[41] In the words of Professor Corwin, " 'that the President is entitled to claim broad powers under his duty to take care that the laws be faithfully executed' has been demonstrated many times in our history."[42]

The expenditure of federal funds (as distinct from the appropriation) is an executive function. In the words of Corwin, The Constitution

> . . . assumes that expenditure is primarily an executive function, and conversely that the participation of the legislative branch is essentially for the purpose simply of setting bounds to executive discretion—a theory confirmed by early practice under the Constitution.[43]

The exercise of executive powers is no less subject to the limitations of the Constitution than the exercise of legislative or judicial powers.[44]

---

39. Burton v. Wilmington Parking Authority, *id.* at 725.
40. 358 U.S. 1, 19 (1958).
41. Cunningham v. Neagle, 135 U.S. 1, 64 (1890).
42. Corwin, The President: Office and Powers—(4th rev. ed. 1957).
43. *Id.* at 127-28.
44. Youngstown Sheet & Tube Co. v. Sawyer, 343 U.S. 579 (1952).

Executive Power Where Congress is Silent.

The power of the President, pursuant to his constitutional duty, to direct appropriate rule making exercises by executive and independent agencies has been exercised on many occasions. On the most recent occasions, the power was exercised expressly to require the eradication of discriminatory practices in areas of responsibility posited with particular agencies under statutes devoid of antidiscrimination provisions. It has been concluded on this basis that:

> The lack of serious challenge to the exercise of this authority by four Presidents in nine executive orders over twenty years lends support to presidential power to prescribe nondiscrimination, at least until Congress acts.[45]

It should be noted that there is no express statutory authorization for this exercise of Presidential power. The absence of such authorization amply serves again to illustrate that the duty of the President under the Constitution is broader than simply the fulfilling of the will of Congress as reflected in congressional enactments. As the Supreme Court held in *Cunningham v. Neagle*,[46] the duty of the President is not limited solely to acts of Congress or treaties made pursuant to the Constitution, but includes "the rights, duties and obligations growing out of the Constitution itself . . . and all the protection implied by the nature of the Government under the Constitution."

Executive Power Where Congress Requires Federal Support of Discrimination.

A definite issue of course would be raised where there is an express congressional direction to the President to administer a statute in an unconstitutional manner. In that event, absent a binding determination by the Supreme Court, the President is obligated to refuse execution of laws of Congress which in his judgment are in violation of the Constitution if such congressional acts are administered in accordance with congressional direction.

The question at this point is whether the President, relying expressly upon his duty to "take care that the Laws be faithfully executed" (United States Constitution article II, section 3) can refuse to administer an act of Congress on the ground that he believes the administration of the Act would result in racial discrimination supported by federal funds, and, consequently, that it violates the fifth amendment of the Constitution, and thus the act as so applied and administered was not "made in Pursuance thereof."[47] It appears to be wholly erroneous to assert that:

> [I]t is not the responsibility of the Executive to pass upon the constitutionality of statutes enacted by Congress, once they have been finally approved by the President.

---

45. Speck, *Enforcement of Nondiscrimination Requirements for Government Contract Work*, 63 Colum. L. Rev. 243, 245-46 (1963).
46. 135 U.S. 1 (1890).
47. U.S. Const. art. VI.

Mr. Justice Story, in his *Commentaries on the Constitution*[48] has provided us with what is perhaps the best articulated assertion of a broad power in the President to refuse to carry out a legislative mandate which he believes to violate the Constitution. In laying the groundwork for a discussion of why the Supreme Court is the final arbiter with respect to constitutional questions, Dean Story made the following observations:

> The Constitution, contemplating the grant of limited powers, and distributing them among various functionaries, . . . whenever any question arises as to the exercise of any power by any of these functionaries under the State or Federal Government, it is of necessity that such functionaries must, in the first instance, decide upon the constitutionality of the exercise of such powers. . . . The officers of each of these departments [executive, legislative and judicial] are equally bound by their oaths of office to support the Constitution of the United States, and are therefore conscientiously bound to abstain from all acts which are inconsistent with it. . . . If, for instance, the President is required to do any act, he is not only authorized but required to decide for himself, whether, consistently with his constitutional duties, he can do the act.[49]

In contrast to some arguments in support of the same conclusion,[50] Story makes it clear that in his eye the President's duty to decide constitutional questions is limited to cases "not hitherto settled by any proper authority," and that a decision by the Supreme Court with respect to the matter in issue would be binding on the President.[51] Counsel for President Johnson in his impeachment proceedings made an argument similar to that of Story in defending President Johnson's refusal to comply with the Tenure of Office Act of 1867 on the ground that it was unconstitutional, but added the additional limitation that the situation be such that only by a refusal to act could the President raise a justiciable issue.[52]

Stated in this form, the argument is not that the position of the President is superior to that of Congress, but only that each of the two branches of the Government owes a duty to obey the Constitution and that the opportunities to act in the light of his duty will occur at different times because of the separate role each has in dealing with matters of national concern. Thus Congress may refuse to enact a law recommended by the President, because of a belief that the law would be unconstitutional, and thus to a certain extent appear responsible for frustrating the aims of the President. The President, on the other hand, when it comes time to execute a law of Congress may refuse to do so

---

48. 1 Commentaries on the Constitution of the United States (4th ed. 1873).
49. *Id.* at 264-65.
50. *E.g.*, Meigs, *The Independence of the Departments of Government*, 23 Am. L. Rev. 594 (1889).
51. See 1 Commentaries 265.
52. Curtis, Argument on Behalf of President Johnson in Impeachment Proceedings, Cong. Globe (Supp.), 40th Cong., 2d Sess. 126-127 (1868), quoted in 1 Freund, Sutherland, Howe & Brown, Constitutional Law 18-19 (2d ed. 1961). See also Story, 1 Commentaries *op. cit. supra* note 48, at 266-67.

because of his belief that the law is unconstitutional. It should be noted that the duty to ascertain constitutionality is an executive duty required by the Constitution itself. Subordinate executive and administrative officials are not directed to "take Care that the Laws be faithfully executed" as is the President. On occasion, however, the courts have recognized that such subordinated administrators may determine the constitutionality of an enactment they are required to administer.[53] In *Little Rock & Fort Smith Ry. v. Worthen*,[54] the Court set forth the reasons why subordinate executive and administrative officials ordinarily are not permitted to determine the constitutionality of statutes they are administering. In a decision which vindicated the action of a state board of railroad commissioners in disregarding, on constitutional grounds, a legislative exemption of certain railroad property from taxation, the Court commented:

> It may not be a wise thing, as a rule, for subordinate executive or ministerial officers to undertake to pass upon the constitutionality of legislation prescribing their duties, and to disregard it if in their judgment it is invalid. This may be a hazardous proceeding to themselves, and productive of great inconvenience to the public but still the determination of the judicial tribunals can alone settle the legality of their action.[55]

Both the President and Congress of course must obey the decisions of the Supreme Court. But, absent such a decision, the President must firstly address himself to the constitutionality of his administration of congressionally approved programs.[56]

Executive Power Where Congress Prohibits Federal Support of Discrimination.

On the other hand, if Congress enacts a nondiscriminatory provision, no problems whatsoever as to the extent of executive power would be raised. Here, in the words of Mr. Justice Jackson in *Youngstown Sheet & Tube*,[57] the executive power is at its maximum.

> When the President acts pursuant to an express or implied authorization of Congress, his authority is at its maximum, for it includes all that he possesses in his own right plus all that Congress can delegate. In these circumstances, and in these only, may he be said (for what it may be worth), to personify the federal sovereignty. If his act is held unconstitutional under these circumstances, it usually means that the Federal Government as an undivided whole lacks power.[58]

The President's Executive Order regarding equal opportunity in housing stands as ample precedent for the exercise of executive power to assure admin-

---

53. *E.g.*, Little Rock & Fort Smith Ry. v. Worthen, 120 U.S. 97 (1887).
54. *Ibid.*
55. *Id.* at 101.
56. *Cf.* Marbury v. Madison, 5 U.S. (1 Cranch) 137 (1803).
57. 343 U.S. 579 (1952).
58. *Id.* at 635.

istration of federal programs in a constitutional manner.[59] The order itself clearly reveals its constitutional basis:

[T]he executive branch of the Government, *in faithfully executing the laws of the United States which authorize Federal financial assistance*, directly or indirectly, for the provision, rehabilitation, and operation of housing and related facilities, is charged with an obligation and duty to assure that those laws are fairly administered and that benefits thereunder are made available to all Americans without regard to their race, color, creed, or national origin. (Emphasis added.)

Among the sanctions which may be imposed for violation of the policy of nondiscrimination is withholding of federal assistance. Section 302 of the Order expressly provides that appropriate departments and agencies may:

(a) cancel or terminate in whole or in part any agreement or contract with such person, firm, or State or local public agency providing for a loan, grant, contribution, or other Federal aid, or for the payment of a commission or fee;

(b) refrain from extending any further aid under any program administered by it and affected by this order until it is satisfied that the affected person, firm or State or local public agency will comply with the rules, regulations, and procedures issued or adopted pursuant to this order, and any nondiscrimination provisions included in any agreement or contract;

(c) refuse to approve a lending institution or any other lender as a beneficiary under any program administered by it which is affected by this order or revoke such approval if previously given.

There is little doubt as to the constitutional authority of the President to issue an order with such provisions.

There would appear to be little doubt that the issuance of the Executive Order in housing is constitutional. It can be concluded that the President has authority to act, based: (1) in part upon the provisions of 42 U. S. C., section 1982 ("all citizens of the United States shall have the same right in every state . . . as is enjoyed by white citizens thereof to inherit, purchase, lease, sell, hold and convey real . . . property"); (2) in part on the constitutional requirements for equal protection of the laws and due process (particularly as interpreted by the Supreme Court in *Hurd v. Hodge*,[60] ruling that a federal court may not lend its aid to enforcement of a private racially restrictive covenant); (3) in part on the precedent of the Executive Orders requiring a nondiscrimination clause in government contracts; and (4) in part on the rulemaking powers conferred on the housing agencies by their basic statutes.

Moreover, the issuance of Executive Orders imposing and renewing prohibitions against discrimination on the basis of race in employment and contract work for the federal government reaffirms the underlying constitutional power of the President to direct the manner of expenditure of federal funds or

---

59. Executive Order 11063, 27 Fed. Reg. 11527 (1962).
60. 334 U.S. 24 (1948).

ultimately to require the withholding of federal expenditures in specified circumstances. The last reaffirmation of this executive power was in President Kennedy's Executive Order 10925.[61] The constitutional foundation for the issuance of the Order has been commented upon extensively in legal literature.[62]

The President in addition to his overriding executive authority pursuant to his constitutional duty to take care that the laws be faithfully executed has by statute the power to direct the manner in which Government business is conducted.[63] Section 22 of title 5 of the United States Code provides that each executive department head

> . . . is authorized to prescribe regulations, not inconsistent with law, for the government of his department, the conduct of its officers and clerks, the distribution and performance of its business, and the custody, use, and preservation of the records, papers and property appertaining to it.

In addition, the present federal budget system makes provision for the withholding of expenditure of appropriated funds. The position of the Bureau of the Budget is:

> In requiring that money be placed in reserve, the Bureau proceeds also on the principle that ordinarily an appropriation is merely an authorization and not a mandate to spend money for the specified purpose.[64]

On matters of defense expenditures, there is a considerable body of executive precedent in withholding appropriated funds.[65]

In considering the power of the executive to assure nondiscrimination in federal assistance, it is important to recognize that a number of significant steps already have been taken toward that objective by heads of executive departments.

For example, former Secretary Ribicoff ruled that beginning in September 1963, racially segregated public education would not be considered "suitable" under the terms of the Impacted Area school program for children residing on federal properties. Several important steps were taken to implement this ruling. First, the Departments of Health, Education and Welfare, and Justice undertook a series of negotiations with school districts in an effort to secure compliance. As a result, fifteen districts said that they would admit on-base children on a nonracial basis, and most have gone beyond this by indicating that they would adopt policies of desegregation which would benefit all students within the district. In five areas where compliance was not forthcoming, the

---

61. 26 Fed. Reg. 1977 (1961).
62. See Speck, note 45 *supra*; Birnbaum, *Equal Employment Opportunity in Executive Order 10925*, 11 Kan. L. Rev. 17 (1962); Bennett, *Non-Discrimination Provisions of Federal Contracts*, Mich. S.B.J. 21 (March 1952); and Pasley, *The Nondiscrimination Clause in Government Contracts*, 43 Va. L. Rev. 837 (1957).
63. Rev. Stat. § 161 (1875), 5 U.S.C. 22 (1958).
64. See Wallace, Congressional Control of Federal Spending 145 (1960).
65. *Id.* at 146.

Department of Justice determined that it had authority and standing to initiate lawsuits (without express statutory authorization) on behalf of Negro military dependents seeking desegregation of federally-aided local schools. In eight other localities where commitments could not be obtained, the Department of Health, Education and Welfare decided to build schools on base in order to provide suitable education for children living on federal property.

These actions, of course, have not come close to solving completely the problem of providing equal educational opportunity for the children of military personnel. They are directed primarily toward families who live on federal property, with only peripheral benefit thus far to the great bulk of military dependents who reside off base. Nonetheless, the actions add up to an affirmative assertion of executive authority to assure nondiscrimination.

Even absent an express statutory nondiscriminatory provision of mandatory nature, the executive obligation compels executive action to assure nondiscrimination in administration of federal programs. Moreover, either the rejection or the enactment of a "nondiscrimination" provision by Congress cannot, under the Constitution, derogate from the constitutional scope of executive power. Therefore, while one would support the objective of legislative nondiscriminatory provisions, it is clear that such provisions are not necessary to establish executive power to reach the same end. But, at the most, such provisions would represent expressions of congressional intent that federal programs be administered in a nondiscriminatory fashion.

HINDSIGHT AND FORESIGHT ABOUT FEPC

John G. Feild*

PEOPLE are asking better questions these days. They used to ask: "Do we need fair employment laws?" Today they are asking: "Are our FEP laws adequate?"

Hopefully, this new question will be answered somewhat more affirmatively with the passage of the Federal Civil Rights Act which includes provisions extending equal employment opportunity on a national basis for the first time in our history. The answer may at best be only partial, however, not only because it is questionable whether the provisions of the new federal law will in fact be adequate to the need, but equally because the continued operation of existing state and local fair employment laws on their present basis is increasingly being challenged.

This challenge, of course, is coming not from those who oppose fair employment laws but primarily from those they are designed to benefit. Ironically, this comes at a time when the operation of these laws has reached unprecedented coverage. Today there are 22 states and more than 50 cities with enforceable fair employment codes. In addition, at the federal level, the strongest executive order ever issued on the subject, signed by President Kennedy in 1961, already embraces that huge portion of the economy that is now involved in federal contracting. It may not be too much to say that fully 75 per cent of all employment is currently subject to some antidiscrimination regulation. Why have these doubts been raised at this time and what validity do they have?

In part, the doubts as well as frustrations expressed in recent direct action demonstrations over job discrimination in the north as well as the south seem verified by recent economic data released by the Census Bureau and the Department of Labor. Dr. Herman Miller, Assistant to the Director of the United States Census Bureau, in his testimony before the Senate Subcommittee on Employment and Manpower last summer testified that his analysis of Department of Labor reports and United States census data indicated that the "economic status [of Negroes] relative to whites has not improved for nearly 20 years."[1] He goes on to say that: "Although the relative occupational status of nonwhites has not changed appreciably in most States since 1940, the income gap between whites and nonwhites did narrow during the Second World War. During the past decade, however, there has been no change in income differentials between the two groups."[2] He testified further: "This conclusion is reinforced by details of the 1960 census which show that in the 26 States (including the District of Columbia) which have 100,000 or more Negroes, the ratio of

---

* Director, Community Relations Service, U.S. Conference of Mayors.
1. *Senate Hearings on S. 773, S. 1210, S. 1211 and S. 1937 Before the Subcommittee on Employment and Manpower of the Committee on Labor and Public Welfare*, 88th Cong., 1st Sess. 321 (1963).
2. *Id.* at 323.

Negro to white income for males increased between 1949 and 1959 in [only] two States (District of Columbia and Florida) and it was unchanged in two others (New Jersey and Oklahoma). *In every other State there was a widening of the gap* between the incomes of whites and Negroes, and in some cases it was fairly substantial."[3] (Emphasis added.)

To underscore further the economic basis for current doubts and dissatisfaction with state and local fair employment laws, it may be well to emphasize the extraordinary impact which automation has had on those occupations which had been sources of relatively stable, even if lower paying, employment for the bulk of Negro workers—agricultural employment and blue collar employment. While the total number of jobs increased by almost 19 million between 1940 and 1960, farm employment decreased by 4 million. In addition, production jobs have declined 600,000 overall since 1947. Documenting the effect this has had on Negro workers, especially in the north, the Labor Department reports that ". . . the proportion of nonwhites employed in blue-collar occupations fell slightly between 1955 and 1962, returning to levels prevailing in 1948."[4] Comparison of unemployment figures may complete the economic list in this discouraging picture. In 1962, for example, the rate of unemployment for white workers averaged 4 per cent, for nonwhite workers it averaged 11 per cent.[5] It is not hard to estimate the impact of an even more shattering statistic: even in the north, unemployment has averaged twice as great for nonwhite workers for *every year since the Korean War.*[6]

Thus, it is apparent that the last two decades have not been witness to the uninterrupted economic progress of the Negro worker that we have tended to believe. To many observers, much of this progress seemed to derive from the fact that a more favorable climate providing "equal employment opportunity under law" had been growing throughout the northern states and that Negroes were inevitably benefiting from this climate as they geographically migrated from the old south into the urban north and west. Certainly, a decline in Negro residence in the southern states from 77 per cent of all Negroes in 1940 compared to 51 per cent today did have a favorable influence on their economic status during the decade between 1940 and 1950, but has apparently had little effect since. In fact, from a national perspective, the economic position of the Negro appears to have been deteriorating since the Korean War.

While the influence of equal employment opportunity laws has apparently been unable to cope with the enormity of this problem, I, for one at least, believe there is ample evidence to demonstrate that conditions today would be far worse were it not for such public policies. To blow up the dyke because the flood crested higher than our bricks seems to me somewhat more foolish than examin-

---

3. *Id.* at 324.
4. Kessler, *Economic Status of Nonwhite Workers, 1955-62*, 86 Monthly Labor Review 782 (1963).
5. *Ibid.*
6. U.S. Dep't of Labor, Manpower Report (1963).

ing our weak points and doing something constructive about them. Thus, while I happen to agree with many of those who contend that we could have done better with our local and state laws and our federal regulations than we have, the basis of our opinion may differ.

Looking backward, it seems to me the reasons for our limited performance with our FEP laws are traceable to at least five kinds of problems. First, there is the limited authority given the local or state administering unit by these laws, either with respect to procedures for invoking that authority or with respect to the coverage or jurisdiction of the law. It is true that administration of such laws by independent, multiple-member commissions is cumbersome and less efficient than that which is possible under a single administrator with more direct administrative power. It is also true that the exemption of large numbers of business establishments employing a significant number of people has tended to be a drag on the effective application of law. Most important, it is evident that those states that have not authorized their administrative unit to *initiate* actions on their own motion—backed up with sanctions—have been less effective. The recent impressive experience of the federal agencies in initiating compliance reviews of contractors and the establishment of requirements for affirmative action designed to extend equal employment opportunity has amply illustrated the desirability of providing the administering unit with "initiatory power."

Secondly, there have been political problems which have shaped the judgment exercised by those responsible for administering these laws. Generally speaking, the state and local fair employment laws have been administered with a high degree of caution if not timidity. Certainly, prudence in gaining public acceptance and in clearing away legal challenges during the early years of the operation of new laws was understandable. Undoubtedly, political considerations have had the effect of both restraining vigorous enforcement activity in many instances and, as during World War II and later with the advent of the Kennedy administration, the effect of stimulating more vigorous action. When President Eisenhower appointed Vice President Nixon to head his FEPC, we perhaps should have realized that the issue had become respectable and that the time to push forward had arrived. On the whole, my personal judgment, witnessed by hindsight, is that politically our enforcement thrust, in contrast to our conciliation efforts, could and should have been more decisive.

Thirdly, there has been the problem of resources. I think the lacks in this area have been more critical and more damaging to our ability to cope with employment discrimination than any other single factor. The budgets and staffs provided local and state commissions, considering the dimensions of their administrative responsibility, have been and are pitifully inadequate. The typical challenge runs something like this. Until recently, the Michigan Commission, for example, had jurisdiction over 38,000 employers which they regulated with a staff of 10 professionals. At such a ratio, even if each staff member were to review two employers a week, they will still not have completed their program for another 30 years. The state of Illinois with an even greater number of employers started its program two years ago on a budget of $50,000 and a staff of five. Even today the state of California, reputed now to be larger than the state of New York, has a total staff of less than 35 compared to about 175 in New York—the only state that seems to be showing any sense of realism about budget.

Moreover, the budget and staff allocations of the federal agencies under their contractor programs make these deficiencies, however inadequate, look rather less so by comparison. For example, there are fewer persons assigned to regulatory activities even in the present federal program dealing with contractors than are currently employed by the New York State Commission alone. The federal agencies are responsible for regulating the staggering total of an estimated 300,000 establishments involving nearly 20 million workers. Few undertakings of such magnitude with such limited resources could expect to succeed. They could not be much more than the "minimum deterrent" which these laws have been and for which they are now being properly criticized.

The political relationship of funds and policy is, of course, self-evident. During World War II, the Federal FEPC had a staff of more than 100 and maintained 15 regional offices. By 1953, under Nixon, we had a federal staff of fewer than 30 and only two regional offices. The Kennedy-Johnson administrations, building on a new political climate at the beginning of the Sixties, have committed more manpower and resources than at any previous time and it still remains, in my judgment, at a token level. (We spend more on a single missile mis-firing at Cape Kennedy, for example, than we do at present on the entire Federal Equal Employment Opportunity Program. I could understand better some of the scatter-shot criticism that is being leveled at state FEP commissions if their alleged "mis-firings" had at least been budgeted as well.)

Finally, I would point to a problem that goes beyond the matter of law and beyond the matter of administration and administrative resources. Those who have been dealing with employment discrimination have always been mindful of the inseparable relationship between our skills development systems and job opportunities. They have been mindful that where and how a person obtains his training is of critical importance to his ultimate job future. They have known that the impact of rural, segregated education was having its cumulative effects in the northern and western cities during these past two decades of massive Negro migration. They have known that the practices of guidance counselors, of placement services, whether public or private, and of recruiting officers are actually a critical part of the employment system and its potential for disadvantage (or benefit) to the Negro worker. They have known that the system of selecting apprentices for the building trades has contained restrictions not greatly different from those involved in the selection of medical interns or junior law partners or accountant trainees. In other words, they have

19

known that the regulation of the practices of employers, unions, and employment agencies has not been enough and that the vocational development system was profoundly involved in their ability to improve the occupational status of non-white workers.

The conclusion which I draw from an examination of these problems leads me, therefore, if I may now look forward, in the following direction. Whether it be at the local, state or federal level, I would like to see both state and federal FEP laws administered by a single, strong administrator with the power to initiate action and with adequate safeguards for appeal and review of his functions and decisions. I would like to see this administrator have comprehensive jurisdiction of those whose practices are affecting employment opportunities including all vocational development institutions, relationships and activities. I would like to see this administrator provided with adequate resources and staff. In this connection I would like to see greater experimentation with and use made of existing regulatory inspection staffs already available to the various levels of government such as building inspection departments, wage and hour units, certification agencies. I have the feeling that the staff resources problem at most levels of government is primarily one of manpower allocation and training and that we should move more in the direction of greater integration of functions rather than establishing new and independent administrative units. The Manpower Development and Training Act and the War on Poverty are as integral to the effective implementation of the Federal Civil Rights Act as they are to each other. The manpower aspects of all three could be unified administratively with considerable benefit. Dozens of illustrations of the same kind could be drawn from present day state and city levels.

Finally, I would like to see this administrator function at a more direct, less independent, political level than has been true of most FEP commissions during the past 20 years. I think we have gone too far in making them bi-partisan. The problem which we confront involves many aspects of governmental coordination that can only be achieved at the highest policy level. It necessarily involves political judgments. It involves the establishment of priorities among functions of government which must be made to be complementary and must be coordinated with one another.

As a footnote, I have the impression that we may have turned another corner as the Sixties unfold. Improvements along the lines I have outlined or any other reasonable improvements, if supported with greater resources, may start us once again on the road toward the widespread enlargement of equal job opportunities that the present situation demands. The impact of automation will clearly be of less significance to today's minority youth than it was to their fathers. Educational opportunities are headed toward greater equalization. The political importance of public policies in the form of better and more comprehensive civil rights laws has never been more clearly or widely recognized than it is today. The time for reform has either arrived or we are dangerously passed it.

20

And finally, I think the experience of those who have been trying to deal with this problem has become in itself a formidable asset. We now have more than 2000 reasonably well trained and experienced professional workers working in the field. Twenty years ago we had less than 100. Given the resources, they ought to know what to do better today than they did when they started. At least, I like to believe that we have learned something in the past 20 years.

TWENTY YEARS OF STATE FAIR EMPLOYMENT PRACTICE COMMISSIONS: A CRITICAL ANALYSIS WITH RECOMMENDATIONS

HERBERT HILL*

I. INTRODUCTION

BEGINNING with the 1940's, civil rights advocates in many states actively campaigned for the creation of state fair employment practice commissions. Stimulated by the dramatic successes of the federal FEPC created by President Roosevelt's Executive Order 8802 in 1941, proponents of fair employment practice laws hoped that rigorous application of the legal power of state civil rights commissions would alleviate the very serious problem of job discrimination, and help open the path to Negro participation in many occupations and industries. Perhaps some advocates of state fair employment practice laws were aware that if employment reached the crisis proportions of a general depression then even the most stringent laws would be ineffective. But it was hoped that the increased hiring of Negroes during periods of full employment and their entrance into stable skilled jobs with union membership would help create a broader occupational distribution that would render the Negro worker less vulnerable to large-scale unemployment.[1]

This concept appeared to be plausible when presented during the period of wartime and postwar industrial expansion. But the analysis did not envision the sharp decrease in Negro employment which was to occur after the wartime demand for labor had subsided. The very serious impact of automation and other technological innovations in many industries was not anticipated. Nor was the intransigence of employers and labor unions in refusing to significantly alter the status of Negro workers realistically evaluated.

Now after almost two decades of experience with state fair employment practice laws, it is possible and indeed necessary to make an assessment of their efficacy. During the period of general affluence and overall prosperity which led to the description of America in the 1950's as "the affluent society," Negro workers experienced the equivalent of a general economic depression.

The period of 1948-1952 was a time of full employment for the nation; the national unemployment rate during this period was about 2½ per cent. In 1950-51 the aggregate demand for goods and services reached a high point for the entire country, but the rate of unemployment among Negro wage-earners was already rapidly increasing. Since 1951, the gap between the average income of Negro and White wage-earners has been growing consistently greater.[2]

---

* National Labor Secretary, NAACP and member of the faculty of the New School for Social Research, New York City.
1. Ruchames, Race, Jobs, & Politics 194-95 (1953).
2. See U.S. Dep't of Labor, Manpower Report of the President and a Report on Manpower Requirements, Resources, Utilization, and Training 106 (1964).

Changes in law and public policy have involved a very small number of Negroes and resulted only in marginal or token integration into some few industries. The occupational pattern of Negro labor has not been changed in states with FEPC laws. "Statutory remedies that rely on individual complaints by aggrieved parties are slow," commented Harold Baron of the Chicago Urban League, "and permit many subtle subterfuges on the part of the discriminators. Relatively few individuals receive better jobs or housing under the protection of these measures, and the basic pattern of second-class status remains unchanged."[3]

Given the significant developments in the American economy during the last twenty years together with the current status of the Negro wage-earner in states with FEPC laws we must conclude on the basis of the evidence that state FEPC laws have failed. They have failed because their potential was in fact never realized. The time has now come to insist upon a fundamentally new approach in the operation of state fair employment commissions and for the adoption of a strong federal fair employment practices law that operates with new standards and enforcement procedures. For the Negro wage-earner the limited and inadequate state FEP commissions are no substitute for broad federal actions to eliminate the deeply entrenched patterns of employment discrimination. If this is not done very soon even the limited gains of the past will be destroyed and the entire Negro community will be in a permanent condition of crisis. Negro wage-earners in vast numbers will either be the working poor or the hard core of the permanently unemployed.

Surely there is great significance in the fact that during the spring and summer of 1963 and again in 1964, the largest and most dramatic public demonstrations against job discrimination occurred in states with FEPC laws as in New York, in Pennsylvania, in California and elsewhere and that the rates of Negro unemployment in several states with fair employment laws are among the highest to be found in the nation.

Herman Miller, Special Assistant, Bureau of the Census, in his book *Rich Man, Poor Man,* states that in the past decade in most states: ". . . there was a widening of the gap between the incomes of whites and Negroes and in some cases it was fairly substantial. In Michigan for example, the ratio of average Negro income to white income dropped from 87 percent in 1949 to 76 percent in 1959."[4]

Several basic propositions will be advanced in this paper. One is that the status of Negro labor in northern states covered by fair employment practice laws has not changed in any basic sense for the past twenty years, and is now further deteriorating. The second is that state FEP enactments have proved unable to cope with the problem of changing the Negro occupational pattern and that FEP commissions do not provide a solution to structural unemployment

---

3. Baron, *Negro Unemployment—A Case Study,* 3 New University Thought 42 (1963).
4. Miller, Rich Man, Poor Man 88 (1964).

problems. Thirdly, that certain industries with expanding job opportunities are beyond the reach of FEP statutes and that a virtual immunity from anti-discrimination laws has been achieved by many important labor unions where Negro exclusion has been traditional and where there is rigid control of hiring by the union.[5] Further, that with some very few exceptions, most state FEP commissions have been administered by timid political appointees, many with little or no professional competence and with an appalling lack of sensitivity to the realities of the Negro workers' life in the racial ghettos of the urban north.

If state antidiscrimination commissions are to become effective and their purpose realized then certain basic changes in the operation of the commissions must be made. These include:

1. *Greater Use of Mandatory Powers*

   The general reluctance to apply statutory enforcement powers must immediately come to an end. In areas where they could function in a positive manner, state commissions most often reject the law enforcement approach. This is because administrators do not regard state FEP commissions as law enforcement agencies and the history of virtually every state agency will indicate that the use of mandatory powers is very rare. This is a basic weakness in the operation of all state FEP commissions.[6]

2. *Affirmative Action Based Upon Pattern Centered Approaches Instead of the Individual Complaint Procedure*

   State commissions have become complaint taking bureaus that very slowly and laboriously—for as long as one or two years or more—attempt to "conciliate" an individual complaint that may or may not result in new employment for one person and do not change the racial employment pattern of a company or an industry. We know that only a very small fraction of all individuals who are the victims of discrimination file complaints and therefore commissions must initiate affirmative action based upon the overall pattern of employment discriminations. The recent decision of the New York State Commission against Local 28 of the Sheet Metal Workers Union[7] comes at least 10 years too late. Had the rigid pattern of overt discrimination in the construction trades in New York and elsewhere been directly attacked a decade ago the status of Negro workers in this important industry would today be very different.

3. *Drastic Reduction in the Number of Rejected Complaints*

   A major characteristic of commission operations is the very high percentage of rejected complaints. Among virtually all state commissions the number of rejected cases is approximately 50 percent.[8]

---

5. Hill, *Racism Within Organized Labor: A Report of Five Years of the AFL-CIO, 1955-1960*, 30 The Journal of Negro Education 109-18 (1961).
6. See *infra* Part V of this study.
7. Lefkowitz v. Farrell, C-9287-63 (N.Y. State Comm'n for Human Rights, 1964).
8. See *infra* Part V of this study.

Taken by itself, it is difficult to say that this figure is necessarily too high. However, as indicated by the discussion below and by other papers presented at this Conference, the record of the state commissions has generally been characterized by a lack of aggressive vigor and by a timid reluctance to root out discriminatory practices in powerful unions and companies. This clear timidity, plus the absence of any indications as to the standard of "probable cause" that is actually applied to these complaints, leads to the inevitable conclusion that these standards are much too rigid, that the number of rejected complaints is much too high. Inevitably, aggrieved persons are discouraged from filing valid complaints. There is clearly a need for revised standards of judgment and the public has a right to know what those standards are.

4. *Public Disclosure of Basis for Settlements*

State commissions must begin to reveal in precise terms what constitutes an "adjusted complaint," and what is meant by a "settlement." From a study of commission reports it is impossible to determine the relation between problem and settlement. In most cases the public does not know what was allegedly "settled." I also recommend that the official reports of the state commissions contain more precise and extensive information and that the atmosphere of secrecy that surrounds FEPC operations be once and for all removed.

5. *Expanded Availability of Commission Facilities*

State commissions have a responsibility to establish an easier access to agency procedures for members of minority groups. In most cases, even after 18 years, where and how to file a complaint remains a mystery for those who suffer the worst discrimination. The burden to eliminate this problem rests upon the various commissions.

Typical of state commissions with very poor records of achievement due to inadequate operations are the Wisconsin and Michigan Commissions, although many other agencies such as the Ohio, Washington and Pennsylvania Commissions might also be cited. The Wisconsin fair employment practices law went into operation on July 25, 1945; thus, the Wisconsin FEP agency was one of the very first state commissions. Revealing indeed are the biennial reports from Wisconsin. In 1956-1958, the Commission received 70 complaints, during 1958-1960, 146 complaints were processed, and in the two year period of 1960-1962, the Commission received 116 complaints which were disposed of as follows: probable cause found in 52, no probable cause in 48, other questionable practices 2, withdrawn 1. Officials of the Wisconsin Commission attributed the "increase" in their case load to the new jurisdictions of age and sex discrimination given the agency.

Michigan is a state wth a large Negro population. Detroit alone has over 500,000 Negroes with a very high rate of Negro unemployment. Michigan has had a state fair employment practice law since 1955. In 1963, the Michigan

Commission received only 280 complaints, in 1962, 303 complaints and in 1961, 250 complaints. The Michigan Commission also has jurisdiction in matters relating to discrimination because of age and sex. Surely there is a connection between a commission's effectiveness and the number of complaints received. Negro workers do not voluntarily file complaints when such actions are believed to bring little or no results. Other state commissions with very small case loads are New Jersey, Minnesota, Oregon and Connecticut, among others.[9]

The state of Pennsylvania has had a fair employment law since 1955 and Philadelphia has had a municipal FEP commission since 1948. After all these years there remains intact a widespread pattern of Negro exclusion from the major building trades craft unions in Philadelphia and elsewhere in Pennsylvania; thus Negro workers are denied jobs in the most important construction projects in the state. The Philadelphia Tribune in its issue of February 12, 1962 stated that: "Philadelphia labor unions have fostered a pattern of racial discrimination that is unsurpassed even in the Deep South."

II. The Economic Status of the Negro

Perhaps the most exhaustive study of the current economic status of Negroes in the United States has been made by Herman Miller of the Bureau of the Census.[10] This report was presented before hearings of the Subcommittee on Employment and Manpower of the Committee on Labor and Public Welfare of the United States Senate. Miller began his study by stating what he believed should be obvious, that "the Negro still ranks among the poorest of the poor and that his economic status relative to whites has not improved for nearly 20 years."[11] Miller disputed the "general impression that the relative economic position of the Negro—particularly with respect to employment opportunities—has improved in recent years."[12]

It is valid to state that for the country as a whole Negroes have raised their occupational levels in the past 22 years at a faster rate than whites. But to make this statement and deduce progress from it is to use the data in a misleading manner. The improvement in the occupational status of the Negro since 1940 is due only to movement from the rural south to urban industrial areas, "rather than to any major improvement in job opportunities," concludes Miller.[13] Negroes who once were highly concentrated in sharecropping and agricultural labor have moved up to urban service jobs or to unskilled and semi-skilled factory work and some few have moved into white-collar employment. But there has been a parallel upgrading of jobs held by whites.

---

9. *Ibid.*
10. *Hearings on S. 773, S. 1210, S. 1211 and S. 1937 Before the Subcommittee on Employment and Manpower of the Senate Committee on Labor and Public Welfare*, 88th Cong., 1st Sess. 321-88 (1963). (Hereinafter cited as *Senate Hearings*.)
11. *Id.* at 321.
12. *Id.* at 322.
13. *Ibid.*

The real question to ask, Miller states, "is whether the relative upward movement has been faster for nonwhites than for whites."[14] The past three census reports show that "although the occupational status of nonwhites relative to whites has improved for the country as a whole, in most States the nonwhite male now has about the same occupational distribution relative to the whites that he had in 1940 and 1950."[15] The results show that there were few significant changes "in the occupational distribution of nonwhite males relative to whites during the past 20 years."[16]

Moreover, during the past decade there has been no change in income differentials between whites and Negroes:

> In 1947, the median wage or salary income for nonwhite workers was 54 percent of that received by the whites. In 1962, the ratio was almost identical (55 percent). Prior to 1957 there was a substantial reduction in the earnings gap between whites and nonwhites. In view of the stability of the earnings gap during the postwar period, however, the reduction during the war years cannot be viewed as part of a continuing process, but rather as a phenomenon closely related to war-induced shortages of unskilled labor and government regulations . . . designed generally to raise the incomes of lower paid workers, and to an economy operating at full tilt.[17]

Concentration in Low Paid Occupations

Even when Negro men are educated and employed in a trade or profession, their earnings are substantially lower than those of whites.[18] More important, however, is the concentration of Negro labor "in low-paid occupations such as laborers and service workers."[19] A Negro man who has not gone beyond the eighth grade has little chance of being anything other than a laborer, porter or factory hand; 8 out of every 10 Negro men with 8 years of schooling worked as laborers, service workers, or in other unskilled jobs—compared with only 3 out of 10 whites with the same amount of schooling!

When Negro college graduates work in professional occupations they do so in almost the same proportion as white college graduates. But unlike the white graduate, they are concentrated in the lower paid professions. Moreover, the earnings of Negroes in these lower paid professions were considerably lower than whites. While 20 per cent of white college graduates were engineers, only 8 per cent of Negro college graduates in professional employment were in this profession. Fourteen per cent of white male college graduates in professional employment were lawyers or accountants, but only 6 per cent of nonwhites. And the average earnings of Negro doctors were half that received by white doctors.

---

14. *Ibid.*
15. *Ibid.*
16. *Ibid.*
17. *Id.* at 323.
18. See Tables 3-8, *Senate Hearings* 324-28.
19. *Id.* at 324.

When Negroes do the same kind of work as whites, they are paid substantially less. Miller showed that study of the lifetime earnings of white and nonwhite men by years of school completed, reveal that "the relative earnings gap between whites and nonwhites increases with educational attainment."[20]

> The lifetime earnings of nonwhite elementary school graduates is about 64 percent of the white total. Among college graduates nonwhites have only 47 percent of the white total. The fact of the matter is that the average nonwhite with 4 years of college can expect to earn less over a lifetime than the white who did not go beyond the eighth grade.[21]

In the north, the Negro with 4 years of college can expect lifetime earnings of $209,000—while the white elementary school graduate can total a lifetime earning of $198,000. In the south, where earnings are lower, the Negro college graduate can expect to earn $154,000, while the white who completed only the eighth grade can expect to earn about 8 per cent more—$167,000.

Education is clearly related to earning power, but the gains of education are not equally distributed between whites and Negroes. The average high school graduate earns more than men who quit school after the eighth grade. But the returns are far greater for whites. In most occupations, Negro men earn less than whites with the same amount of schooling. Miller notes that among "carpenters, bricklayers, factory workers, almost any occupation you turn to—there is a very substantial difference between white and nonwhite earnings."[22]

Miller's data revealed, to sum up the evidence, that improvement has resulted only because many more Negroes now live in the north in 1963 than twenty years ago. "It would be incorrect to infer from this fact," Miller pointed out, "that job opportunities in the North have improved relatively faster for Negroes than for whites."[23] Job opportunities in New York for example, "have not changed for about 20 years, according to census data."[24] The data shows that in both occupation and wages, there "has been no improvement in the economic status of Negroes relative to whites since the end of World War II."[25]

Miller concludes "that the Negro has a dual handicap. He works at far lower paid jobs than the whites and even when he works at the same kind of job he is payed far less. As a result the figures show that the Negro college graduate makes less than the white who has had only 8 years of elementary school."[26]

Concentration in Lower Income Brackets

Miller's presentation was strikingly confirmed in a recent study made by Dr. Vivian W. Henderson, professor of economics and business administration

20. *Id.* at 325.
21. *Ibid.*
22. *Senate Hearings* 379.
23. *Id.* at 375.
24. *Ibid.*
25. *Id.* at 377.
26. *Id.* at 380.

at Fisk University.[27] The issue is not whether Negroes have made any progress, but whether it has been rapid enough to enable the Negro to adjust to an economy whose rate of change is cumulative and intense and undergoing revolutionary changes in the mode of production.[28]

The truth is, as Professor Henderson points out, that "Negroes are on a treadmill and time is in reality 'running out' on them as a group, in their pursuit of parity with whites. The group has to run exceptionally fast in order to stand still."[29]

While the proportion of Negro families with incomes between $4,000 and $6,000 tripled between 1945 and 1961, 60 per cent of Negro families maintained an income of less than $4,000 annually, compared with 28 per cent of white families. Moreover, white families were abandoning the lower income bracket at a faster rate than Negro families. Conversely, Negro families reached the higher brackets at a much slower rate than white families.

Seventy-five per cent of Negro families have incomes lower than $5,981, the medium income for white families. In 1960, the wage and salary income of Negro males was only three-fifths of that earned by white males—the same proportion as existed in 1955. Dr. Henderson states:

> Two characteristics stand out. On the one hand, relative growth in wage and salary income of Negroes since 1940 has been greater than that of whites; on the other hand, the absolute, or dollar difference, has widened considerably.
> White males have stretched the "dollar gap" between their earnings and that of Negroes over three times since 1939. White families similarly have increased the differential between their employment income and that of Negro families.
> People spend and save dollars. It is this dollar difference that counts. Pronouncements regarding economic progress which are confined to acceleration concepts and percentage change obscure the real predicament—Negroes are losing ground rapidly in gaining dollar parity with whites. The "dollar gap" trend . . . means very simply that earnings are increasing for whites at a faster pace than for Negroes.[30]

The number of Negroes employed in better paying semi-skilled and white collar jobs has increased. Yet this fact is not a basis for an optimistic view of the Negro employment pattern. The rate of improvement has not closed the large differential between the Negro and white, and "in dollars and cents the position of Negroes has deteriorated."[31] Negroes have not overcome their marginal position in the work force. Negroes continue to be confined to the lowest occupational categories.

Henderson states that: "Whites are acquiring the highest paying jobs in

27. Henderson, The Economic Status of Negroes: In the Nation and in the South (1963). (Document published by Southern Regional Council, Atlanta.)
28. *Id.* at 9.
29. *Id.* at 11.
30. *Id.* at 13.
31. *Ibid.*

the higher occupational classifications. The benefits of general economic expansion and technology, therefore, have only 'trickled down' to the Negroes, putting more of them into wage and salary jobs. These benefits automatically produced high acceleration in the income change, but were restricted tightly to lower occupational classifications."[32] Despite the growth in income among Negroes, their relative position has become worse. More than twice as many Negroes as whites are in the lower income brackets, and the differential continues to widen. "Accordingly," states Henderson, "it .is still difficult for Negroes to purchase health, education, and the amenities of life on the same level as other members of the population."[33]

Adverse Effect of Changes in Labor Market Requirements

The nature of the profound changes in technology and manpower requirements suggest that Negroes can no longer depend upon national economic expansion to generate improvements in employment opportunity. Technology has changed in a most fundamental sense the kind of manpower needed by the American economy. The need for unskilled labor has drastically declined—while highly skilled labor in a variety of crafts finds more employment. The very slow pace of manpower change and development among Negroes means that the colored worker is in an unfavorable position in relation to the requirements of the labor market. Between 1947 and 1961, the number of employees in mining, manufacturing, contract construction and agriculture decreased, while the number in wholesaling, insurance and service industries increased. "Noteworthy," warns Dr. Henderson, "is the fact that the industries with a declining rate of employment are the industries which have absorbed Negroes."[34] The source of Negro "improvement" in the past has been the movement out of agriculture and into mining, manufacturing and construction where unskilled and semi-skilled jobs as laborers and operatives were once plentiful. "These are the industries which since 1957 have had either declining employment or relatively little growth. Excluding government, the areas of growth in employment are not the areas in which Negroes have traditionally found employment."[35]

At the same time, there has been a shift from plant to office in manufacturing industries. Between 1950 and 1961, the number of persons employed in manufacturing increased by over 1 million while the number of production workers declined by almost one-half million. "This means that increases in manufacturing employment were in nonplant and nonproduction jobs, a shift . . . to office work and white collar jobs, areas of employment which have never absorbed many Negroes."[36] Automation means there will be a further sharp decline in the need for semi-skilled and unskilled workers. "It will, therefore,

---

32. *Ibid.*
33. *Id.* at 25.
34. *Id.* at 16.
35. *Ibid.*
36. *Ibid.*

become increasingly difficult for Negroes to attain higher or retain previous levels of employment in those occupations and industries which they had penetrated during the 1940's and 1950's."[37]

Data analyzed by Harold Baron confirms that the Negro is especially vulnerable to technological displacement and long term unemployment. The rate of Negro unemployment is more than twice that of white, and in heavily industrialized areas the differential is significantly larger.

Baron writing of Chicago, states that:

> From 1947 to 1957, long-term unemployment (fifteen weeks to six months) remained about 10 percent of total unemployment; very long-term unemployment (six months or over) varied in the neighborhood of 8 percent of the total. From 1957 to 1962, long-term unemployment rose by 100 percent and very long-term unemployment by almost 150 percent. While nonwhites comprise 20 percent of the unemployed, they comprise 26 percent of the long-term unemployed and 28 percent of the very long-term unemployed; and these proportions have been increasing in recent years."[38]

In 1960-1961 in Chicago, where 813,000 Negroes constitute 23 per cent of the population, there were 320,000 Negroes in the city's labor force—20 per cent of the total labor force—but Negroes made up 43 per cent of Chicago's unemployed. The Negro unemployment rate was 11.5 per cent, or to put it simply, one out of every nine Negroes was out of a job. The white unemployed comprised only 3.5 per cent of the labor force, showing that Negro unemployment is four times as great as white unemployment. If one adds to this figure those who would be in the labor market if they thought they could obtain a job, Baron adds a total of 12,000 "discouraged" Negro workers and concludes that Negro workers in Chicago are more than half the unemployed in the city. He writes:

> Using a social definition of unemployment which includes the discouraged workers, we arrive at an adjusted 1960 unemployment rate for nonwhite males of 16 percent. When the estimate is made on the basis of data for the metropolitan area, the figure rises to 17 percent. A further adjustment for the racial differential in part-time employment would add about 1 percent to the above figures. This is hardly prosperity for the Negro community, with over one out of every six men who could be working out of a job![39]

In contrast, the white worker is relatively untouched by unemployment in Chicago. During 1960-1961, white males between the ages of 25 and 44 had an unemployment rate only of 2.2 per cent—minimal unemployment. In the Chicago Negro ghetto, as elsewhere, unemployment has become a way of life. In 31 all-Negro census tracts, the unemployment rate is over 15 per cent, while only 3 white tracts have a ratio that high. Negro unemployment in Chicago

---

37. *Ibid.*
38. Baron, *op. cit. supra* note 3, at 43.
39. *Id.* at 45.

has not changed for the better since 1950, and the concentration among Negroes has remained constant. Labor force projections indicate that there will be 450,000 more workers in Chicago's metropolitan area in 1970 than there were in 1960. One-third of these will be Negroes. Yet the trend of employment potentiality indicates that only 150,000 new positions will be created by 1970. The future indicates only the prospect of increasing long-term unemployment for the Negro wage earner.

The entire Negro community throughout the United States is today faced with a crisis of unemployment. What for the white worker has been a mild or temporary recession has become for the Negro worker a major depression. Negroes now constitute a very large part of the hard-core permanently unemployed group in American society.

As a result of automation and other technological changes in the economy, unskilled and semi-skilled job occupations are disappearing at the rate of 40,000 a week or two million a year. It is in these job classifications that there has been a disproportionate concentration and displacement of Negro workers. The economic well being of the entire Negro community is directly and adversely affected by the generations of enforced overconcentration of Negro wage earners in the unskilled and marginal sectors of the industrial economy. A continuation of this pattern will cause even greater crisis in the years to come unless fundamental and rapid changes take place in the occupational characteristics and mobility of Negro labor in the United States. Negroes may be slowly winning the broad legal and social struggles for full citizenship rights but are currently losing their battle for economic equality and job opportunity. "In 1963 there were more than 22 million nonwhites in the United States, most of whom were Negroes. Nonwhites comprised 11.7 per cent of the population, 11 per cent of the labor force, and 21 per cent of the unemployed. These stark figures serve to dramatize the disadvantaged status of Negro workers, for their disproportionately high rate of unemployment is essentially the climax of all the discriminatory forces shaping the lives of Negroes. . . ."[40] To quote the New York Times, "Unemployment of these proportions were it general, would be a national catastrophe."

III. THE OPERATIONAL APPROACH OF STATE ANTIDISCRIMINATION COMMISSIONS

Twenty-five states now have fair employment practices commissions in operation. Their domain covers 41 per cent of the Negro population in the United States. Provisions in state fair employment practice laws make it unlawful to refuse to hire, employ, bar, discharge or promote individuals because of race, creed, color or national origin. The provisions cover labor unions and employment agencies as well as employers. The commissions have the

---

40. U.S. Dep't of Labor, Manpower Report of the President and a Report on Manpower Requirements, Resources, Utilization, and Training 95 (1964).

power to receive, investigate and pass upon complaints which allege the existence of unlawful racial practices. They are empowered to hold hearings and compel attendance, secure enforcement of subpoena and production of records, and to gain and enforce such power through the state courts.

The enforceable state statutes have the following provisions in common according to Konvitz and Leskes:

> they declare discrimination in public and private employment on racial, religious, or ethnic grounds to be illegal; they authorize a state administrative agency to receive and investigate complaints; they empower the agency to eliminate, by persuasion and mediation, any discrimination found to exist; if unsuccessful in such efforts, the agency is authorized to proceed by public hearings, findings of fact and law, and cease and desist orders, which are enforceable by court decree; judicial review is available to a person claiming to be aggrieved by an agency ruling; and finally, the state agency is responsible for an educational program intended to reduce and eliminate discrimination and prejudice."[41]

On the face of it, the powers enumerated above seem to indicate that FEPC is a worthwhile mechanism for eliminating job discrimination. Early studies of the state FEP commissions, however, reveal that from their very inception, they were ineffectual agents of social change. Berger's study of the New York State Commission Against Discrimination,[42] the first state FEP agency (it became effective on July 1, 1945) revealed that in its first 18 months the Commission found insufficient evidence to uphold 57 per cent of the complaints filed. In 1947, SCAD found no evidence of discriminatory practice in 62 per cent of cases filed, in 1948 in 72 per cent, in 1949 in 63 per cent and in 1950 in 68 per cent. "The Commission itself," Berger wrote, "does not present the data in precisely this way and has not commented on the large proportion of complaints (65 percent) in which it found insufficient evidence to support the specific charge of discrimination, and the small proportion of cases (25 percent) in which it did sustain the complainants's claim."[43]

Berger pointed out that SCAD's disposition of complaint cases was not likely to encourage other workers to file complaints. Regardless of whether or not SCAD was able to rule in any other way than against the 65 per cent of complainants who charged discrimination, "when two out of three complainants find their charges not sustained . . . it is probable that few workers come away from an experience with SCAD in a mood to recommend the same procedure to their friends among minority groups."[44]

Moreover, the length of time it takes to settle a case is a discouraging factor to potential complainants. To the end of 1947, the average time required to dispose of a case was three months. Berger states that, "This is

41. Konvitz and Leskes, A Century of Civil Rights 203 (1961).
42. Hereinafter cited as SCAD.
43. Berger, Equality by Statute 128-29 (1952).
44. *Id.* at 135.

33

obviously too long a period to be effective for a worker who has experienced discrimination, since it is not likely that he can afford to remain unemployed for more than a few weeks while his complaint is being handled. If many weeks go by and the Commission has not yet come to a decision, the worker [who has experienced discrimination] probably has to get another job. When he does, the chances are he is no longer interested in the one where he experienced the discrimination."[45] SCAD's first chairman told a United States Senate subcommittee that less than 243 persons had actually obtained jobs as a result of filing complaints with the Commission between 1945 and 1947.[46] "Such a record," Berger notes, "is not one to encourage the filing of complaints."[47]

Berger is critical of three months as being "too long a period" for the disposition of a complaint, but recently in New York state important cases have been filed which have taken a year or two or more to resolve.

On September 27, 1962, Harold Mitchell, a member of the NAACP branch in Spring Valley, New York, filed a complaint against Local 373 of the AFL-CIO Plumbers Union in Rockland county with the State Commission for Human Rights (previously SCAD). The union, he alleged, had forced him out of a job he had held for more than 10 years with the R&S Plumbers and Mechanical Systems Company, after the Plumbers Union had entered into a collective bargaining agreement with his employer, and they refused to admit him into membership. Mr. Mitchell also charged that the union was "lily white" in its membership and had never admitted a Negro into the Union-controlled apprenticeship program. On February 21, 1964, the New York State Commission handed down an order requiring re-employment of Mr. Mitchell, payment of some back wages and admittance into the union.[48] *Seventeen months after the filing of the complaint, the Commission issued its determination.* (The significance of this important decision will be discussed below.)

On April 4, 1961, a complaint was filed against Local 10 of the International Ladies Garment Workers Union with the New York State Commission for Human Rights. On May 18, 1963, *25 months later in the case of Ernest Holmes, a Negro worker,*[49] the ILGWU entered into a stipulation upon which the complaint was finally withdrawn. In the agreement obtained by the Commission the union agreed to admit Holmes into the Cutter's local of the ILGWU, to assist him in seeking employment and in gaining training experience as an apprentice cutter.

This is precisely what the State Commission had ordered the ILGWU to do a year before when a finding of "probable cause" was issued by the investigating commissioner. I quote from *The New York Times*, July 2, 1962, in a report headlined "Union Told to Get Job For A Negro":

---

45. *Ibid.*
46. *Id.* at 136.
47. *Ibid.*
48. Mitchell v. R & S Plumbers & Mechanical Systems, Inc., C-9092-62 (N.Y. State Comm'n for Human Rights, 1964).
49. Holmes v. Falikman, C-7580-61 (N.Y. State Comm'n for Human Rights, 1963).

A garment cutters' union has been ordered by the State Commission for Human Rights to arrange for employment of a Negro at union rates commensurate with his skill and to admit the Negro into union membership if his work is satisfactory.

The *Times* story also states "With regard to the union, the decision found that 'the evidence raises serious doubt as to its good faith to comply with the State Law Against Discrimination in the matter of this complaint; and that there was "probable cause" to credit the allegations of the complaint.' "

On September 14, 1962, Rupert Ruiz, Investigating Commissioner, New York State Commission for Human Rights, in a letter to Emil Schlesinger, Attorney for Local 10, stated that the Commission had "repeatedly requested and for a period of eight months tried to obtain data pertinent to a resolution of the charges of discrimination against Amalgamated Ladies Garment Cutters Union—Local 10. These efforts were unsuccessful. The failure of representatives of that local to cooperate in the investigation despite their promises to do so, left me no alternative but to find 'probable cause to credit the allegations of the complaint.' " However, eight more months were to elapse before the Commission finally acted to secure enforcement of the law.

It is of some significance to note that this was not the first encounter by the ILGWU with the New York state antidiscrimination agency. In 1946, an action was brought by a Negro member of Local 22 who was barred from higher paying jobs controlled by Local 89, an Italian local.[50] After the Commission called the union's attention to relevant portions of the state antidiscrimination law and informed the ILGWU that the existence of nationality locals was a violation of the statute, a conference was held on January 22, 1947, at the offices of the State Commission Against Discrimination in New York City. Frederick Umhey, Executive Secretary of the ILGWU represented the union and Commissioner Caroline K. Simon, the State Commission. The ILGWU entered into an agreement with the Commission that it would not bar Negroes, Spanish-speaking or other persons from membership in the all-Italian locals. Today, eighteen years later, not a single Negro or Spanish-speaking person holds membership in the two Italian locals which have control of some of the highest paying jobs in the industry and no action has been taken to comply with the state law forbidding such practices. These cases are important because the garment industry is the major manufacturing industry in New York City and of great importance in the economy of the entire state.[51]

In its early years, SCAD relied on the technique of conference, conciliation and education as the basic approach in ending employment discrimination. The

50. Hunter v. Sullivan Dress Shop, C-1439-46 (N.Y. State Comm'n Against Discrimination 1947).
51. For a documentation of the status of nonwhite workers in the ladies garment industry in New York City and in the ILGWU see Herbert Hill, Testimony Before the House Committee on Education and Labor, 88th Cong., 1st Sess. 1569-72 (1963); see also Hill, *The ILGWU, Fact and Fiction*, 2 New Politics 7-27 (1962).

Commission anticipated danger in utilizing the threat of punitive measures, and therefore sought only voluntary compliance. The Commission resisted the demands of those who sought pressure to enforce compliance and frequently claimed that the alternative to its timid approach was to administer the law in an atmosphere of hostility and conflict. It presented an either/or alternative of conciliation or conflict, disregarding that a possible middle path between conciliation and harshness could be achieved. The Commission was extremely reluctant to enter into public hearings or to issue cease and desist orders because of the fear that employer and labor union opposition would then increase resistance to SCAD's conciliatory efforts. By the end of 1950, SCAD had only twice invoked its powers beyond the conciliation stage.[52] In its early years, SCAD handled complaints which were very few in number compared to the established pattern of employment discrimination. This evidently suited the overly cautious administrators of the Commission, who were apparently concerned that frequent processing of many cases would produce hostility. Thus, Berger concluded, SCAD carried a very small caseload and took too long to settle complaints.[53]

Louis Ruchames of Smith College reached similar conclusions. Absence of the issuance of cease and desist orders was described by Ruchames as "symptomatic of a weakness in the commission's policy." SCAD gained the reputation of being willing to settle for less than full compliance with the law. Employers would be likely to continue discriminatory practices if they knew that doing so did not involve any penalty or other difficulty, but merely entailed a promise to obey the law in the future or at worse suffer the adjustment of an individual compliant. "This has created in the minds of many of New York's citizens the impression that it is possible to evade the law and that the filing of a complaint with the Commission will not necessarily bring satisfaction to the complainant."[54]

In 1951, SCAD declared that settlement of cases involving discrimination in hiring did not entail compulsory hiring of the complainant at once or at the next available opportunity. SCAD felt even less impelled to demand partial or complete back pay from an employer who was found guilty of discriminatory practices. Its main function seemed to be the promotion of an "educational message" rather than the satisfactory settlement of complaints based upon enforcement of the law. That weakness was aggravated by the small number of complaints which the agency found to be valid. Either many complaints filed with the commission are weak—an assertion that can only be questioned because the existence of widespread discriminatory employment patterns is sustained by ample data—or the standards of adequate evidence required by the Commission are too severe and unrealistic. "In either case," commented Ruch-

---

52. Berger, *op. cit. supra* note 43, at 117.
53. *Id.* at 127, 133.
54. Ruchames, Race, Jobs, & Politics 173 (1953).

ames, "its rejection of two thirds or almost three fourths of all complaints is hardly calculated to increase its stature in the eyes of the average worker."[55]

SCAD's policies contributed to the impression that it accomplished little, that its scrutiny is easily evaded, and that individuals filing complaints are not likely to emerge with any gain. The result is that only a small number of complaints are filed each year, "far smaller than prevailing discriminatory practice would seem to call forth."[56] In 1949 there were 315 verified complaints, 257 in 1950 and 243 in 1951. It is the number of complaints filed and the extent and rapidity of enforcement that determines the law's effectiveness. "As a result of the current small number of complaints being received," Ruchames concluded, ". . . and the fact that they do not reflect existing discriminatory practices, the commission's efforts must ultimately prove inadequate."[57]

IV. FEPC ADMINISTRATORS SPEAK

Information given by FEPC administrators and others involved in the operation of state commissions indicates that the criticisms advanced by Berger and Ruchames more than a decade ago remain quite valid. Mr. Walter H. Wheeler, Jr., Chairman of the Board of the Pitney Bowes Company of Stamford, unintentionally demonstrated one of the major causes of the ineffectiveness of the state FEPC. Mr. Wheeler's Company, a medium-size office equipment manufacturing concern, cooperated fully with the Connecticut State FEP Commission after it was created in 1947 and has publicly supported the concept of FEP legislation. The Connecticut Commission has the power to initiate complaints, order public hearings, issue cease and desist orders and petition courts for enforcement of its orders if it becomes necessary. Yet, as Wheeler testified before the Senate Hearings on Equal Employment Opportunity in 1963, "the Commission has had to order hearings in only three instances in 16 years."[58] According to the Commission's Reports, 1,137 complaints had been processed in 16 years and 48 per cent of these were found to be valid. All of these were adjusted by conciliation. Forty-four per cent were dismissed for insufficient evidence, and the remaining 8 per cent had been withdrawn.

The Connecticut FEPC "has used its 'big stick' scarcely at all," Wheeler commented, but the knowledge that it does exist has "undoubtedly helped obtain employment for many victims of prejudice." Wheeler acknowledged that the Commission does not pretend to control all employment discrimination, but that its activities are "educational weapons" and are backed by legal compulsion when no other course is open. Wheeler felt the Commission was effective because employers experienced "little or nothing in the way of new personnel

---

55. *Id.* at 175.
56. *Ibid.*
57. *Ibid.* Significant changes in the operation of the N.Y. State Commission, together with important recent decisions, are noted below.
58. *Senate Hearings* 210. Mr. Wheeler's statement may be found on pp. 208-11. Other testimony referred to in this section was presented at the same Senate hearings.

problems because of the law, and that none of the dreadful happenings predicted to take place by opponents of FEP had occurred."

Wheeler's conclusions sustain Ruchames' observation that the very high percentage of complaints rejected by state commissions was responsible for the minimal opposition to such laws. Ruchames states that in 1948 New York's SCAD had reported that its efforts proved "beyond the preadventure of a doubt that such a law can be administered without confusion, recrimination . . . and without threat to the stability and order of business enterprise." It is evident that state commissions are much too concerned with avoiding hostility from businessmen, too careful to refrain from interfering with the stability of manufacturing enterprise or union power, and insufficiently concerned with the welfare of the Negro job seeker.

Wheeler, by saying that "no dramatic upheaval has followed the enactment of FEP legislation in Connecticut," has testified to the fact that the Commission has really succeeded in changing little or nothing. Applications for new employment by Negroes have not increased substantially nor "has [the businessman] been forced to spend the best part of his time in court as an alternative to hiring every minority group member who presents himself for employment . . . He is not hounded unjustly, as evidenced by the fact that discrimination actually has been found in about half the cases investigated." This, however, is exactly the fact which reveals how little the Commission has accomplished. Although under the statute the Connecticut Commission is empowered to initiate complaints and in 1953 the Supreme Court of Connecticut sustained the Commission's authority to issue enforceable cease and desist orders, the Commission has consistently refrained from using these powers.[59]

Moreover, the data cited earlier by Herman Miller show that the occupational status of Negroes in Connecticut has not changed appreciably since 1940.

The testimony of Mr. Wheeler reveals the inadequacy of FEPC to deal with the broad patterns of employment discrimination as stated by an employer who advocates the creation of these Commissions. In fact, Mr. Wheeler cites with approval the fact that "no employer need maintain any sort of percentage or ratio of minority group employees within his organization." But what is the criteria used to determine compliance with the state antidiscrimination law? This is not indicated. Thus, an employer may often feel his company is abiding by a nondiscriminatory policy if the Commission's poster is exhibited and one or two Negroes are employed. Actually, Mr. Wheeler has inadvertently focused on the real problem—the fact that FEPC in Connecticut and elsewhere is not meant to change the Negro occupational pattern by widespread and fundamental changes in racial employment practices.

Edward Howden, Executive Officer of the California Fair Employment

59. Int'l Brotherhood of Electrical Workers v. Comm'n on Civil Rights, 140 Conn. 537, 102 A.2d 366 (1953). In this case the Supreme Court of Errors of Connecticut protected the job rights of Negro workers by sustaining a cease and desist order against the IBEW.

Practice Commission revealed other limitations inherent in state FEP commissions during his testimony at the Senate Hearings. The compliance program which stems from receipt of miscellaneous individual complaints is a piecemeal, "wholly inadequate method of operation," he stated. There is no correlation between the existence of restrictive practices and the filing of complaints, Howden admitted; and an FEP agency is often "obliged to close its eye to practices which flout the law."[60]

Howden was pleased that his own Commission was entitled to undertake and initiate investigations—but his own testimony showed a dependence on what he termed an "atmosphere of confidence and good will, with full protection of the rights of all parties."[61] Howden denied any "punitive" aim to FEPC, and noted that in only "a handful of cases" was it necessary to move beyond conciliation and persuasion to the evidently forceful procedure of a "formal public hearing." Mr. Howden seemed more concerned with attainment of a proper educational environment than with the full use of commission powers to gain new jobs for Negro workers. Rather than operate as a policing and enforcing agency as Mr. Howden put it, FEPC is a service institution, "assisting those who provide employment and those previously denied equal access to jobs to find each other." But the evidence proves that the two parties have not met, and that the responsibility for law enforcement should not depend upon the Negro complainant. It is no wonder that FEPC is inadequate to eliminate broad patterns of job discrimination, since the California Commission undertook corrective action in only one-third of the cases submitted to it. It is perhaps well for Mr. Howden to talk of the educational process which "flows freely" as a by-product of handling a case, but the process has meant little if anything for the Negro worker in California.[62]

The General Counsel of the New York State Commission, Henry Spitz, asserted in his testimony at the Senate hearings, that job discrimination, while still existing in New York, was being eliminated due to administrative application of the state anti-discrimination law's educational and regulatory procedures. Yet Spitz's testimony revealed that the New York Commission has a very limited record of achievement, although by contrast with other state FEP agencies, it appears far better than most. From July 1, 1945, when the Commission went into effect, through December 31, 1962—7,725 verified complaints were filed alleging discrimination in employment. Of these, 4,198 were dismissed by the Commission for lack of jurisdiction or lack of probable cause. In 1,620 cases, no cause was found as to the specific complaint, but other discriminatory practices or patterns were found and adjusted. Throughout these years only four complaints were not adjusted by conciliation and proceeded to public hearings and eventually to the issuance of cease and desist orders. Twenty-

---

60. *Senate Hearings* 231. Mr. Howden's statement may be found on pp. 227-33.
61. *Id.* at 228.
62. *Id.* at 228-29.

seven complaints ordered for public hearings were settled before the hearing date.[63]

The record of the New York State Commission fully sustains the criticisms of the early studies. The Commission evidently takes great pride in refraining from a vigorous and broad application of powers which the Commission is legally entitled to use. Its reluctance to hold public hearings and issue frequent cease and desist orders, instead of being regarded as a sign of weakness is viewed as a positive standard which supposedly justifies enactment of more FEP statutes. Spitz made clear that the Commission's preference was to resolve cases "through conference, conciliation and persuasion" although it has the power, after public hearings, to issue cease and desist orders which are enforceable through the courts. The status of Negro wage-earners in New York clearly requires a more dynamic and vigorous approach.

In Missouri, where an FEP Commission has existed only since 1961, attempts to cope with the deep and traditional pattern of employment discrimination are rather pathetic. Milton Litvak, Vice-Chairman of Missouri's Commission on Human Rights, acknowledged in his Senate testimony that "a general pattern of discrimination against Negroes"[64] exists in Missouri. This is true in public and private employment, is a common practice in labor unions, employment agencies, offices and public agencies of Missouri itself. As of July 23, 1963, the Commission had received only 45 complaints. Six were adjusted by conciliation, 11 were dismissed for no probable cause, 2 for insufficient evidence, 3 were withdrawn by the complainant, and 4 were judged to be out of the Commission's jurisdiction. Nineteen were still under investigation. Litvak frankly stated that although the Commission had "a three pronged program of education, research, and enforcement, the 'primary task' was 'education.'"

The record proves that the individual complaint approach is totally inadequate and is incapable of dealing with the fact that "the great mass of Negro workers remains in the lowest levels of employment," that few are employed in public agencies and that most Negroes occupy "unskilled or menial positions, with little jobs open and available to the general labor force." Public conferences, discussions of "human relations" and the seeking of "voluntary action between employers and labor unions" as a basis for ending the deeply entrenched pattern of job discrimination are ineffectual.

Mr. Litvak revealed that the Missouri Commission held "the general power to foster mutual understanding, eliminate discrimination, and the power to make studies and research." As a result of this power it undertook a study of civil rights in Missouri. The Commission found that 390,853 Negroes lived in Missouri out of a total population of 4 million—comprising almost 10 per cent of the population. Ninety per cent of the Negro population was found in

---

63. *Id.* at 234. Mr. Spitz's statement may be found on pp. 233-35.
64. *Id.* at 236-43.

the St. Louis-Kansas City and southeastern Missouri area. The Commission disclosed that "there was discrimination against Negroes in the entire State of Missouri in all areas and particularly employment." Mr. Litvak states that his Commission has enforcement powers under the law but he repeatedly emphasizes education and persuasion although the record indicates that they are of little value. Litvak says "I want to stress that we still consider our primary task to be education." In his testimony before the Senate Committee, Mr. Litvak produced sufficient evidence to prove that the approach of the Missouri FEPC is basically irrelevant to the problem of ending widespread job discrimination. Its basic program is education and complaint taking—a process which is extremely limited in bringing gains to the Negro community. It is no wonder that Negroes are resorting to militant mass protest in St. Louis and are increasingly engaging in public demonstrations elsewhere in Missouri, instead of filing complaints with a Commission that regards its "primary task to be education."

The truth was bluntly stated by Mr. Litvak in an exchange with Senator Joseph S. Clark of Pennsylvania. What FEPC has created, according to Litvak was "a climate or atmosphere of the idea of equal job opportunity." This did not mean, however, that Negroes would be readily hired by industry. "I would not say statistically that we have made any substantial progress," Litvak admitted, "but nonetheless we feel like we are creating this atmosphere of acceptance. . . ."[65]

This atmosphere was allegedly created in part we are told by the appointment of biracial committees to discuss public accommodation problems. Negroes, however, do not care whether FEPC administrators detect some vague atmosphere of acceptance when FEPC has not resulted in new, tangible jobs. The white liberal may have his conscience eased by talk of an atmosphere of equality, but the unemployed Negro prefers reality to psychological wish-fulfillment.

A major point to consider in the study of state antidiscrimination commissions is what the definition of "satisfactorily adjusted" really means. Data produced by the Minnesota State Commission Against Discrimination reveal that adjustment of individual complaints, often involving acquiescence in the hiring of the solitary Negro complainant, is taken as proof that the company which previously refused to hire Negroes has now eliminated its racist practices. In one case a Negro woman who applied for the position of an electrical assembler had not been hired although she had the necessary qualifications. The Minnesota State Commission's investigation found that the particular company never employed a Negro on production work and feared that the applicant would not be accepted by fellow employees. After conferring with the Commission the company agreed to offer the complainant the next position open. She was then

---

65. *Id.* at 268.

hired, and because she turned out to be a "very satisfactory employee," the commission closed the case as "satisfactorily adjusted."

According to the record, no effort was made, to determine if a total pattern of employment discrimination continued to exist. Because the company avoided difficulty by hiring the one Negro complainant this does not provide evidence that this un-named company has ended its discriminatory employment policy throughout its various operations. In fact, the granting of a "satisfactorily adjusted" determination in this case could possibly be interpreted by the company that it can continue its discriminatory policy by merely agreeing to take one or two Negro workers into a limited part of their operation. The pressure was immediately removed, because the company engaged the one complainant. This practice repeated many times over during the years is responsible for the fact that the Minnesota Commission has failed to change the occupational status of Negro workers in that state.

In yet another case, a Negro man was refused referral by an employment agency. The agency referred the man to the company and mentioned that the job applicant was a Negro. The company maintained that they did have a non-discriminatory employment policy, but feared that if a Negro were hired for this particular job there would be "trouble." The Commission found the agency to have violated the law by stating the applicant's race, and found the employer to have practiced discrimination as the applicant was not hired because he was a Negro. The Commission told the employer that since the applicant was qualified it should offer him the next available job. In the meantime, the Negro applicant had taken another job. The Commission then had the company publicly state its nondiscriminatory hiring policy, and closed the case as "satisfactorily adjusted." One wonders in what manner this solution constitutes "satisfactorily adjusted." By the Commission's own testimony, the company previously announced a nondiscriminatory policy but still refused to hire Negroes. The company was cleared by the Commission merely on the strength of the company's statement that it did not discriminate; it was not requested to hire any Negro employees.

The Commission's administrators did not concede that their efforts were relatively meaningless. James C. McDonald, director of Minnesota's SCAD, testified before the Senate hearings that it was not true that evidence existed that FEPC has been ineffective.[66] McDonald claimed that FEPC had "been of major importance." He did not present evidence to sustain his conviction. Rather, he attributed lack of knowledge of the beneficial results of FEPC to the fact that "commissions must work on cases quietly and without public knowledge."

But the Negro community and Negro civil rights organizations increasingly believe that in order to open up the job market, publicity must be given to the activities of corporations and unions which refuse to admit Negroes, and that

---

66. Mr. McDonald's statement may be found on pp. 244-252 of the *Senate Hearings*.

sharp public exposure of racist practices is essential in eliminating such policies. The practice of commission chairmen in holding quiet, secret meetings with employers and unions indicates their desire not to offend, which is apparently greater than their desire to take the most effective means possible to eradicate discriminatory hiring practices. How much more effective it would be if public hearings were held, the case laid out before the public, and pressure exerted on recalcitrant employers or unions by all interested parties. Such a publicly oriented policy would accomplish more toward ending discriminatory patterns than the friendly little discussions that often go on interminably and bring little or no tangible benefits to Negroes.

Most revealing of the actual effect of FEP legislation was the statement submitted by Governor Endicott Peabody of Massachusetts to the Senate Committee on Labor and Public Welfare.[67] By 1963, Massachusetts had a fair employment practice commission in existence for 17 years. Like the other commissions, the Massachusetts Commission Against Discrimination had not processed many complaints—only 2,819 since its inception. Only one of these had proceeded beyond the conciliation stage! The law had eliminated what Governor Peabody had called "outward signs of discrimination, "—such signs saying that Negroes need not apply. Personnel offices now had to display "at least outward courtesy" toward Negroes. Above all, the law allowed those who administered the FEP commission to undertake "effective education of employers and employees." The Governor attributed this to the enforcement provisions in the Act, which made the law effective.

Yet the Governor admitted that *"the law has not achieved the broad equality in economic status for Negroes which its supporters once envisioned."* (Emphasis added.) This criticism is perhaps the most devastating and accurate made by any state official concerned with an FEP commission's operations. And this is the result of a law which has "teeth" in it! In Massachusetts, the Governor stated, the Negro is still twice as likely to be unemployed as the white. "In Metropolitan Boston he earns 50 percent less than the average white, and even after attending college, he earns no more than the median income earned by a white person with 3 years of high school."[68]

The Governor indicated that it is hard for FEPC commissions to judge whether or not discrimination has occurred. A head count could be taken in lower ranks of employment in large companies, but when other types of jobs and professional positions were in question, such methods could not be used. Where hiring and promotional decision is accorded on a subjective basis, it is doubly hard to prove discriminatory intent. The FEP agency finds it has to judge whether the Negro applicant is qualified for the job, and whether or not he was dismissed because of race. The result is that "it is harder to be certain that the law has been broken." The law, Governor Peabody admitted, once considered a

---

67. *Senate Hearings* 281-83.
68. *Id.* at 282.

"potent remedy," had "lost some of its curative power." And many types of employment discrimination were not even reached by law.

Governor Peabody noted that elimination of open hostility to Negroes has resulted in the substitution of covert and subtle forms of discrimination—not in conversion to a real nondiscriminatory hiring policy. The astute Governor understands that "neutrality is not enough and that we must do more." It is unfortunate that the Governor does not question the operating procedures of those who administer the Massachusetts antidiscrimination law.

V. The Record of State Fair Employment Practice Commissions

By making a close examination of the records of various state fair employment practices commissions, it is possible to evaluate more fully the consequences of their past operations and to indicate the need for new policies by federal and state agencies in the future.

California

In 1959, the California state legislature enacted a fair employment practice act. From September 18, 1959, the date the new law was put into effect through December 30, 1960, 565 complaints were received. Eighty-nine per cent of these cited alleged discrimination because of race. Out of these 511 cases, 502 or 87 per cent involved discrimination against Negroes. Fifty-seven per cent of the 502 involved refusal to hire, 24 per cent dismissal from employment, 8 per cent involved refusal to upgrade, 14 per cent the withholding of employment agency referral, and 35 per cent involved union discrimination. Sixty-seven per cent of the cases charged private employers, 24 per cent cited public employers, 18 per cent, agencies, and 26 per cent named labor unions.

In 287 of the cases, or 86 per cent, the Commission was able to make a determination as to whether or not discrimination had occurred. Forty-five cases, or 14 per cent, were dismissed because of lack of jurisdiction or failure of the complainant to proceed. Only 96 cases, or 33.5 per cent of complaints filed were found to be valid and were corrected by conference and conciliation. One hundred and ninety-one cases, or 67 per cent of those filed, were dismissed because of insufficient evidence.

Of the 96 cases in which the Commission found discriminatory practice, 29 cases or 30 per cent were settled by offers of immediate hiring of the complainant. But 64 per cent involved agreements that the respondent would comply with the state law and would issue a merit employment policy and also declare an intent to cease discriminatory practices. It is quite evident that the mere issuance of a nondiscriminatory statement does not assure equal opportunity for Negroes. Twelve cases in fact were adjusted by a commitment to consider hiring or promoting the complainant at the first opportunity. Why a firm commitment was not demanded in the specific case before the Commission is not explained.

Records of the Commission further reveal the limited nature of FEP settlements. In one case, a Negro saleman in an automobile agency was finally granted the opportunity to sell on the floor and thereby earn higher commissions. The Commission noted that the salesman was re-instated, given equal floor time, and his performance was evaluated after 90 days. It was found he had the third best sales record on the floor. The Commission concludes that equal opportunity led to rising sales and thereby showed the company that they too would profit by a nondiscriminatory policy. One asks whether the Negro salesman would have the right to make a low sales record on some weeks, and if he had, whether he then would have been dismissed. The Commission acknowledges that a city-wide check found that only six Negro salesmen were allowed to sell cars on the floor. No effort was made to provide the same right for other Negro salesmen in other automobile agencies. (During March 1964, 102 persons were arrested in the course of mass demonstrations organized by the local branch of the NAACP, at the General Motor Showrooms in San Francisco. On April 11, 226 persons again were arrested during demonstrations at auto showrooms.)

In another case, a young Negro was rejected after trying to file a job application with gas stations of a large oil company. The Commission learned that the company's standing policy was to accept applications from all potential employees. The firm's 36 stations in the area had 180 attendants, but not one was Negro. The FEP Commission persuaded the company to accept the complainant's application, evaluate it, and hire the respondent if he were qualified. "His qualifications were better than average," it noted, "and he got the job." This is what the Negro community today regards as token integration—the granting of one job to a highly qualified Negro, and is not acceptable as such, but is regarded by the California FEPC as proof of successful adjustment—although the Commission itself admits that the company has no other Negro employees. That such token standards are accepted as progress further indicates that the traditional approach of FEPC is obsolete and that the statute is not enforced in a manner that would make possible the fullest gains for nonwhite workers under the law.[69]

The rather anxious desire to appease business concerns that are guilty of discriminatory employment practices rather than to use all available powers to open new job opportunities for Negroes is attested to by the attitude of Commission executives. John Anson Ford, California FEP Commission Chairman, emphasized that its work is accomplished mainly by conference, conciliation, education and persuasion. "We have never yet had to invoke the enforcement power provided by the law," he commented. Ford, in a press release aimed at gathering support for FEP emphasized that "our sincere attempt to find the facts is shown by the number of cases—well over half—which have been closed

69. 1959-1960 Cal. F.E.P.C. Ann. Rep. 9-10, 19-27, 31-34.

on the basis of 'insufficient evidence' or 'no evidence' of discrimination."[70] The fact that the Commission has ruled against defendants in only approximately half the cases filed is not a record of which to be proud, especially when it is admitted that the entire number of complaints filed does not adequately indicate the serious extent of racial discrimination. Even if one claims that the Commission could not have ruled in any other manner in these cases, the decisions are geared to gain the confidence of the business and trade union community and the scorn of the Negro worker.

The Commission has chosen to answer conservative critics by claiming that FEPC action will not really alter the status quo. This tactic succeeds in placating the business interests that originally opposed FEPC, but it also reveals the actual character of FEPC to the Negro worker and his community. Thus there should be no cause to wonder at increasing Negro disillusionment with antidiscrimination commissions and the frequent recourse to direct mass action.

By 1961-1962, in California, 1,321 employment cases had been completed and closed by the Commission. One hundred and eighteen cases were dismissed for being outside the Commission's jurisdiction, and 414 were corrected after discriminatory practices were found. Seven hundred and eighty-seven cases however were closed for insufficient evidence or no evidence of discrimination. Three public hearings were held for respondents who did not make what the Commission accepted as a satisfactory settlement. But the courts set aside Commission orders in two cases and the third was pending at the end of the year.[71]

The FEP Commission in California takes it as a strong point that public disclosure of the identity of a respondent is prohibited on the assumption that this protects the accused against implications of guilt and might impair settlement efforts during the conciliation process. I believe that disclosure would facilitate reaching the goal of eliminating discrimination if this were the sole purpose of the Commission. The public would be able to exert pressure upon discriminatory company and union practices and also to judge whether the FEP Commission was an effective agent of social change.

Events occurring in March and April of 1964 reveal that extra-legal militant action for jobs has been more successful in attacking overt employment discrimination in some areas than the years of FEPC operations in California. On March 6 and 7, 1964, 1000 demonstrators picketed the Sheraton-Palace Hotel in San Francisco, and demanded that the hotel honor its avowed equal opportunity policy and hire 15 to 20 per cent of its total staff from the Negro and Mexican population in the area. At first representatives of the Hotel Employers' Association refused to negotiate with "irresponsible" groups and claimed that their hotels had always had an "equal opportunity" policy. But when 135

70. Cal. Dep't of Industrial Relations, Div. of Fair Employment Practices, *News from FEPC* (April 29, 1962).
71. Cal. Dep't of Industrial Relations, 1961-1962 Employment Relations Agency Biennial Rep., *Fair Employment Practices* 15-16.

persons staged a sit-in during the midst of the evening hours and when the demonstrators let it be known that the mass demonstrations would continue, the Hotel Employers agreed to the demands of the civil rights organizations.

A two-year agreement was signed in which the civil rights groups pledged to halt demonstrations, and the hotels agreed to refrain from pressing charges against those arrested, and further they agreed to hire the same percentage of Negroes as demanded before July 20th of the same year.[72]

The two-day demonstrations forced the hotels, which previously denied the existence of discriminatory employment practices to change the previous standard of judgment, by recognizing that the small percentage of Negroes they had hired in the past was not sufficient proof that they actually had a nondiscriminatory policy. The method used by the FEP Commission—that of judging intent and evaluating individual complaints—was also proven to be useless in changing the discriminatory practices of the Hotel Employers' Association. The standards used by the FEPC Commission in fact were virtually the same as those employed by the Hotel Association. Negroes in California will increasingly engage in mass action and participation in the militant Negro civil rights movement to effect significant change in the racial situation—with or without FEPC.

Massachusetts

The record of the Massachusetts Commission Against Discrimination is a dismal one especially since the Massachusetts Commission is one of the oldest in years of operation and is given extensive powers under the statute, powers which it uses only very rarely. Thus, like many other state FEP commissions, it can not be regarded as a law enforcement agency. The Massachusetts Commission has been in existence since 1946 and has the authority to initiate investigations and to invoke its compliance procedures without the filing of complaints by aggrieved persons in instances where "trouble is manifest and can be traced to race." Conciliation and conferences are used in these investigations, but in 15 years, only 5 cases were brought to the stage of public hearing from the Massachusetts FEP docket. From November 10, 1946 to December 31, 1961, 2,149 complaints were initiated and received. Of these, 722 were dismissed for lack of probable cause, 76 for lack of jurisdiction, and 101 were withdrawn by complainants. The Commission found evidence of discriminatory practices in 1,186 cases, and closed them as satisfactorily adjusted. The Commission initiated 864 cases; 847 of these were closed after conciliation.[73]

Although the Commission found probable cause of discrimination in 1,186 cases, the reasons why Governor Peabody found that the Commission did not eliminate employment discrimination is quite clear after an examination of some typical cases which were "settled."

In an employment case, a Negro just recently discharged from the Air

---

72. The New York Times, March 8, 1964 § 1, p. 53.
73. 16 Mass. Comm'n Against Discrimination Ann. Rep. 35 (1961).

Force applied for a position as an IBM tabulator operator. Although he had been trained to operate the 407 tabulator and had successfully completed seven courses of study in IBM machine operation, he was not hired. The company claimed that it did not hire him because he did not have enough experience, but then decided that he would qualify for another lessor position and hired him.[74] No information was gathered as to how many Negroes are employed by the company, or what is the occupational distribution of nonwhites, nor is such information used as a basis of determining discriminatory intent. The employment of the individual Negro complainant by the company in a position lower than that for which he applied and had been trained, evidently provided enough justification for the state FEP Commission to close the case. In my opinion this is not adequate.

In another case, a complainant declared that she had not been hired because she was Negro. The Commission found that the company employed 75 people and that only one employee was colored. It was determined that three white women had been hired two days after the Negro complainant applied for the job. Hence the Commission asked the company to hire the Negro applicant, and "the complainant was given the next vacancy as a means of conciliating the matter."[75] By agreeing to hire the Negro complainant, after having been caught in a clear example of discriminatory racial practices, the company avoided the shame of exposure in a public hearing and the possibility of facing a court enforcement order. The Commission, however, made no effort to inquire how many other Negro applicants may have applied for a job and been refused. It made no recommendation that the company basically alter its racial employment practices nor did it determine that the hiring of two Negroes did not constitute compliance with the state anti-discrimination law. Because the data show that unemployment is much higher for the Negro than for the white worker in Massachusetts, the possibility exists that other Negroes might have applied and been turned down by the same company. It is also possible that many Negro applicants felt a sense of futility in filing a formal complaint with the Massachusetts Commission. Yet the Commission made no attempt to have the company publicly pledge to hire all qualified Negro applicants in the future—and to affirmatively seek and train Negroes in an effort to remedy and compensate for its previous record of discriminatory racial practices.

In yet another case, the Commission revealed that some investigations took longer than one year, a period quite long, so that a worker in need of employment is not able to wait for the verdict of the Commission. A Negro applicant had been interviewed by a company and was advised by the personnel department to try and find employment elsewhere. After applying two more times for a job, the Negro complainant charged the company with unlawful discrimination because of race. Investigation by the MCAD revealed that the company's em-

---

74. 15 Mass. Comm'n Against Discrimination Ann. Rep. 4-5 (1959-1960).
75. 17 Mass. Comm'n Against Discrimination Ann. Rep. 5 (1962).

ployees were "numbered in the hundreds" and that although "there were colored persons living in the same community and surrounding areas, none was employed." The particular Negro applicant had applied for a production job, a category in which the yearly turnover amounted to 6 per cent. Two hundred applications for production positions were on file with the company, but the personnel director said that few Negroes applied for employment. Investigation of the company's files revealed that the Negro applicant's card was distinctly marked to separate it from the others, and was dated three months after the actual date of application.

Two months after the Negro applicant first applied, when the MCAD began investigation, 130 persons were hired. Ninety-two of these were new employees. The company adamantly denied that the Negro applicant had been discriminated against because of her race. Yet the MCAD noted that its file showed that "no Negroes were employed despite information" and that "a few had applied." MCAD had the company give another test and interview to the applicant, upon completion of which her application was put into the active file. In the meantime, the Negro complainant took another job and notified the MCAD that she was no longer interested in working for the respondent company. In this case, where the MCAD took into consideration the fact that many other Negroes were unemployed in the nearby area and that some *had* applied for jobs, the Commission evidently dropped the case upon receipt of the information that the particular complainant had taken another job. The fact that a most clear discriminatory pattern existed throughout this company's operations did not lead the MCAD to take the necessary action obviously indicated by all the available evidence.[76]

New Jersey

Other state commissions reveal a similar potential of unused powers. New Jersey's Division Against Discrimination reports that "monumental" tasks still have to be accomplished. In the period from July, 1957 to June 30, 1958, the New Jersey Commission investigated 123 employment cases. Out of this number only 53 cases were adjusted and declared to be based upon valid complaints. Fifty-nine per cent of cases registered were dismissed.[77]

In one case, Puerto Rican workers complained of discriminatory working conditions and charged their union with failing to give them proper protection and representation. Fifty-five per cent of the workers in the shop were Puerto Ricans. The union responded by accusing the Puerto Rican workers of holding anti-union attitudes. The Commission settled the grievance by arranging conferences between the Puerto Rican workers, the union leadership and employer representatives. The union agreed to promote better communication with the workers and to print material in both English and Spanish. The Puerto Rican

---

76. 11 Mass. Comm'n Against Discrimination Ann. Rep. 8-9 (1955-1956).
77. 1957-1958 N.J. Dep't of Education, Div. Against Discrimination Ann. Rep. 12-13.

leaders agreed "to place greater emphasis on the understanding and acceptance of responsibility to the union."[78]

The manner in which the case is described in the Commission's *Annual Report* for 1958 supports a rather idyllic view of how the Commission restores harmony and prevents tension from erupting. Yet, the report shows only that Puerto Rican workers, angry at their union's refusal to represent their interest, were forced to stop their protest and accept the judgment of the union leadership. No evidence is presented to enable the reader to learn the nature and accuracy of the Puerto Rican workers' charge against the union and no reasons are offered as to why the workers should accept the position of the union's leadership and stop their protest. Especially suspect is the involvement of the employers in a case where workers protest the collusion of the union with the employer against the workers' interests.

Like other state commissions, New Jersey's takes pride in the fact that the majority of cases are resolved in a "satisfactory" manner without resort to holding formal hearings and that the law enjoins the commission to use conference, conciliation and persuasion before resorting to legal sanctions. Yet from July 1, 1950 through June 30, 1953, out of 201 employment complaints which were investigated, 110 were dismissed for no probable cause, 9 others were dismissed for other reasons, and only 82 were judged to be valid and then adjusted. Over 54.7 per cent of complaints filed were found to be invalid.[79]

Other cases brought before the New Jersey Commission indicate the Commission's inability to deal with problems arising from the low occupational status of the Negro worker. A group of Negro workers complained about a company's discriminatory discharge policy. The men were dismissed in accordance with union seniority agreements and in the light of production requirements. But in this plant, only the Negro workers, who constituted less than 20 per cent of all employees, were dismissed. This occurred because there was in effect a plantwide system of segregation in which Negro workers were restricted to certain menial and unskilled jobs. Segregation was thus declared by the Commission to be discriminatory in intent and result, and the company had to give evidence that it would abandon such practices and rehire the Negro workers "whose skills permitted employment in other processes."[80] In this case, Negro workers were actually displaced because of technological innovation. But their vulnerability as a group to job loss was a direct result of racial discrimination, *i.e.*, they were segregated in all-Negro job classifications and limited to menial and unskilled occupations. Thus a disproportionate displacement of Negroes occurred as a result of their disproportionate concentration in unskilled jobs with no promotion rights. The State Commission was unable to cope with the "legal" explanation invoked to justify the mass dismissal of the Negro workers. Increasingly, Negro workers are experiencing large scale dismissals especially in the mass

---

78. *Id.* at 14.
79. 1951-1953 N.J. Dep't of Education, Div. Against Discrimination Biennial Rep. 4.
80. *Ibid.*

production industries as a result of automation and other technological change; state FEP commissions are impotent to deal with this very serious problem.

Minnesota

Another state commission which shows a poor record is the Minnesota Commission. This body has been in existence since 1955, but in seven years of operation it has handled only 205 cases through 1962. Of these, 136 dealt with employment discrimination. Out of the total of 205 cases, 81 were dismissed for no probable cause, 9 for lack of jurisdiction, 3 were withdrawn by the complainants, 4 were dismissed for insufficient evidence and only 32 were judged to be valid and then adjusted. If conciliation is found to be unsuccessful in Minnesota, the Commission may ask the Governor to appoint a three member hearing body from a 12 man Board of Review. This Board may then hold a public hearing, and determine whether an unfair discriminatory practice does exist. If it finds this is the case, the Board may then issue a cease and desist order. This absurd and unwieldy procedure is clearly unsuited to meaningful action against recalcitrant companies and labor unions and certainly explains the very small number of complaints filed with the Commission.[81]

However, even when cases are brought before the Minnesota agency, there is evidence to show a general reluctance on the part of the Commission to take affirmative action. In one case, a Negro woman had applied for the position of airline stewardess and had been rejected. The Commission took four years to complete the investigation, at which time they recommended that the case be held over pending further investigation.

In another case, a Negro man was not hired as a salesman by a department store in a small Minnesota community. The local manager informed the Commission that he believed company policy forbade the hiring of Negroes. The company stated that this interpretation was not correct and proceeded to inform all local managers of the company's nondiscriminatory hiring policy. This affirmation of a nondiscriminatory policy was evidently enough to settle the case, although the firm had still not hired a Negro. No investigation was made to determine how many Negroes, if any, were employed in the future with this firm.[82]

The Minnesota Commission stated that it is aware that the pattern of complaints filed does not indicate the actual pattern of discrimination. Actually most people seek employment where they know that they have a chance to be hired. Firms which do not have Negro employees may seldom get an application from one. The FEP commission may be the least likely agency to receive complaints based upon attempts to gain jobs in these firms. "Thus, the Commission is least likely to receive complaints against the very firms, industries, unions and employment agencies which may be most discriminatory in their employment

81. 7 Minn. Comm'n Against Discrimination Ann. Rep. 1-9 (1962).
82. *Id.* at 4-5.

practices."[83] Minnesota proposes an "educational" program as an answer. But we already know that this approach has become quite meaningless and that much more than education is necessary.

Minnesota, in fact, seems to rely to such a great degree on so-called "education and persuasion" to resolve complaints that requests for Review Board hearings are seldom made. In 1956, one case was not "settled" during the process described as "education and persuasion" and a hearing was requested. But this action "was not taken until after the Commission had tried unsuccessfully for fourteen months to secure a satisfactory adjustment of the complaint through the process of conference and conciliation."[84]

In another complaint, a Negro truck driver who weighed over 220 pounds was informed that he could not be employed because he was overweight. The management presented evidence to show that it was concerned about the over-all weight of men and produce on its trucks. However, the Commission was not persuaded that overweight was the real disqualifying factor, because white drivers working for the company in some cases also weighed over 200 pounds. The Commission asked that the applicant be given another test. The applicant, having obtained another job during the protracted negotiations between the Commission and the company, failed to appear. Because the company agreed to affirm a nondiscriminatory policy—although they had not hired a Negro for 6 or 7 years—the "Commission made a finding of no discrimination," and the company was asked to put the policy into practice by employing Negro drivers when the opportunity presented itself in the future. The Commission's standards, so vague and indefinite, point to the conclusion that much more is needed to clear a company, which does not hire Negroes, of the charge of discrimination than a mere promise to hire Negroes sometime in an indefinite future when and if there are job vacancies and if Negroes apply. The Commission's judgment in this case was really absurd as the Commission saw fit to accept a mere statement of alleged nondiscriminatory policy, although the company obviously employed no Negroes. Nor did the Commission take action to provide for compliance with the state law in the future.[85]

New York State—The Test of FEPC

The experience of the New York State Commission Against Discrimination, later re-named the State Commission for Human Rights, is most important to evaluate. New York was the first state to enact an FEPC law. Beginning in 1945, its Commission has had the largest staff and highest budget of all state FEP commissions. Unlike some other commissions, the New York agency does investigate discriminatory *employment patterns* and attempts to correct them.

---

83. 4 Minn. F.E.P.C. Ann. Rep. 9 (1959).
84. 2 Minn. F.E.P.C. Ann. Rep. 10 (1957).
85. 3 Minn. F.E.P.C. Ann. Rep. 7-8 (1958).

The Commission is empowered to investigate discriminatory patterns even if no individual complaint is filed. If discriminatory patterns are found to exist and the accusation is accompanied by reasonable factual support, the Commission may authorize the start of an informal investigation and may seek to remedy the discriminatory pattern through education, conciliation and persuasion. Although the Commission may not call a formal hearing in these cases, the State Industrial Commissioner or the State Attorney General may file a formal complaint with the Commission against the respondent.

In 1962, the New York State Commission received 1,171 complaints; 740 verified complaints from the previous year had not been settled, making a total of 1,911 cases under consideration. This figure represented the greatest number of complaints filed with the Commission in its 17 year history. Of these, 611 or 52.2 per cent pertained to employment. This amounted to a drop from 660 filed in 1961, a drop of 7.4 per cent. Sixty-six and two-tenths per cent of the employment complaints were based on discrimination because of race. Refusal to hire was alleged in 235 complaints (38.5 per cent of the employment complaints.) One hundred and fifty-four concerned dismissal from employment, 113 conditions and privileges of employment and 48 concerned the withholding of employment agency referral. The remaining charged refusal of union membership and other forms of labor union discrimination and pre-employment inquiries.[86]

Of the 1392 complaints closed in 1962, probable cause was found to sustain charges of discrimination in 340, or 24.4 per cent of cases filed. Another 111 cases, or 8 per cent disclosed other unlawful practice which was adjusted. Thus, in 32.4 per cent of cases closed some discriminatory practices were found and adjusted. This means, however, that in nearly 70 per cent of cases filed by complainants, no evidence of discrimination was found. The percentage of cases rejected remains close to the amount which Berger studied in 1950. In that year, Berger noted that SCAD had ruled against 65 per cent of the cases filed. It is interesting to note that in 1962 the percentage of rejected cases is very close to what it was in 1950; thus the pattern of Commission rulings does not give the Negro worker confidence in the ability of FEPC to eradicate job discrimination, that is to help solve his employment problem. Probable cause was found to sustain the allegations in only 12.3 per cent of the employment complaints, 40 per cent of public accommodation complaints, and 45.1 per cent of housing complaints.

The Commission is authorized to make informal investigations of potential discriminatory situations. Since 1945, 1,463 of these were conducted. Three hundred and six were conducted in 1962 alone; 301 of these dealt with employment discrimination.[87]

New York's FEPC record reveals that more complaints were filed with

86. 1962 N.Y. State Comm'n for Human Rights Ann. Rep. 2-4. (Mimeo ed.)
87. *Id.* at 4-5.

the Commission as the years moved on. From 1945 through 1949, 1,583 employment complaints were filed. Two hundred and fifty-six were filed in 1950, 321 in 1955, 650 in 1957, 794 in 1959 and 611 in 1962.[88] Of the 611 employment cases filed in 1962, 405 (or 66.2 per cent) alleged discrimination on grounds of race. For 1945 through 1962, a total of 5,244 employment complaints alleging racial discrimination were filed. Thus, discrimination based on color was charged in 67.9 per cent of the employment cases brought before the New York Commission during this seventeen year period.[89]

Out of the 611 filed in 1962, 235 cases concerned refusal to employ, 154 alleged dismissal from employment, 113 cited conditions of employment, 48 agency referral and 46 concerned trade unions. Out of the 7,725 employment complaints filed from 1945 through 1962, 3,365 concerned refusal to employ, 1,732 dismissal, 1,054 conditions of employment, 493 employment agencies and 743 involved labor union discrimination.[90]

What was the disposition of the employment cases for the year 1962 and for the period from 1945 to 1962? The record is clearly revealed in the statistics presented by the Commission itself:

COMPLAINTS CLOSED BY TYPES OF CLOSING[91]

Closing	Employment Cases	
	1962	1945-1962
1. Probable cause—specific complaint sustained		
a. Adjusted after conference and conciliation	103	1,405
b. Ordered for hearing or consent order issued	1	64
2. No probable cause found as to specific complaint but other discriminatory practices or policies found and adjusted	96	1,620
3. No probable cause found—specific complaint dismissed and no other discriminatory practices or policies found	588	3,811
4. Withdrawn by complainant	19	171
5. Lack of jurisdiction—specific complaint dismissed	36	387
Total	843	7,458

Translated into percentage distribution figures, the Commission's analysis of closings shows that for category two above, no probable cause was found as to the discrimination charged by the complainant in 11.4 per cent of 1962 employment cases and in 21.7 per cent of 1945 to 1962 employment cases. No discrimination *of any kind* (category three above) was found in 69.7 per cent of 1962 cases and in 51.1 per cent of 1945 to 1962 employment cases. In generalized terms, therefore, the Commission found no probable cause to credit the specific discrimination alleged in the complaint in 81.1 per cent of employment cases in 1962 and in 72.8 per cent of employment cases from 1945

88. *Id.* at 10, Table 2.
89. *Id.* at 12, Table 4.
90. *Id.* at 13, Table 5.
91. *Id.* at 14, Table 6.

to 1962. The over-all record substantiates the fact that the same pattern exists as that studied by Morroe Berger five years after the New York Commission came into existence; the large percentages of cases invalidated still does not tend to create confidence in the Commission among Negro workers, and that given the enormity of the problems of the very large Negro community in New York state, the actual number of complaints received by the New York Commission is very small indeed.

New York's Commission—despite the fact that it rejects half of the complaints which are filed with it—is the only Commission with a substantial annual budget and a fairly adequate staff. Its 1960 budget was $950,000 and the Commission had a working staff of 80 people. California, a state that had two-thirds as large a Negro population, had a Commission budget of only $203,000 and a staff of 15. Pennsylvania, a state with a sixteenth as many Negroes had a budget of $100,000 for its FEPC commission and a staff of 3. Yet even the large budget and staff for New York's agency is not sufficient to cope with the very serious problems of racial and other forms of discrimination. Hence it is obvious that the other state commissions would be extremely understaffed and ill-equipped to function properly. The other commissions are forced to limit their activity to processing complaints. Only the New York Commission has a budget that is large enough to enable it to conduct activity on a pattern-centered compliance basis.

During its eighteen years of existence, New York's FEPC concluded agreements with over 2,000 separate firms. This is but a small fraction of companies which have six or more employees—but they do account for business operations in which the Commission found proof of discriminatory practices. If all the firms revised their previous discriminatory policy, the result would have to be some general improvement in employment opportunity. The Commission's post-settlement investigations reveal that many of the firms did hire an increased number of Negro employees after settlements took place, as a direct consequence of revised employment policies. Therefore New York's Commission did demand and secure some significant enforcement of the law, a step which other state FEP settlements did not entail. In 1951, for example, SCAD had studied 334 cases for follow-up review. In 85 per cent of cases investigated it found that there was "a definite improvement in the employment pattern as compared with the conditions which existed at the time the original complaints against them were filed. These changes were reflected in substantial increases in the number of members of different racial . . . groups employed in professional, technical, skilled, semiskilled and unskilled job categories."[92]

But this very improvement delineates the actual inability of the Commission to make meaningful changes in the total pattern of employment discrimination. By the very nature of the process used by the Commission—investigation of the employment pattern of respondent firms—the Commission can influence only a

---

92.   1951 N.Y. State Comm'n Against Discrimination Ann. Rep. 7-8.

small minority of business firms operating in the state. The change in employment patterns achieved by later investigation of agreements is certainly to be commended—but unfortunately it touches only a small minority of New York's manufacturing and other industries. Thus, as Herman Miller pointed out, the occupational status of Negroes in the 1960's in New York remains close to the levels reached in 1940.

In 1958, some relative progress in specific industries for Negro "white collar" employees can be noted. The Commission made an analysis of reviews of Negro employment in several important industries—banking, insurance companies and department stores. These institutions traditionally excluded Negroes from all but menial jobs. Comparison of the findings of their follow-up investigations with the original employment pattern revealed that originally Negroes held only menial jobs in these firms. In the middle 1950's, however, 7 banks which had been respondent firms had more than 100 Negroes in white collar positions, and 2 of the banks had 300 Negroes in each. The progress appears to be great, however, because for a Negro, any job above a menial position is regarded as a significant change in occupational status.

Of 20 insurance companies investigated by the Commission, 8 firms showed that they had no Negro employment; 1 showed that Negroes were employed but that no general increase in Negro employment had been registered. Ten firms had no Negro employees at the time of the analysis. The largest firm studied had no Negro employees in 1945, at the time of the original investigation. By 1956, it had employed 750 Negroes in many different positions, and 200 Puerto Ricans. Similarly, few retail stores had Negroes employed in any but menial jobs in 1945 and most had no Negro employees at all. By the 1950's, Negroes comprised approximately 10 per cent of the work force of New York department stores. However, these gains for Negro middle class white collar workers are more than offset by losses in employment opportunity for Negro industrial workers especially in mass production manufacturing. Although increases in Negro employment have taken place, they appear to be significant only in contrast to the complete exclusion which was the standard 20 years ago. In the communication industry in New York state, Negroes may now comprise 5 per cent of the total work force, compared to only 2 per cent in the 1940's, but the percentage of change does not signify a great increase in the actual number of Negroes whose occupational status has changed. A few Negroes have been employed, but the demand for jobs is much higher than the number of Negroes who are working at them or who are qualified for such positions. As automation begins to eliminate many of the jobs in these industries, the ability of Negroes to gain entrance becomes even more difficult. Racial bias in the allocation of jobs has changed slightly, and this change reflects the positive aspects of New York's FEPC. But it also reveals the inability of FEPC as an institution to cope with the over-all pattern of job discrimination. Even when FEPC has worked most effectively compared to other states—and it has worked most effectively in

New York—it is simply unable to fundamentally alter the Negro employment pattern.

New York's FEPC commission has tried to avoid the defects inherent in the other state FEPC agencies. It has tried to do more than rectify the situation of an individual complainant. One Negro man charged that he had received no referrals for a job as a front elevator operator in an East Side luxury apartment. The Commission failed to find evidence to support the contention that he was not employed because of his color. Nevertheless, it investigated to determine whether a combination of geographic area factors and the specific category of employment acted to discriminate against Negroes. It found that no Negroes had ever been employed as front elevator operators in the expensive East Side apartment buildings. The Commission then had the specifications for jobs in the area changed. It would no longer be acceptable for employers to ask for "East Side apartment house experience" or "comparable experience" as a prerequisite for employment. Because Negroes never held the job, this type of qualification automatically excluded them. The Commission emphasized that such "localized prior experience is certainly not the only way to acquire the necessary training."[93] This ruling does not insure Negro employment as front elevator operators, but it certainly sets the basis for ending their absolute exclusion.

Nevertheless, the Commission's efforts to affect the employment pattern are not always successful. In 1953, 228 respondent firms were involved in complaints which were closed that year. One hundred and seventy-nine companies were first complaint cases; 49 had previously been investigated in connection with other complaints. Checking on the latter group is a method of examining whether changes had taken place in employment patterns and of testing how effective earlier conciliation agreements were. Of these 49 firms, 13 were found to be no longer practicing any discrimination. Fifteen were found to have nondiscriminatory employment policies currently, although in previous years they did not. Fourteen companies were found still to be engaged in discriminatory practices, indicating that "the earlier conciliation agreements had not been completely effective."[94] Adjustments made with these 14 companies were proved to have been based upon meaningless agreements, for the employers did not end their discriminatory pattern of employment. Promises are not always kept, and satisfactory adjustment does not mean that respondent firms will always act upon the agreements they sign. The remaining 7 firms were found to have a discriminatory policy which had not been disclosed during earlier investigations. This result shows that companies may often avoid scrutiny of their policies, despite an FEPC investigation.

New York's Commission tries to prevent lack of compliance by undertaking a review of complaints six months after they have been closed. In 1953, 103 reviews were made. Field representatives visited respondents, made inquiries

93. 1961 N.Y. State Comm'n Against Discrimination Ann. Rep. 60.
94. 1953 N.Y. State Comm'n Against Discrimination Ann. Rep. 15.

about employment practices, policies and patterns as well as general compliance with the terms of the conciliation agreement. The Commission found that in one Long Island defense plant there was a steady increase in Negro employees. At the time of the original investigation the plant had 900 employees and no Negro workers. At the first review, it employed 1,600 persons and 19 Negroes. At the second review, it employed 1,800 employees and 32 Negroes. A large bakery employed 1,000 people, but used Negro sales people only in Negro neighborhoods. At the first review, the Commission found that Negroes sold goods in 9 shops where they had not been previously employed. A Fifth Avenue department store had 2,900 employees. Of the 135 Negroes employed, only 1 was in sales work. At the first review, the store was using 18 Negro salespeople.[95] The Commission thus notes an increase in the use of Negro workers—but it cannot do anything about the small percentage which this increase comprises. This kind of limited increase against the background of Negro unemployment and underemployment does not effect a change in the Negro's occupational status, and is of benefit only to the few who are fortunate enough to have been chosen for the token advance. It is necessary to observe that this kind of progress might have been very important as symbolic achievement 20 years ago, but today given the reality of Negro life in the north, it can be regarded only as token compliance with the law at best.

New York's Commission has indicated a serious effort to attempt a review of its cases and to secure compliance. This has amounted to an increase in the number of Negroes employed by industries in which investigations have been made. But in all the categories cited, only a very small percentage of Negroes has benefited. There has been no general increase that would match the increased percentage of Negroes in the population and give them equality in employment on the same terms as that enjoyed by whites. Moreover, most Negro migrants are unskilled, having been accustomed to life and work in rural areas. No significant training programs involving large numbers of workers have been initiated to make them eligible for clerical, professional and skilled craft jobs in which employment opportunities are available.

In one case, the Commission received the complaint of a Negro welder that he had not been referred for employment by a local craft union because he was Negro. This local union controlled all hiring for welding operations on the St. Lawrence Seaway construction project. The local had 800 members, all of whom were white. Negroes were denied the opportunity to work because in practice the union was the exclusive hiring agent and refused to refer Negroes for work. After the Commission acted, the complainant and two other Negroes were sent out for work by the Union. "These men represented the first Negroes in this job category to be employed on the seaway."

In this case, SCAD made no effort to establish the permanent right of Negroes to belong to a union which rigidly controlled the hiring hall operation

---

95. *Id.* at 16-17.

and to make certain that all qualified Negroes seeking jobs in the future would be referred for employment by the union. Thus they achieved the goal of getting a job for the complainant, but did not initiate action to change the over-all pattern of discrimination by craft unions which control the hiring process and which exclude Negroes from membership.[96]

VI. TECHNOLOGICAL CHANGE, TRAINING PROGRAMS AND LABOR UNION RACIAL PRACTICES

The 1948 Annual Report of the New York State Commission notes that "the extent of integration depends not only on the absence of a discriminatory hiring and employment policy, but also on the number of people in the discriminated group possessing the requisite skills who are available for employment as well as the state of a given industry and the condition of the labor market."[97] This is much more true in 1964 than it was in 1948. Increasingly, the central issue of fair employment practices involves the availability of new training opportunities for nonwhite wage earners.

The American economy is characterized by a great paradox in the area of manpower utilization, for in the midst of a serious rise in unemployment, many jobs are going begging because of a lack of skilled workers. Even in an area of critical unemployment such as Detroit during 1961-1962, and in other industrial communities where there has been a very high rate of unemployment, industry has been unable to find an adequate supply of skilled workers in a variety of crafts. There is every indication that this pattern will continue.

For every 100 skilled workers that the nation had in 1955, it will need 122 in 1965 and 145 in 1975; yet all of the available data clearly indicate that the nation's training programs are not even turning out enough new craftsmen to replace those who retire. It is now clear that in the next decade, the entire American economy will be faced with a crisis because of the lack of skilled manpower.

A major factor contributing to the irrational, wasteful and socially harmful operation of the nation's apprenticeship, vocational and other training programs is the color discrimination and racial exclusion which characterize training programs in major sectors of the economy in the north as well as the south. For many occupations the only way a worker can be recognized as qualified for employment is to successfully complete apprenticeship or other established training programs.

Studies such as that made by the New York State Commission Against Discrimination,[98] as well as by the National Association for the Advancement

---

96. For a discussion of trade union racial practices see Hill, *Labor Unions and the Negro*, 28 Commentary 479-88 (Dec. 1959) and Hill, *Has Organized Labor Failed the Negro Worker*, 11 The Negro Digest 41 (May 1962).

97. 1948 N.Y. State Comm'n Against Discrimination Ann. Rep. 11.

98. N.Y. State Comm'n Against Discrimination, Apprentices, Skilled Craftsmen and the Negro: An Analysis (1960).

of Colored People, clearly indicate that no significant advances have been made by Negroes in those craft union apprenticeship training programs which have historically excluded nonwhites. An examination of available data makes evident that less than one per cent of the apprentices in the building and construction industry throughout the United States are Negro. In the ten year period, 1950-1960, in the state of New York, Negro participation in building trades apprenticeship programs increased from 1.5 per cent to 2 per cent.[99]

Open access to plumbing and pipe fitting apprenticeship controlled by the Plumbers Union is a very rare experience for young Negroes in the north as well as the south. Similarly, Negro youth are completely excluded from apprenticeship programs controlled by the Sheet Metal Workers Union, the International Brotherhood of Electrical Workers, the Lathers and Plasterers Union, the Ornamental and Structural Iron Workers Union and from other important craft unions operating in the construction industry.

Almost equally exclusive are the printing trades unions. In a survey made by the National Association for the Advancement of Colored People of the seven major New York City newspapers in 1962, we find that with the exclusion of building services and maintenance personnel, less than one per cent of those employed on the major New York newspapers are Negro. Virtually, all of the Negroes employed on these newspapers are in the "white collar" jurisdiction of the New York Newspaper Guild.

We estimate that less than one-half of one per cent of those currently employed in the newspaper crafts outside of the Guild's jurisdiction are Negroes. This includes printing pressmen, compositors, photo-engravers, stereotypers, paper handlers, mailers and delivery drivers. As far as apprenticeship training for these crafts is concerned, we have been unable to detect a single instance where Negroes have been recently admitted into a training program in the newspaper crafts in the City of New York or in other major cities in the United States.

In the study entitled *Made in New York: Case Studies in Metropolitan Manufacturing,* published by Harvard University in 1959, we are told that "Negro and Puerto Rican women who are on the lower rungs of the city's economic ladder, have become important in the New York garment industry, but they work mainly in the more established branches and with few exceptions . . . they do not become highly skilled tailor system workers on dresses or 'cloaks.' As a result a shortage of skilled sewing machine operators is developing."[100]

In most of these programs the role of the labor union is decisive because the trade union usually determines who is admitted into the training program and therefore, who is admitted into the union membership. Labor unions also exercise control over apprenticeship programs through hiring hall procedures in

---

99. Hill, The Negro Wage Earner and Apprenticeship Training Programs (1959).
100. Made in New York: Case Studies in Metropolitan Manufacturing 95 (Hall ed. 1959).

de facto closed shop situations. In these circumstances, craft unions have the power either to promote or prevent the admission of individuals or of an entire class of persons.

By means of a variety of formal and informal controls, craft unions are frequently the decisive factor in the recruitment process in many apprenticeship programs and often directly prevent Negro youth from becoming skilled craft workers via the established route of apprenticeship.

A careful analysis of most apprenticeship training programs currently operating in many skilled craft occupations will clearly indicate the utter lack of a system of objective standard criteria for admission into apprenticeship training. At the present time there is no objective basis for determining admissions. Persons are admitted or not admitted because of nepotism and caprices of certain union officials acting in collusion with management.

On the level of the small shop and local union, the tradition of racial discrimination has now become deeply institutionalized. A form of caste psychology impels many workers to regard their own positions as "white man's jobs," to which no Negro should aspire. These workers, and often their union leaders, regard jobs in their industries as a kind of private privilege, to be accorded and denied by them as they see fit. Often Negroes are not alone in being barred from such unions which have much of the character of the medieval guild, but Negroes as a group suffer the most from these practices. On the local level, the tradition which sustains discrimination is to be found among skilled workers in heavy industry as well as in the craft occupations and in the north almost as commonly as in the south.

FEP commissions clearly have the authority to function in this decisive area but with very few exceptions they have not invoked their powers against discriminatory apprenticeship training programs and against skilled craft labor unions directly responsible for maintaining a rigid pattern of Negro exclusion.

If Negroes do not possess the skills required by modern technology, fair employment practice commissions cannot help them. They can only ask that those few Negroes who do have skills be treated equally. If a given industry is in decline or experiencing a depressed condition, FEPC cannot help to gain an increase in the rate of Negro employment. It can only call for equal opportunity, and this becomes a meaningless abstraction.

Recent decisions of the Pennsylvania State Commission and the New York Commission indicate that mass demonstrations and other forms of organized public pressure from the Negro civil rights movement have influenced some state commissions to invoke their authority against institutions that previously enjoyed a virtual immunity from fair employment practice laws. Equally significant is the nature of the findings and the substance of commission orders in these few recent cases which represent a significant departure from the limitations of past practice.

Dramatic public exposure of anti-Negro practices can create an atmosphere which is conducive to effective action by state FEP agencies. As in the San Francisco hotel case which was previously discussed, eradication of discriminatory practices and action by the California Commission came only after the intensification of independent mass action by civil rights organizations.

Early in May of 1963, mass demonstrations stopped construction of an $18,000,000, twenty-one story municipal service building in Philadelphia. On May 27, 1963, NAACP members began mass picketing at the construction site of a school in the Negro district of Philadelphia, because building trades unions affiliated with the AFL-CIO refused to admit skilled Negroes as members, and thus denied them access to employment controlled by the unions. In June and July of 1963, construction in Harlem and elsewhere in New York City was stopped because of the refusal of labor unions to admit Negroes into craft occupations. During the summer months, Negro civil rights groups conducted mass demonstrations to dramatize the pattern of Negro exclusion from training programs and jobs in the building and construction trades in many cities across the country.

After years of avoiding conflict with the politically powerful building trades unions, the Pennsylvania State Commission, beginning on July 9, 1963, held public hearings involving six major unions and finally issued a series of orders against these unions that had long engaged in anti-Negro practices. On February 24, 1964, the New York State Commission for Human Rights made its first important step forward in prohibiting employment discrimination by building trades unions. On that date it found Local 373 of the Plumbers Union of Spring Valley, New York guilty of maintaining a pattern of anti-Negro practices. The significance of the Harold Mitchell case against the Plumbers Union is in the nature of the Commission's decision. After finding that the membership of Local 373 was composed exclusively of Caucasians and that it maintained a policy of excluding Negroes from membership, the New York Commission directed the union to place Mitchell at the head of its work referral list, giving him priority on the job referral list, whether or not he joined the union. It further directed that Mitchell be allowed to take the journeyman entrance examination and that the examination be graded fairly. It also directed the union to treat all apprenticeship applicants equally and to disregard race. The local was ordered to submit an affidavit outlining the manner in which it was complying with the order. The plumbing company in question was ordered to send Mitchell a letter offering to rehire him at full union wages and to restore all seniority rights that would have accrued had he been continuously employed since his date of dismissal. The company also was ordered to give him three hundred dollars in back pay for partial loss of wages following illegal dismissal.[101]

The decision in the Mitchell case represents a fundamental departure by

---

101. Mitchell v. R & S Plumbers & Mechanical Systems, Inc., C-9092-62 (N.Y. State Comm'n for Human Rights, 1964).

the New York Commission from the traditional limited settlements which in the past only benefited the individual complainant. The Commission for the first time touched upon the power of those craft unions, which control the hiring process and deliberately exclude Negroes from skilled craft occupations. Although the New York Commission had been in existence for 18 years, it was not until the Negro mass movement began an intensive public attack on union discrimination in the building trades that the Commission acted to reach the source of the union's power, *i.e.*, exclusive control of assignment to jobs.

The provisions of the state antidiscrimination law are such that they empower the Commission to deal with union discrimination. The law makes it illegal for unions to deny or withhold membership from any qualified person because of race. This is a serious difficulty for colored people nationally and New York State has one of the most rigid patterns of overt discrimination against Negroes in the building trades industry. This pattern of discrimination was extensively studied for the New York State Advisory Committee to the United States Commission on Civil Rights by Dr. Donald F. Shaughnessy of Columbia University.[102]

Some critics have called the attempt to gain admission for Negroes into the construction trades ill-advised, because allegedly there is not enough work for those already in the industry. What good is a call for Negro participation, so the argument goes, when whites as well as Negroes are in danger of losing their jobs?

The logic is good, but it does not apply to the construction industry. Dr. Shaughnessy's report, as well as other studies revealed that there is a huge backlog of work that will take decades for the construction industry to complete. Exclusion of Negroes from participation in this industry is *not* a reflection of economic stagnation. Building construction is not an industry in which there are fewer jobs for both Negroes and whites. The construction industry represents a segment of the economy which is not declining. General contractors and the employers associations believe that there is a severe shortage of both residential and nonresidential construction in New York and elsewhere. New York, with twice the population of Chicago, has over four times the need for office space. Data indicate that the construction demand is growing.

Dr. Shaughnessy has pointed out that the fear of unemployment by construction workers must be set aside due to reliable estimates of forthcoming construction activity. New construction is scheduled to increase by 57 per cent between 1960 and 1964, and double between 1970 and 1975, according to Commerce Department estimates. The volume of construction and new repairs is also expected to grow. Thus the skilled manpower necessary in 1970 will be 35 per cent above the present labor supply.

The *Wall Street Journal*, April 10, 1964, in a front page story states

---

102. Shaughnessy, A Survey of Discrimination in the Building Trades Industry, New York City (April 1963). Dr. Shaughnessy's study was the basis for the Report of the New York Advisory Committee to the U.S. Commission on Civil Rights (August 1963).

"Booming construction activity will provide strong support this year for the nation's economy." The report concludes by noting that ". . . the general contractors who build highways, housing, office structures, and utility facilities generally agree they will have record volume." Although the industry is expanding, Negro workers have not been able to enter into the construction industry. This occurs because, as Shaughnessy notes, "the economic characteristics of the industry have created a condition wherein the decision making power is concentrated in the local union."

It is the economic structure of the building industry which concentrates in the local unions the power to decide who obtains employment and who gets admitted to the craft. The men who are engaged in construction work are recruited from labor pools controlled exclusively by the various unions in the craft jurisdictions of building trades. The union is the sole employment agency and the men who appear on the jobs are those whom the union has referred to the job site. Because the volume of operation of individual contractors and subcontractors in the industry is too small to allow them to employ steadily a large number of skilled workers in a given area, contractors must depend upon a pool of available craftsmen in each trade. Contractors are thus completely dependent upon local unions for their labor supply. This factor further increases the power of local craft unions to control the employment process.

The worker, in turn, is dependent upon the union for his source of job security. Since he works on many different jobs for a variety of contractors, his sole sense of loyalty is to the union which dispatches him to various jobs. His attachment is to the source which gives him his job security, in this case, the specific building trades union to which he belongs. The economic characteristics of this industry provide fertile soil in which racial discrimination can and does flourish.

Rather than admit Negro members, the unions frequently encourage the use of out-of-town labor. Based upon direct interviews, Shaughnessy found that commuters travel as much as 120 miles per day from Connecticut and elsewhere to find steady employment in New York, when the available local union membership supply is exhausted. But local sources of skilled Negro manpower are deliberately ignored. During the spring and summer of 1963 there were approximately 1200 plumbers with "travelling cards" from other cities working in New York City.

Thus the New York State Advisory Committee of the United States Commission on Civil Rights stated in its 1963 report that ". . . the building trades unions continue to maintain an effective shortage of labor. One way that shortage is preserved in the face of continuing high demand is the use of commuters like those from Bridgeport who represent an auxiliary source of manpower that can be cut off at any time." Out-of-town construction workers commute over 100 miles daily to jobs in New York City while local Negroes and Puerto Ricans are denied employment and entry to union controlled jobs and apprenticeship programs.

Apprenticeship programs provide from one-half to two-thirds of all the skilled workers who are needed to replace older craftsmen and to meet new needs of industry. The unions, however, have the power to fix the number of apprentices. Thus, they deliberately maintain an effective shortage of the skilled labor supply on the theory that this enhances their power at the bargaining table. Twenty-two vocational high schools exist in New York City. Five of these teach skills used in the building trades. But qualified Negro graduates are limited to low-paying non-union jobs, or are forced to leave the trade entirely. Negro youth taught a skilled craft at public expense, find that they are deprived of the opportunity to practice it. Parenthetically it should be noted that this contributes to the high rate of Negro school drop-outs, drop-outs that are an expression of a sense of futility and alienation among Negro youth in relation to job opportunities.

Yet as Shaughnessy puts it, the "swollen myth" exists that discrimination in training and employment has been effectively prevented by law in New York City. Section 296 of Article 15 of the Executive Law of New York State is most clear. The law prohibits discrimination by employers in hiring, compensation, employment privileges, working conditions and discharges, prohibits union discrimination in membership and bars discrimination by unions in admission to apprenticeship training, on the job training, and in other vocational training programs.

However, the state FEPC cannot act until a complaint has been filed by an aggrieved party, and only after a public hearing in which the respondent is found to be guilty. The Commission has the power to establish and maintain an office, meet and function at any place within the state, appoint attorneys and amend and rescind rules, receive, investigate and pass upon complaints, hold hearings, and act upon the results. "It has, in fact, every conceivable power such a commission might need except the power to initiate investigations." But as Dr. Shaughnessy put it, the New York Commission "has been singularly ineffective in preventing or eliminating discrimination in apprenticeship programs in the building trades industry."

In 1948, SCAD had ordered the New York Sheet Metal Workers Union to desist from "executing and/or maintaining constitution or by-law provisions which exclude Negroes." Yet seventeen years later no progress had been made in that area although the "Caucasian only" clause was removed from the union's constitution, apparently for public relations purposes only.

In December of 1963, the New York City Commission on Human Rights investigated the problem, and found "a pattern of exclusion in a substantial portion of the building and construction industry which effectively bars non-whites from participating in this area of the city's economic life."

A major factor in perpetuating Negro exclusion is the union's use of father-son clauses and preferences for relatives, plus the need to be recommended by a group of *union* members. When the right to become an apprentice is limited to sons and relatives of members, Negroes are automatically excluded since none have ever belonged to these unions. Union members may view this provision as a source of job security and claim that they are not discriminating against Negroes, but only against people who are not related to members. Yet the logic of the arrangement is to exclude, on a systematic basis, all Negroes as a class. The situation is analogous to the exclusion of Negroes from the all-white southern primaries in the 1920's. According to defenders of the "white primary," it was not anti-Negro, it merely allowed only those citizens whose grandfathers had voted to take part in primaries. But in effect the rule prevented all Negroes as a group from voting. Only when the courts ruled that the "white primaries" were unconstitutional and in fact were a device meant to bar Negroes, did the exclusion of Negroes from voting in primary elections come to an end in southern states.

The analogy suggests that what is needed is a new definition, a new standard by state FEP commissions. It is necessary to recognize that father-son clauses and preference to relatives is *prima facie* evidence of a discriminatory position; that, in effect, their use as a basis of admittance to apprentice programs is as anti-Negro as the more overt discriminatory clauses which used to be in many union constitutions until the law forced them to be removed. The same standard should be applied to the more common sponsorship clauses. When union practice requires that a youth be sponsored by two members of five years good standing, a Negro almost never can obtain such sponsorship.

On March 4, 1964, the Commission ruled that Local 28 of the Sheet Metal Workers Union had "automatically excluded" Negroes over the entire 78 years of the unions' existence. This was held to be a violation of New York State Law Against Discrimination. The Commission announced that it would issue an order for the union to "cease and desist" from such discriminatory practices and would demand affirmative action to guarantee an end to job discrimination.[103]

The decision was called "revolutionary" by the Commission's chairman, George H. Fowler, because "it takes into account a historical pattern of exclusion and not merely a specific complaint." Thus the Commission ruled against the union as an institution functioning within a given racial situation and with a history, and not on the basis of the "validity" of an individual complaint. The decision was based on public hearings against the union conducted by three commissioners. They had been called to investigate charges against Local 28 of the Sheet Metal Workers Union filed by the Civil Rights Bureau of the State Attorney General's office. The Bureau, which has been quite effective in this area, charged that the union and a contractors committee responsible for selecting apprentices had systematically discriminated against Negroes. The contractors committee had refused apprenticeship to a qualified Negro applicant. The State Commission charged that Local 28's admission program bore "a remarkable resemblance to the medieval guilds" by maintaining a father-son

---

103. Lefkowitz v. Farrell, C-9287-63 (N.Y. State Comm'n for Human Rights, 1964).

admission standard. The Commission noted that in a provision of its International Union constitution, which was deleted in 1946, the union declared that "no Negro could ever become a full member."

Observers agree, as The New York Times put it, that the ruling by the Commission was "a key harvest of the seeds planted by the massive civil rights protests at construction sites here last year. Local 28 has been a prime target of the rights groups."[104] What the decision demonstrates is that despite years of a state FEPC law and a previous ruling against Local 28, discrimination in the building trades continued unabated. Voluntary union programs, investigations, exposure, education, interminable negotiations and conciliation brought no results to Negroes. The historic pattern was retained and the union leadership, supported by the Building Trades Council of the AFL-CIO bitterly defended its anti-Negro practices. The state antidiscrimination law was not enforced and for the Negro job seeker in the building trades, for all practical purposes, it just did not exist in New York City and state. Therefore, civil rights demonstrations took place in a state with the oldest and strongest FEP Commission in the nation. Another factor is the litigation initiated by the NAACP currently pending in the New York State Supreme Court against Local 28 and eight other building unions and against the city and state of New York.

What the ruling also indicates is that if FEPC is to work, it must change the entire basis of its function. No longer can FEPC serve merely as a complaint taking agency or remain content to settle cases on an individual level, often agreeing to token settlements. It must be able to rule against respondents on the basis of a broad pattern of racial practices even when the respondent avows a nondiscriminatory policy in some vague future. It must take into account what Mr. Fowler called the "historical pattern of exclusion" and not only individual complaints. And then, it must take affirmative actions to assure that the pattern is really ended. Later, on March 23, the State Commission announced that it had given Local 28 sixty days to discard the old apprentice list of some 900 names of white persons and that it had ordered the Local to "cease and desist" from excluding Negroes from membership and to abandon the practice of requiring that an applicant be sponsored by a union member. The order is, in effect, a significant breakthrough for Negro workers and can have far reaching consequences. What is now necessary, as Roy Wilkins, Executive Secretary of the NAACP, requested, is that Governor Rockefeller and Mayor Wagner take immediate steps to order the cancellation of any contracts for public construction in which the hiring of apprentices and journeymen is controlled by Local 28 and other AFL-CIO craft unions guilty of similar practices. The state and city governments must abide by the State Commission's ruling by cancelling all contracts, and refusing to enter into new ones, in which hiring is controlled by unions that engage in discriminatory racial practices. The State Commission's ruling, Mr. Wilkins stated, in his letters of March 6, 1964 to Governor Rocke-

---

104. The New York Times, March 5, 1964.

feller and Mayor Wagner, has now "removed whatever justification existed, and we contend that there was none, for failure of city and state officials to cancel such contracts." Moreover, authorization of new contracts should be withheld until a realistic policy of nondiscrimination has been effected. Wilkins also called for "the institution of foolproof practices and procedures to insure the policing and affirmative enforcement by the city and state of their policies of nondiscrimination in employment." Unfortunately, in his reply to Roy Wilkins, Governor Rockefeller stated that it has been his "consistent policy . . . to encourage voluntary compliance with the laws against discrimination." In declining to act immediately, the Governor stated, the union would be given a "reasonable time within which to comply." The Governor also noted that ". . . Local 28 is still entitled to test the recent opinion of the Commission in the Courts." Mayor Wagner did not reply to the request of the NAACP Executive Secretary.

State FEP commissions could function more effectively if in addition to the development of new criteria, other law enforcement agencies worked in close conjunction with them. In New York, the state Attorney General, Louis J. Lefkowitz, has proposed an amendment to the state antidiscrimination law, making it illegal under an apprentice program, registered with the state, to select persons, "on any other basis than their qualifications as determined by objective criteria which permit review." The proposal was enacted into law in March 1964[105] over the vigorous opposition of the state AFL-CIO Council and the bitter objections of the Building Trades Unions. Now that new standards are established, and the FEP Commission performs the review, the means by which discriminatory practices can be legally ended is at hand.

The decision of the New York State Commission for Human Rights in the Sheet Metal Workers Union case holds great importance insofar as it influences FEPC operations throughout the nation. The decision, if its implications are carried to their logical conclusion, clearly indicates that state FEP commissions need not be obsolescent. State commissions however must qualitatively change their operational assumptions by using a new public standard based upon the realities of the social situation. Individual complaint settlements must now become a secondary function of the commission and for the first time, FEP commissions should demand that employers and labor unions change their entire institutional pattern in relation to Negroes and other nonwhite citizens.

Negro militancy in the north has created a new set of conditions for state FEP commissions. Now they must proceed boldly to the attack upon discriminatory patterns in entire industries and crafts, with new standards of evidence and new concepts of permanent affirmative compliance and above all, a far greater use of mandatory measures including the frequent issuance of cease and desist orders and court enforcement of commission rulings.

If state FEP commissions continue instead to operate with timidity and a general reluctance to broadly and rapidly enforce antidiscrimination statutes

---

105. L. 1964, ch. 948. The New York Times, March 21, 1964.

then they are obsolete, for the rising Negro mass movement will proceed to the attack in its own way. What state antidiscrimination commissions do within the next months and years and how rapidly they go about doing it will determine in large measure the nature of the racial confrontation in the northern states. This is now especially important as it becomes clearer each passing day that the next great crisis in American race relations will be in the north.

COMMENT

Louis H. Pollak*

D EAN HYMAN, friends: It is a great privilege to participate in a conference honoring Judge Halpern. And it is of course deeply fitting both that we honor him by meeting to discuss problems of civil rights—problems which so deeply engaged the Judge's mind and heart—and that this conference is held under the auspices of the Law School with which the Judge was so closely identified. As this conference bears witness, Buffalo Law School is one of those centrally dedicated to fostering those uses of law which can help to realize our democratic commitments. The character of this School is one of the lasting memorials to Judge Halpern. But it also testifies to the distinguished leadership of Dean Hyman. As the Dean nears the end of his decanal term, I am happy to have this opportunity to salute him.

Dean Hyman has indicated, in his very generous introduction, that my role as commentator on this evening's papers—however that role may have been originally conceived—has been skewed a little. Let me explain why: Up until yesterday morning I was quite hopeful that, as commentator—whatever that may be—I would be permitted an advance view of the papers I was to commentate (if you will excuse the expression) upon. To be sure, none of the papers was in hand. But at least I had a phone call yesterday morning from Dean Ferguson's secretary promising me that a massive tome was on its way to New Haven. Yet when I stopped at my office this morning, en route to the airport—no tome.

Well, how would you feel? I felt discriminated against. But, remembering that the law proceeds only upon due inquiry, I sent out my field examiners to the New Haven Post Office to track down the Ferguson manuscript. A few minutes later they were back with a reply from the Postmaster: "If Dean Ferguson sent Pollak a paper through the mail, we'll produce it or write one ourselves." And, sure enough, five minutes later one of those red-white-and-blue mail wagons trundled up to the Yale Law School door and delivered what was alleged to be the Ferguson opus. I grabbed it, drove to the airport, and settled down to read Dean Ferguson's text on the flight to Buffalo. And a splendid text I found it to be, all garnished with fifty-eight numbers designating footnotes. But there were no footnotes. So, once again, I felt discriminated against. After all, I'd received only one of the three papers, and only the text of that. But then, still in mid-flight, I reasoned it out to myself that I'd misunderstood the dimensions of the role Dean Hyman and Professor Schwartz had contemplated for me. It was sheer megalomania that had led me to suppose I was to commentate upon the Ferguson *and* Feild *and* Hill papers. My assignment was the Ferguson paper, and only the text of that; and another heavy-domed scholar was to commentate upon the footnotes.

But when I arrived at this dinner I discovered I was in error. Dean Hyman

* Professor of Law, Yale Law School.

70

indicated that he expected me to deal with all three papers—and he made it fairly clear that he didn't think my contribution would be any the less meritorious for not having seen two of the papers. I was trying to decide whether the Dean's observation was just routine courtesy (and if so, to whom) when John Feild came over to greet me—a document in one hand and a bourbon in the other. I'm afraid I mixed them. What I'm trying to say is that, though I absorbed a good deal of the Feild paper, I'm not sure that the absorption process was wholly useful.

At that point Professor Schwartz came in bearing on his back what turned out to be the collected works of Herbert Hill. I sampled pages; then chapters; and then, in my desperation, whole volumes. And, as I was trying to think of how to locate and climb the central summit of the Hill, I was reminded of an experience which befell my colleague, Boris Bittker, some nine thousand years ago when he was law clerk to Jerome Frank. One Friday afternoon Judge Frank handed Boris a draft opinion which he proposed to hand down the following Monday. Boris said, with law clerkly diffidence, "Judge, this is a pretty substantial opinion—sixty-eight pages long. I wonder whether you would be willing to let me take it home over the weekend and see if I could whittle it down a little bit." Judge Frank said, "Of course, Boris, if you want to spend your weekend that way." Boris did and came in proudly on Monday morning with a seventeen-page restatement compressing the Judge's opinion. He handed it to the Judge and the Judge said, "Give me a little while to look at it, won't you?" He retired to his chambers and emerged ten minutes later: "Boris, what you've done is first-rate. We'll add it on at the end of the opinion."

And now that you know the legislative history of my appearance here this evening, I shall proceed to commentate. First, I'd like to address myself to Dean Ferguson's paper:

Dean Ferguson has strongly emphasized the paramountcy of federal interest in the whole question of racial discrimination in employment. He's exactly right, of course. We start with the integrated nature of our economy—if not of our employment picture. We are compelled—if we really mean to deal with these problems seriously and with substantial effect—to rely heavily on the national power in all of the aspects which Dean Ferguson so clearly articulated; so I'm not disagreeing with anything I understood him to say.

My qualifications are only with respect to what he did not say—at least what I did not hear him say. Actually, I doubt that he will disagree with what I will add by way of addendum—and it may sound like a small thing, but it seems to me a reservation of considerable consequence. In stressing the importance of federal regulation, whether through the President's executive power unaided by legislation or through the whole elaborate programmatic regulation that a federal fair employment practices law would give us, I would urge that we not forget, or sort of discard as not worth bothering about, the segments of the employment picture which are beyond federal control. I mean "beyond" in two senses:

First, I suppose there is an area that's constitutionally beyond federal control. If we think hard enough—or if we get our students in Constitutional Law I to think hard enough—it is possible to isolate certain kinds of businesses that probably don't have any impact on interstate commerce at all. There are ice-cream parlors that are not on interstate highways. There are barbershops that have three chairs which do not cater to people moving back and forth across state lines. And I think it worth being concerned about barbershops. (Tonight I'm not talking about whom the barbershop caters to. We all remember hearing *ad nauseam* how difficult it is for a white barber to learn to cut Negro hair. But I can't believe we whites are wholly incapable of learning this skill. This seems to me a technological problem that we ought to be able to lick in time. Tonight, however, I'm more concerned about the converse of the problem.) In most cities, barbers' scissors do not seem to be handled by people who are not white. And the barbershop is only one of many very small businesses throughout the country which, collectively, employ hundreds and hundreds of thousands of people—far too few of whom are Negroes.

Moreover, even within the range of what the federal government constitutionally can reach, the most vigorous programs conceivable—programs designed by Clyde Ferguson and John Feild and administered by Herbert Hill—are not going to cover anything like the full sweep of possible federal fields of control. That, after all, is why the National Labor Relations Board set up jurisdictional limits.

My point is that "the limits of effective legal action" may be far broader when policed at the state level and yet again at the municipal level.

Now Mr. Hill has very challengingly asserted the ineffectiveness of local regulation—at least the ineffectiveness of state regulation. He hasn't really addressed himself to—although I'm sure it's included in his general indictment —the possibilities of municipal regulatory action. I respond immediately to this. I live in a city which is at this moment considering the establishment of a municipal commission which, among other things, would administer—within the city limits of New Haven—the state of Connecticut's fair employment, public accommodations, and fair housing laws. And the chief reason why it should be possible to persuade the New Haven Board of Aldermen to do this is because the Connecticut Commission on Civil Rights has not been able to do the statewide job that we would want it to do.

Why? Perhaps for many of these reasons adduced by Mr. Hill. But assuredly for the reason that nobody can police Connecticut on a biennial budget of $190,000.00 with a staff of four field investigators. Now those figures, I thought, were fairly pathetic, but they certainly don't look so bad when measured against the figures compiled by Messrs. Feild and Hill as to states which claim to be even larger than Connecticut. California, for instance.

Now are these meager budgets the fault of the California Commission or of the Connecticut Commission? Of course not. These budgets are, instead, an apt measurement of our inability, as political communities, to elect legislators who will commit a meaningful quantity of tax dollars to support regulatory programs of this sort.

In short, if California has a staff of only 35 to 50 or whatever to administer its state antidiscrimination laws, that's because, collectively speaking, California doesn't really care very much about this kind of a program. Now there may be added problems—there may be internal problems of administration such as those Herbert Hill and John Feild have discussed, and my guess would be that much of this criticism is justified. For example, everything that John Feild said about how he would want to structure a state commission or a national commission seems to me entirely right. On the other hand—and here I am particularly concerned with the Hill paper—I want to file one important caveat.

Mr. Hill finds it significant that Pennsylvania and New York are—and are increasingly—centers of mass Negro underemployment and unemployment. The significance which Mr. Hill sees is that these are states which have been purporting to enforce their fair employment practice laws. The apparent "ergo" is that such laws are useless, or perhaps even counter-productive. But surely that is not the actual lesson to be drawn. Surely the existence of these agencies derives from the lack of employment opportunities—not vice-versa. And surely the lesson to be drawn is that the kind of regulatory apparatus we now have, structured in the fashion we're presently accustomed to, may be able to cope with certain symptoms, but not with deep-seated disequalibria in the labor market. Actually, I doubt that Mr. Hill seriously contends that his data support a graver indictment—*i.e.*, that the law is generically incapable of developing institutions adapted to meeting these exigent moral and economic issues. Indeed, the *Sheet Metal Workers* case,[1] to which Mr. Hill devotes considerable attention, is itself a demonstration that, properly activated, the existing New York Commission can act with significant impact at least at the level of symptomology.

Now, having said that, there is, of course the very real possibility that Herbert Hill is right in the larger sense, namely, that we are talking about a range of problems that are only partially, and haphazardly, within the effective limits of the law at whatever level we are applying the law—federal, state, municipal, or what have you.

And I suspect that this is true. I suspect that we are talking about problems which, since most of us gathered here are lawyers, we would like to analyze and criticize in terms of how can we sharpen up administration, how can we get more administrators—more mine inspectors as John Feild put it so well—and get the job done better. But surely, when we are talking about a major reorientation of our economy, we are really talking about problems that go beyond the scope of regulatory law as conventionally conceived.

We are looking, in short, for new kinds of initiative, not to supplant but to supplement our ordinary regulatory institutions. Now, to give one closest to

---

1. Lefkowitz v. Farrell, C-9287-63 (N.Y. State Comm'n for Human Rights, 1964).

the governmental standard, I refer you just by chance to the fact that Yale University, under its new President, Kingman Brewster, has established its own private equal opportunity panel. This panel—which is, I may add, still awaiting the filing of its first complaint—is charged with the duty of adjudicating complaints about discrimination in the employment practices of the University, and also in the employment practices of contractors working on substantial Yale building programs. In short, we have a fair-sized corporation engaged in policing its own employment practices and those of enterprises over which it has significant economic leverage. And this private apparatus supplements the existing governmental machinery operative in Connecticut.

But all this, you may properly say, is just another form of governmental mechanism—differing from standard models only in the sense that it happens to be run by a nominally private entrepreneur.

So, you may argue, it is not enough to lengthen our stride a few inches; what we must do is to walk in different paths up steeper mountains. And in a very real sense this is incontrovertible: Today we have to devise new techniques of teaching scores of new skills and disciplines—and we must radically improve existing techniques of teaching the established ingredients of a good education. We have to accelerate the pace of our thinking about the impact of automation on those already in the labor market. And—hopefully—we have to plan the phased readjustment of a defense-oriented economy to one which is at once more variegated and more generally productive. All these, surely, are economic adaptations which are far beyond the scope of anything that the New York State Commission or the Connecticut Commission can decree or that the President of Yale or the President of the United States can by executive order ordain and establish.

In short, we're looking for imaginative, creative action—public and private —which requires legislation or money (and probably both) and which has as a chief objective fitting people to the useful and rewarding jobs likely to exist one and two decades hence. To revert to a single mundane example on the local level I happen to be familiar with, New Haven now has in being a real retraining program producing the kind of technicians John Feild mentioned the growing need for. Under this program men and women, both white and black, who now have neither skills nor jobs, are acquiring both in a matter of months. Today this is a pilot program administered by Community Progress Inc. and financed by the Ford Foundation. But if it proves itself—and there is good reason to believe it will—I have little doubt that New Haven and hundreds of comparable communities will, with federal support, undertake programs of this kind as long-term municipal endeavors. (Please understand that my frequent references to New Haven are not solely the product of a parochial pride fertilized by wider ignorance. My real point is that programs manageable by one medium-sized city are duplicable by hundreds of others).

What conclusions do we come to, then, as to the effective limits of the law in dealing with the problems of racial discrimination in employment? We know, from what Messrs. Hill and Feild have taught us, something of what needs to be done to improve the fair employment practice commissions which are already in being. The fact that improvements—very likely radical improvements—are in order should not surprise us: after all, in terms of our political-historical perspective, these two-decade old regulatory mechanisms are still very new. But what of the apparent fact that all the innovations we can think of will not enable these commissions to make serious inroads on the dearth of good jobs which confronts millions of Negroes now in and shortly to enter the labor market? When we reach the conclusion that we must, simultaneously, pursue far bolder and far more comprehensive programs, are we saying that the law as we have conventionally understood it is ineffective? Not at all.

I think the more accurate assessment is this. The process we are witnessing —and participating in—is the extension and ramification of law. Thus, I think we can agree that chief among the antecedent causes of this conference is the fact that ten years ago the Supreme Court decided the *Segregation Cases.* To be sure, that was, strictly considered, law of a very different order from the detailed and systematic regulatory legislation which is the focus of our present agenda. That was law speaking in the simple, non-meticulous idiom of the Constitution—law saying to government, "You can't treat people this way any longer." But it was law which has implications far beyond that negative command. That negative command has forced back on all of us collective political responsibility to go out and do affirmative things to right the ills of our democracy. That's why, at the national level, there have been two Civil Rights Acts— in 1957 and 1960;—and why this summer we will get a far more comprehensive Civil Rights Act; and why, in turn, the Civil Rights Act of 1964 will in three or four years time seem ripe for amendment.

Paralleling this positive regulatory legislation there must and will be a wide range of supplementary efforts, both public and private: poverty programs in Harlem and Appalachia; Ford grants to community colleges in Yakima, Sheboygan and Raleigh; self-starting neighborhood groups in Buffalo, Washington and Chicago's South Side.

It's very easy for us, as lawyers, to sit and devise better ways of structuring existing political institutions such as the state antidiscrimination commissions. I hope we do it. I hope we can follow this up by persuading legislators to bet some tax money on it. I hope we can get some better legislators and some re-apportioned legislators. (In fact, while we're talking about discrimination in employment, perhaps state legislatures would be a good place to start widening Negro job opportunities.) Better and more responsive legislatures can be expected to provide not half or three-quarters of a million dollars but five or ten million to back up the efforts of a state commission policing a medium-sized state.

It may prove far harder to move our political communities in the ways they must be moved to invest hundreds of millions of dollars in education and retraining programs and the whole gamut of other necessary ameliorative programs. These, it seems to me, are the things we have to do in addition to the things we are talking about tonight. I have no recipe. In closing I suggest only that there is a paramount fact we cannot escape: as we enter the second century of the Negro's emancipation the most important problem he confronts is how to get back in the labor market.

The discussion following the presentation of the prepared papers on Friday evening focused on several themes which recurred throughout the conference.

The first of these themes is that the Negro community has lost faith in the FEPC system as an effective device for getting jobs. This was emphasized by a representative of the New York State Commission, who, replying to Mr. Hill's paper, pointed to a crisis in confidence—Negroes just do not believe that the state commissions generally can do much for them. A joint effort—by the civil rights groups and the commissions—is required. In confirmation of this, Mr. Hill noted on Saturday morning that his highly critical paper was simply an articulation of what the Negro community feels. Dean Ferguson stressed, however, that there was little any agency could do to achieve equal job opportunities until employers begin to concentrate on this problem as a matter of administrative routine. It seemed to him that there should be some way to build a concentrated and institutional concern for the problem, perhaps through the use of economic incentives and pressures.

This feeling was shared by many at the conference who pointed out that most employers simply want to operate profitably and, as one speaker noted, did not consider themselves in business to try social experiments. Only if they faced economic loss would they be willing to focus their energies on this problem.

A second recurrent theme was whether and why few Negroes applied for various jobs, apprenticeships and other programs. Mr. Hill and Mr. Joseph Easley, President of the Buffalo NAACP, replied that: (1) there have been numerous applicants over the years; and (2) if the number of applicants has declined recently, this is because many Negroes have become reluctant to undergo the continual and frustrating refusal which almost inevitably meets such applications. In the printing trades, noted Mr. Hill, the procedures for applying had been kept secret for a long time.

The third recurring theme was that of preferences for Negro applicants. Citing an example from Dean Ferguson's paper, where a Negro post office employee had been elevated to supervisory status despite the seniority of several white employees, Professor Pollak asked whether this amounted to preferring an unqualified applicant because of his race. Dean Ferguson replied that the Negro was indeed less qualified because less experienced on an objective basis *as of the moment of choice.* But this lack of experience was based on a historical discriminatory pattern which had prevented the Negro from getting the requisite experience. The key question for decision in such matters is therefore: What would have been this Negro applicant's qualifications had there been no discrimination?

---

* These summaries were prepared by Associate Professor Herman Schwartz, Co-Chairman of the Conference, and checked by the named participants who made corrections and amplifications where they thought it necessary.

The approach would determine individual rights on the basis of membership in a group and Dean Ferguson recognized that it raised constitutional problems, though he did not think it unconstitutional. He also recognized that the white employee may have had nothing to do with depriving the Negro of the opportunity to become qualified, for he may have joined a discriminatory union long after the discriminatory policy had been firmly established. In Dean Ferguson's mind, one ameliorating factor in the problem is that such hardship cases are likely to be infrequent for usually only a few Negroes will be involved and thus few jobs will be determined on such a basis. This did not, however, dispose of the academic question of the conflict in rights between the specific Negro applicant who gets the job and the specific white employee who loses it.

PART II: STRENGTHENING ENFORCEMENT BY COMMISSION

TAILORING THE TECHNIQUES TO ELIMINATE AND PREVENT EMPLOYMENT DISCRIMINATION

Henry Spitz*

The New York State Law Against Discrimination was enacted in 1945.[1] It declared the "opportunity to obtain employment without discrimination because of race, creed, color or national origin . . . to be a civil right"[2] and created the State Commission Against Discrimination (now State Commission for Human Rights) as the administrative agency to enforce the law.[3] On July 1, 1964, the Commission will mark its 19th year of existence.

This paper is a discussion of the techniques devised by the Commission to eliminate and prevent discrimination because of race, creed, color or national origin[4] in the fields of employment and apprentice training. Since its inception, the Commission has sought to eliminate and prevent racial and religious discrimination against apprentices as employees.[5] In 1962, the Commission's enforcement jurisdiction over this subject area was made explicit[6] and was extended to include discrimination in guidance programs and other occupational training and retraining programs.[7] The Commission's jurisdiction extends also to the elimination and prevention of discrimination because of race, creed, color or national origin in the fields of public accommodations, education, housing and commercial space.[8] This paper does not deal with the techniques employed by the Commission in these areas, though experience gained in one field of jurisdiction can frequently be applied to problems in other fields of jurisdiction.

This paper is further limited to the sole consideration of those techniques utilized by the Commission in the course of processing verified complaint cases and Commission-initiated investigations. These limitations are dictated by the program of this Conference, and do not reflect any limitation of the activities

---

* General Counsel, N.Y. State Commission for Human Rights.

1. L. 1945, ch. 118, adding art. 12, §§ 125-36 to the Executive Law. By L. 1951, ch. 800, these provisions were renumbered as art. 15, §§ 290-301. [The Law Against Discrimination will be cited herein as "the Law" or as "LAD"].

2. Section 126, later amended and renumbered as § 291.

3. The name was changed by L. 1962, ch. 165.

4. L. 1958, ch. 738 vested the Commission with additional jurisdiction to eliminate and prevent discrimination in employment because of age.

5. See 1960 N.Y. State Comm'n. Against Discrimination Rep. of Progress 55. These annual Reports of Progress will be cited herein as Report.

6. See 1962 Report (Mimeo. ed.) 15.

7. LAD § 296.1-a, added by L. 1962, C. 164.

8. The Commission's jurisdiction was extended to public accommodations by L. 1952, ch. 285, to publicly-assisted housing by L. 1955, ch. 340, to tax-exempt nonsectarian educational institutions by L. 1958, ch. 960 and to private housing and commercial space by L. 1961, ch. 414 and L. 1963, ch. 481.

of the Commission, which also engages in broad educational and research programs, sponsors studies of discrimination "in all or specific fields of human relationships,"[9] and issues publications "to promote good-will and minimize or eliminate discrimination."[10]

COMMISSION PROCEDURES

Any person who claims to be aggrieved by an unlawful discriminatory practice may file a verified complaint with the Commission. When such complaint is filed, the Chairman assigns one of the seven Commissioners comprising the State Commission for Human Rights to conduct an investigation to determine whether "probable cause exists for crediting the allegations of the complaint." If no "probable cause" is found, the complaint is dismissed. However, if the Investigating Commissioner finds "probable cause", he attempts to eliminate the discriminatory practice by conference, conciliation and persuasion. Cases which are closed as adjusted by conciliation are subject to later review to determine whether the respondent has complied with the conciliation agreement.

However, if the respondent is unwilling to adjust the case on terms acceptable to the Investigating Commissioner, the complaint is directed to be noticed for public hearing before three other Commissioners, designated by the Chairman to sit as Hearing Commissioners. If, upon all the evidence at the hearing, the Hearing Commissioners find that the respondent has engaged in any unlawful discriminatory practice, they issue an order requiring the respondent to cease and desist and to take such affirmative action as, in their judgment, "will effectuate the purposes" of the Law.[11]

The Commission may petition the supreme court to enforce the order of the Hearing Commissioners, and the complainant, respondent or other person aggrieved by the order may obtain judicial review thereof. The Court on such application may make "an order enforcing, modifying, and enforcing as so modified, or setting aside in whole or in part the order of the commission."[12]

In addition to its jurisdiction initiated by verified complaints, the Commission has a "general jurisdiction",[13] which includes the power to investigate the problems of discrimination even in the absence of a verified complaint.[14] If apparently credible information about alleged discriminatory practices or patterns is received from a responsible source, or if it is accompanied by a reasonable degree of factual support, the Commission may initiate an investigation. In such cases, there is no formal hearing and no judicial enforcement. The investigatory process and the following steps of conference and con-

---

9. LAD § 295.8.
10. LAD § 295.9.
11. LAD § 297.2.
12. LAD § 298.
13. LAD § 290, after setting forth the purposes of the Law, states: "the commission established hereunder is hereby given general jurisdiction and power for such purposes."
14. Board of Higher Education of City of N.Y. v. Carter, 14 N.Y.2d 138 (1964).

ciliation are carried out by an Investigating Commissioner, who endeavors to work out a conciliation agreement.[15]

The Law lists several measures of permissible affirmative relief which may be incorporated in an order after public hearing, but does not limit the Commission to them.[16] The Law is silent on the terms which may be included in a conciliation agreement.[17]

Basically, every conciliation agreement and cease and desist order of the Commission is structured to achieve four results: (1) to do equity to the complainant who has been wronged, (2) to eliminate all existing unlawful discriminatory practices engaged in by the respondent, (3) to prevent the commission of any future unlawful discriminatory practices by the respondent and (4) to assure compliance with the terms of the order or agreement by the respondent before the case is finally closed. Underlying these four stated objectives, there is the additional leit-motif of accelerating the integration of the members of hitherto excluded minority groups into the main stream of our economic life. This calls for a high degree of creativity by the Commission because the elimination and prevention of discrimination does not necessarily equate with accelerated integration. History, custom, usage and countless other factors have built barriers into the system which may not have been motivated by prejudice in their inception, yet today constitute effective roadblocks to the rapid integration of the members of excluded groups.

Underlying Problems

Although the "particular circumstances of each case determine the terms of conciliation",[18] no case exists in a vacuum. There are a number of underlying problems of which the Commission must take account in order to deal realistically with the cases before it. One of these problems is that "discrimination . . . has had the sanction of time and custom"[19] and become a part of the traditional pattern of many industries.

Past customs of discrimination have resulted in "[f]ailure by minorities to train or apply for jobs through fear, ignorance, tradition, or their unwillingness to sacrifice immediate higher-paid jobs for the longer-range better op-

---

15. 1951 Report 26.
16. LAD § 297.2 authorizes the hearing commissioners to order "such affirmative action, including (but not limited to) hiring, reinstatement or upgrading of employees, with or without back pay, restoration to membership in any respondent labor organization, admission to or participation in a guidance program, apprenticeship training program, on-the-job training program or other occupational training or retraining program, or the extension of full, equal and unsegregated accommodations, advantages, facilities and privileges to all persons, as, in the judgment of the commission, will effectuate the purposes of this article, and including a requirement for report of the manner of compliance."
17. For an earlier discussion of conciliation agreements see Spitz, *Patterns of Conciliation Under the New York State Law Against Discrimination.* This work published by the Commission, originally appeared in the N.Y.L.J., April 6, 9, 10, 11, 12, 1951.
18. 1948 Report 10.
19. *Id.* at 7.

portunities."[20] The Commission endeavors to overcome the effect of these discriminatory traditions by measures designed to raise the aspirational sights of the disadvantaged and encourage them to acquire the skills which will enable them to compete effectively for new job opportunities.

Experience requirements can have a similar blocking effect. Since few, if any, Negro elevator operators in New York City have "East Side apartment house experience", a requirement of "*prior* experience in that particular job area may be used effectively to limit or prevent the entrance of Negroes into it for an indefinite period." Since such localized experience was not essential to the ability "to run a front elevator in an East Side luxury apartment", the Commission prevailed upon the New York State Employment Service to consider such a job specification unacceptable.[21]

The tradition of discrimination was reflected in a number of the constitutions and practices of international unions. International union color bars or requirements of segregation were obstacles to the observance of the Law by New York union locals in the railroad and maritime industries. The Commission finally secured changes in these provisions.[22]

When the Commission has to decide upon the relief to be demanded of a respondent, it is often confronted with the fact that existing employees have retention or recall rights based on their seniority. These are a great protection against unemployment.

Disregard of these seniority rights would, of course, open up more jobs for which the victims of discrimination might compete on equal terms. The Commission has adopted the policy of recognizing employees' seniority rights in a respondent's firm. However, while respecting seniority within a firm, the Commission has expressed misgivings about the establishment of industry-wide seniority where it would perpetuate a pattern of discrimination. The Chairman of the Commission made this point in 1959 in a letter written concerning the so-called Jensen Award. The Jensen Award was an award in an arbitration case between the New York Shipping Association and the International Longshoremen's Association. It established a system of seniority or priorities in various geographical areas of the New York City waterfront. The Chairman stated the Commission's position that nothing in the Jensen Award can limit the Commission's power to take affirmative action to effectuate the purpose of the Law.[23]

In a recent case, a complainant charged the members of the Seniority Board, set up under the Jensen Award, with transferring his seniority rights because complainant had opposed discriminatory practices.[24] The Commission

---

20. 1957 Report 72.
21. 1961 Report 60.
22. 1948 Report 33; 1951 Report 87; 1952 Report 92.
23. 1959 Report 30.
24. LAD § 296.1(d) makes it an unlawful discriminatory practice:
For any employer, labor organization or employment agency to discharge, expel or otherwise discriminate against any person because he has opposed any practices

ordered the union co-chairman of the Seniority Board to schedule a meeting of the Board to reconsider its action in changing the geographical section in which complainant had his seniority rights. The Commission's order was enforced by the supreme court and complainant's seniority rights in the section where he had worked were restored.[25]

Sometimes a union refuses to admit new members because a large percentage of its members are out of work. In these circumstances, Investigating Commissioners have required the unions to consider complainants for admission when the membership books are again open. Of course, the closing of membership books to keep out persons of a particular race is another matter.

The practice of nepotism in the apprenticeship and exercise of various crafts can be traced back to the medieval guilds. In a current case decided by the Commission, the respondent argued that the discrimination was nepotic, not racial.

Local 28 of the Sheet Metal Workers International Association and an employers' association had set up a joint apprenticeship committee to conduct a program for training apprentices. The local union designated the apprentices from a waiting list, and did not adhere strictly to chronological selection. The local union has no Negro members and, until November, 1946, the constitution of the International union denied Negroes full membership privileges and limited them to auxiliary locals. Virtually the only way of gaining admission into Local 28 is through apprenticeship, and the only way of getting an apprenticeship is by being a son, nephew or other close relative of a union member. Negroes as a class are thus automatically excluded. The Hearing Commissioners found that an unlawful discriminatory practice had been committed. Although neither a chronological list, nor a monolithic pattern, nor a nepotic system is discriminatory *per se*, when a combination of these devices is used to bar equality of employment opportunity because of color or race, it does become violative of the Law.

In 1957, the Commission reported the results of an interdepartment study of the problem of poverty. "Sixteen obstacles were shown to prevent the economic advancement of minority groups."[26] In addition to the obstacles associated with tradition and unemployment previously discussed, the Commission listed certain other obstacles associated with migration, deficiencies in education and with environment. The obstacles associated with migration include language difficulties, the absence of original trades acquired at the source of migration, transience and lack of leadership. The deficiencies in education include defective operation of the educational system for minorities, and failures of apprenticeship systems, counseling services and trade schools. The environ-

---

forbidden under this article or because he has filed a complaint, testified or assisted in any proceeding under this article.

25. Delany v. Conway, 39 Misc.2d 499, 241 N.Y.S.2d 384 (Sup. Ct. N.Y. County 1963).

26. 1957 Report 71.

mental difficulties include deficiencies in home life, absence of housing, and unfavorable community attitudes. Some of these obstacles have been attacked by extension of the Law to reach certain of the educational[27] and environmental difficulties.[28] However, the obstacles associated with migration remain to be overcome. In discussing the "increases in numbers of nonwhites and Americans of Puerto Rican descent" in this state, the Commission said:

> The important task of integrating these rapidly expanding minority groups into the economic, educational, and social milieu presents a challenge of formidable proportions which will demand the utmost in energy, ingenuity and commitment from this Commission and all other public and private agencies devoted to the goal of creating equal opportunities for all people. In brief, the Commission must utilize all available resources, both internal and external, to maintain and further the gains which can be achieved through an enlightened and dynamic administration of the Law which gives this Commission its mandate.[29]

REDRESS TO COMPLAINANTS

Provisions for redressing complainants depend on the facts in particular cases. Sometimes no direct redress will be accorded a complainant even though he may have been the victim of an unlawful discriminatory practice. Thus, a complainant who has suffered no monetary loss as a result of an act of discrimination and who has found other employment which he now prefers to the job from which he was precluded, may help to eliminate and prevent discrimination by filing a complaint, without getting any direct personal benefit.

On the other hand, where warranted by the facts, Investigating Commissioners have frequently required respondents to offer employment to qualified complainants as part of the terms of conciliation.[30] In one case, an employer was required either to offer complainant employment or to give him two weeks pay.[31] In another, the employer was required either to employ complainant or to explain why not. Promotion of a complainant has also been made a term of conciliation.[32] Where the alleged discriminatory practice was the employer's failure to certify complainant's competence to the union, the employer agreed to do so as a term of conciliation.

An employer is always entitled to consider an applicant's qualifications and competency. Thus, the Temporary State Commission Against Discrimination, which drafted the Law, stated in its report:

---

27. The Commission's jurisdiction was extended to tax-exempt nonsectarian schools by L. 1958, ch. 960, and to guidance programs and other occupational training and retraining programs by L. 1962, ch. 164. See text accompanying notes 5-7 for discussion of apprenticeship.
28. The Commission's jurisdiction was extended to the bulk of housing accomodations by L. 1961, ch. 414 and L. 1963, ch. 481.
29. 1960 Report 15.
30. The Commission may order "hiring, reinstatement or upgrading of employees, with or without back pay." LAD § 297.2.
31. Yard v. Bond Sewing Stores, 1951 Report 65.
32. Cave v. Delaware & Hudson R.R., 1953 Report 39.

Other employers fear that they may be compelled to employ, or retain in employment, persons of inferior efficiency. The administrative body contemplated by the Commission will have no charter to protect the inefficient or the unfitted in jobs they are incapable of handling.[33]

Therefore the Commission often limits its requirement of the respondent to a consideration of the complainant for training,[34] union membership or employment without regard to race, color, creed, religion or national origin. Terms of conciliation have at times required that the complainant's qualifications be assessed by the Commission or a neutral consultant.[35]

The Commission has required unions to admit complainants to membership.[36] Agreements have been reached to admit a complainant to membership upon his employer's recommendation and to admit a complainant unless a nondiscriminatory reason for ineligibility is discovered.[37] Unions have agreed to reassign complainants from segregated lodges to lodges of their choice.[38] In one case, the Hearing Commissioners ordered a union to reinstate a complainant and to withdraw challenges to his return to his former area of work.[39]

In a case involving discrimination in admission to union membership, the respondent agreed to adopt and administer uniformly a reasonable and fair examination which was to be submitted for confidential evaluation by a competent authority selected by the Commission. In another case, the Hearing Commissioners ordered a union to give an admission examination to complainant, to fix as passing mark a score no higher than the lowest mark made by any member admitted in the last ten years, and to submit the examination for confidential evaluation in the event complainant should fail the examination.

Some respondents have been required to make efforts with third parties on behalf of complainants. Respondent employment agencies have been required to make sincere efforts to place the complainant or to refer him to the first available job for which he is fitted.[40] One union arranged for the complainant's admission into another union. A third union agreed to assist a complainant to become a qualified cutter. A respondent county sanitorium agreed to submit the problem of complainant's residence waiver to the county civil service commission.[41]

---

33. P. 49.
34. Carter v. Aschenfelder, 1949 Report 21. (Respondent trained singers, organized them into groups and arranged for performances.).
35. Byams v. N.Y., N.H. & H. R.R., 1956 Report 57.
36. Workman v. Bottlers & Drivers Union, 1955 Report 94. Miller v. Checkers & Clerks Union, 1959 Report 106. (Complainants given seniority status commencing with date of entry into industry.)
37. Case C-4824-57, 1958 Report 53.
38. Valentine v. Brotherhood of R.R. and S.S. Clerks, 1952 Report 34. Brown v. Brotherhood of R.R. and S.S. Clerks, 1957 Report 81.
39. See note 25 *supra* and accompanying text.
40. Brown v. Jones & Clark, 1949 Report 35. Westreich v. Wall St. Employment Bureau, 1952 Report 53. Mitchell v. Greater Syracuse Employment Agency, 1956 Report 33.
41. Case C-5466-58, 1958 Report 47.

The Law expressly authorizes the Commission to order "admission to or participation in a guidance program, apprenticeship training program, on-the-job training program or other occupational training or retraining program."[42] In one case a Negro complainant charged a university's placement service with aiding and abetting discrimination. Respondent's representatives seemed to believe that they were doing a service to Negro students by not referring them to communities where they might encounter discrimination. This discriminatory practice was eliminated and the dean communicated with complainant, offering to refer him if he is interested.

Whether or not to award any back pay is discretionary with the Commission. Terms of conciliation have provided reinstatement without back pay where the service of the complainant had been marred by drunkenness or absenteeism. Once the Commission has determined to award back pay, the amount thereof must have reference to a particular period of unemployment suffered by the complainant. In a cease and desist order after formal hearing, the amount of the back pay award must represent the actual losses sustained by the complainant. In a conciliation agreement, the amount of back pay may represent the actual losses sustained by the complainant,[43] or may be a compromise amount less than such actual losses. An estimated amount may be included for tips.[44] Terms of conciliation may lawfully require an employment agency which had discriminatorily refused to refer a complainant to make him whole for his loss of earnings during the remainder of his period of unemployment. The Commission does not have the power to impose a penalty or fine or punitive damages against a respondent or to assess costs against him.

ELIMINATING DISCRIMINATORY POLICIES AND PRACTICES

The cessation of existing discriminatory policies and practices is required in all cases. However, in a society where discrimination has had the sanction of time, law, custom and usage, a high degree of sophistication may be needed to make the cease and desist provisions of an order or conciliation agreement meaningful and to prevent future acts of discrimination. A respondent's commitment that he will cease discriminating is generally insufficient to bring about changed employment patterns. There is often a need for affirmative action to carry conviction to the hitherto excluded members of minority groups of the employer's changed policies and practices. The new policy must be publicized to potential job applicants. It must be filtered down to lower echelon employees who are charged with responsibility for administering its new policy. Changed recruitment procedures and personnel practices may be required to eliminate inbreeding and to overcome indigenous barriers to integration. Encouragement to the members of minority groups to acquire the skills and

---

42. LAD § 297.2.
43. Calvin v. Calmar Steamship Corp., 1953 Report 44.
44. Sweet v. Towers Hotel Corp. 1953 Report 44.

apply for the new job opportunities as well as on-the-job training opportunities may all be called for to effect a change in existing patterns. The Commission has secured the elimination of policies limiting the employment of Negroes by means of a quota[45] or excluding them entirely from many job categories, including those of telephone operator, dining car steward, and railroad grill car worker.[46]

Terms of conciliation have required the abandonment of union restrictions limiting membership to white workers or to workers of Italian ancestry.[47] A union official's refusal, contrary to union policy, to let a Negro work in a theatre catering to Puerto Ricans was corrected. A fraternal association of employees of fashionable hotels and restaurants voluntarily eliminated rules limiting membership to white males. That association was deemed to be an "employment agency"[48] since its employment department filled job orders.[49] Its elimination of this color bar constituted "the first important break in an almost exclusively white employment pattern within the service departments of the fashionable restaurants and hotels of New York."[50]

It is an unlawful discriminatory practice to deny to "any qualified person because of his race, creed, color or national origin the right to be admitted to or participate in a guidance program, an apprenticeship traning program, on-the-job training program, or other occupational training or retraining program."[51] At a hearing, an agreement was procured from a union to process all applications for membership in training programs on the basis of qualifications only.

An elevator company was charged with requiring Negro job applicants to take a test that was not required of white applicants.[52] In another case, a union of iron workers was charged with requiring a Negro complainant to take a difficult written test for membership, although several white applicants had been admitted to membership without being required to take or pass the test. In each case the Commission secured an agreement from the respondent to give tests on a nondiscriminatory basis. The Commission has required the abolition of a separate "Negro organization" in a sales force[53] and of policies limiting Negroes employed as investigators to Negro neighborhoods.[54]

---

45. Saunders v. Knickerbocker Construction Corp., 1950 Report 38 (carpenters).
46. Thomas v. N.Y., N.H. & H. R.R., 1948 Report 25.
47. LAD § 296.1(b) prohibits discrimination by labor organizations.
48. The Law prohibits discrimination by employment agencies. LAD § 296.1 (c).
49. "The term 'employment agency' includes any person undertaking to procure employees or opportunities to work." LAD § 292.2.
50. International Geneva Association, Inc., 1952 Report 95.
51. LAD § 296.1-a(a). Effective Sept. 1, 1964, this paragraph will be renumbered to LAD § 296.1-a(b) and the word "qualified" deleted. Furthermore, it will be an unlawful discriminatory practice "(a) To select persons for an apprentice training program registered with the state of New York on any basis other than their qualifications, as determined by objective criteria which permit review." L. 1964, ch. 948.
52. Case C-4147-56, 1957 Report 44.
53. Simmons v. The American Tobacco Co., 1957 Report 44.
54. Williams v. The Hooper-Holmes Bureau, Inc., 1956 Report 57; Ingram v. Benton & Bowles, Inc., 1960 Report 116.

The Commission has required the elimination of policies of segregated training. A barber school agreed to eliminate a policy limiting students to practicing on "customers" of the same race; a dancing school agreed to hire instructors and to assign students without discrimination; and, a respondent in the business of forming and training singing groups and securing employment for them agreed to abandon a policy against racially mixed groups.[55]

The Commission has required labor organizations to eliminate policies of segregating Negroes in auxiliary locals,[56] barring them from serving as convention delegates and relegating them to segregated hiring halls.[57]

As part of the terms of conciliation, employers and supervisors have been directed to discontinue their habitual use of vile language referring to persons of particular races, religions or national origins.[58] A similar approach has been taken toward co-workers' remarks of that sort.[59] Likewise, employers have agreed to refrain from less base remarks evincing discrimination, such as a statement that Jewish persons had no chance of advancement or a "joking" threat to discharge colored employees. An Investigating Commissioner instructed a respondent that a supervisor's attempts to convert a complainant from his religion should be promptly discontinued.[60]

The Law Against Discrimination contains provisions prohibiting employment advertisements and inquiries that specify race, color, creed or national origin.[61] The Commission has required various types of respondents to desist from violating these provisions. Employment agencies have agreed to discontinue using the proscribed specifications in advertisements, on job order forms, on applicant record forms, and in statements to applicants[62] and employers.[63] The New York State Employment Service made a similar agreement concerning household job placements, although they are not covered by the Law.[64] Employers and unions[65] have agreed to cease discriminatory inquiries and magazines have agreed not to print discriminatory advertisements. Similar terms of conciliation have been accepted by a university placement office, placement offices operated by business training schools,[66] and a public school teacher.

Explicit notations and inquiries concerning race, national origin and religious preference, whether made of employers[67] or of job applicants,[68] are prohibited by the Law and have been eliminated by terms of conciliation.

55. Carter v. Aschenfelder, 1949 Report 21.
56. Kinard v. Walsh, 1955 Report 92.
57. Carey v. Hall, 1951 Report 61.
58. Martinez v. Lido Toy Co., 1956 Report 89.
59. Schlesinger v. Andrea Candy Co., Inc., 1962 Report (Mimeo. ed.) 56.
60. Denker v. W. E. Dean & Co., 1954 Report 23.
61. LAD §§ 296.1(c), 296.1-a (c).
62. Smith v. Sims, 1951 Report 67.
63. Westreich v. Wall St. Employment Bureau, 1952 Report 53.
64. LAD § 292.6.
65. Raglund v. O'Dowd & Kelvin Engr. Co., 1950 Report 39.
66. Brown v. Felt & Tarrant Comptometer School, 1956 Report 35.
67. Bowen v. Ross, 1954 Report 32.
68. Mitchell v. Greater Syracuse Employment Agency, 1956 Report 33.

Confidential inquiries and coded notations about these matters are likewise unlawful. An employment agency was required to give back pay to an employee it had discharged for refusal to use racial codes. Terms of conciliation have required the elimination of questions which directly or indirectly tend to elicit information revelatory of race, creed, color or national origin. Among the proscribed inquiries have been those pertaining to place of birth, change of name[69] and whether a person was married by a minister. Likewise, the required presentation of documents revelatory of birthplace or religion, such as birth certificates, baptismal certificates and references from clergy[70] have been eliminated. Specifications that job applicants have attended an "out-of-town college" are considered subterfuges for discrimination and have been eliminated by terms of conciliation.[71] Notations or advertisements that a job is in a "Negro neighborhood" have been eliminated also.

As photographs are revelatory of color and, sometimes, of national origin and religion, a requirement that an applicant for employment submit a photograph is unlawful. Terms of conciliation have required unions[72] and employment agencies to discontinue the policy of requesting or requiring the submission of photographs with applications.[73]

The Law Against Discrimination makes an exception in cases of "bona fide occupational qualification."[74] Such a qualification, however, must be "material to job performance."[75] Thus, terms of conciliation have eliminated discriminatory policies, where an attempt had been made to justify them on the basis of specious job requirements. An employer was required to offer employment to a worker whom he considered too heavy and too "dark", and a dress manufacturer agreed not to limit his job orders to those national origins considered by him to include "traditional needlewomen". A requirement, designed to exclude Negroes, that a foot-press operator speak Italian was eliminated. Discrimination against workers of a particular creed may not be justified by a need to have work performed on religious holidays, or by a legal requirement that children be placed with probation officers of their own religion.[76] An inquiry concerning religion may not be justified by the need for an employee of absolute honesty. However, it is permissible to inquire whether a job applicant regularly attends a house of worship. A religious educational organization which is exempt from the law and which customarily holds devotional services for its employees voluntarily eliminated an inquiry about creed.

---

69. Holland v. Edwards, 116 N.Y.S.2d 264 (Sup. Ct. N.Y. County 1952), *aff'd*, 282 App. Div. 353, 122 N.Y.S.2d 721 (1st Dep't 1953), *aff'd*, 307 N.Y. 38, 119 N.E.2d 581 (1954).
70. Safron v. Home Ins. Co., 1955 Report 50.
71. Tobison Employment Agency, 1950 Report 40.
72. Raglund v. O'Dowd & Kelvin Engr. Co., 1950 Report 39.
73. The Allied Teachers' Bureau, 1952 Report 39.
74. LAD §§ 296.1(c), 296.1-a (c).
75. Rulings on Pre-Employment Inquiries, p. 10 (published by the Commission).
76. American Jewish Congress v. Hill, 1956 Report 27, 1 Race Rel. Rep. 971 (1956).

Terms of conciliation have eliminated policies against the hiring of all Negroes based on unfavorable experiences with some Negro workers.[77] Such terms implement the individual right to be free from discrimination. "No person," the state constitution states, "shall, because of race, color, creed or religion, be subject to discrimination in his civil rights . . ."[78] The Commission has stressed that "no entire group should be characterized as unreliable or unqualified because of the poor performance of some of its representatives."[79]

The Commission has required the elimination of discriminatory policies, despite alleged difficulties, in compliance with the Law. A policy against hiring Negroes may not be justified by a belief that they will be unable to secure lodgings in the area. A foreign nation's policy against granting entry visas to Jews does not justify the making, in New York, of discriminatory inquiries by a company doing business in the foreign nation.[80]

The Commission has required the elimination of discriminatory policies based on fear of disharmony. A discriminatory hiring policy based on neighborhood racial tension[81] and an inquiry to ascertain if applicants were of the "same general type" as a bakery store's customers and employees[82] were eliminated. When employees refused to work with a Negro, the Investigating Commissioner sent a field representative to persuade them to do so.[83] An employer who expressed a general fear of colored people agreed to eliminate a policy against hiring them.

Preventing Discrimination and Promoting Better Human Relations

Terms of conciliation have required the alteration of existing procedures to avoid any possible future discrimination. This does not mean that the existing procedures constituted unlawful discriminatory practices, although they may have been susceptible to being so used. The procedural alterations are required to minimize frictions and reduce complaints of discrimination. Among the procedures so altered have been those pertaining to referrals. Thus a school placement service agreed to make referrals in order of scholastic standing. In several cases, unions have agreed to advise all persons of the referral procedures, to keep the rotary referral list on display,[84] to refer members in order of registration or to furnish reasons for by-passing them,[85] or to install machines to facilitate referrals in rotation.[86]

---

77. Mason v. Sidney J. Bernstein, Inc., 1959 Report 78.
78. N.Y. Const. art. I, § 11.
79. Jule Jacobs, Inc., 1952 Report 33.
80. American Jewish Congress v. Carter, 19 Misc.2d 205, 190 N.Y.S.2d 218 (Sup. Ct. N.Y. County 1959), *modified*, 10 A.D.2d 833, 199 N.Y.S.2d 157 (1st Dep't 1960), *aff'd*, 9 N.Y.2d 223, 173 N.E.2d 788, 213 N.Y.S.2d 60 (1961).
81. Sawyer v. Whelan Drug Co. Inc., 1953 Report 39.
82. Armstrong v. Cushman's Sons, Inc., 1954 Report 27.
83. Schenectady Venetian Blind Co., 1952 Report 52.
84. Allen v. Bricklayer's Tenders' Local Union No. 59, 1952 Report 55.
85. Williams v. Waiters & Waitresses Union, 1955 Report 56.
86. MacMillan v. Plasterer Helpers Local Union, 1956 Report 59.

A constricted recruitment procedure, where information about job openings is largely "inside information" can perpetuate a traditional discrimination.[87] Thus, in cases of employment discrimination, the Commission has required respondents to change their methods of recruitment of personnel to insure minority groups of better opportunities.[88] It has even furnished a respondent with the names of individuals and organizations willing to assist it in its new recruitment program.[89] The Commission has required respondent employers to add to the list of high schools where they recruit employees,[90] to set up a central employment office and to place job orders with the New York State Employment Service.[91]

Some terms of conciliation have required that respondents place job orders with organizations or agencies identified with a particular racial or religious group.[92] Others have required advertising in Jewish and Negro newspapers.

Requirements that ethnic or sectarian recruitment sources be used are practical measures designed "to eliminate the unlawful discriminatory practice complained of."[93] They are designed to prevent perpetuating the existing discriminatory pattern brought about by long-continued unlawful discriminatory practices. The Commission has consistently opposed token employment, quota employment and proportional representation.[94]

Terms of conciliation have also required alterations in hiring procedures. Employers have agreed to post notice of vacancies on bulletin boards or at the entrance to the job site.[95] Respondents have been required, in several cases, to have job interviews conducted by the manager instead of subordinates,[96] to interview all applicants,[97] to interview them without unreasonable waiting,[98] to interview them in the order of their applications, to advise unsuccessful applicants of the reasons for their rejection, or to keep applications for future use. Vague questions about "physical characteristics" and "personality" were eliminated from an interviewer's screening forms.[99] The completion of a form asking information about color and birthplace required by a government agency was deferred until after hiring.

---

87. See the "sandhog cases", 1949 Report 69.
88. Drakes v. O'Neill Motor Corp., 1955 Report 51.
89. Fulton v. Sears Roebuck Co., 1961 Report 100.
90. N.Y. Life Ins. Co., 1949 Report 35. Bowen v. Marine Midland Trust Co., 1955 Report 53.
91. Feuer v. United Press, 1955 Report 32.
92. Perry v. Krug Baking Co., 1956 Report 25 (Urban League); Johnston v. Victor Beinfield, 1954 Report 52 (Archdiocesan Vocational Service, Federation Employment Service).
93. See LAD § 297.
94. 1953 Report 73; Teddy's Shanty, 1951 Report 39, Moe v. H.R.H. Construction Corp., 1950 Report 38.
95. Byams v. N.Y., N.H. & H. R.R., 1956 Report 56.
96. Hardy v. Schenectady Hotel Co. Inc., 1954 Report 52.
97. Barnes v. Newark Electric Co., 1949 Report 34.
98. O'Kelly v. Longine-Wittnauer Watch Co., Inc., 1950 Report 57.
99. Carroll v. American District Telegraph Co., 1953 Report 31.

As part of the terms of conciliation, employers have agreed to make changes in working arrangements, including the elimination of insanitary conditions and the practice of searching employees.[100] Applicant preference has been considered in the initial assignment to a work place, clothing lockers have been assigned on a seniority basis, and work schedules have been arranged to permit time off for religious observances.[101] An employer agreed to give employees exact and clear reasons for dismissals.

Unions have agreed to terms of conciliation altering their procedures. Some have placed nondiscrimination clauses in their by-laws, or have adopted fixed rules for the processing of membership applications,[102] or have agreed to administer uniform tests to applicants for journeyman status or apprenticeship and to establish review procedures. One union appointed to its executive board a person who spoke Spanish in order to create a better relationship with its Spanish-speaking members who were inarticulate in English.[103] At least one union included a nondiscrimination clause in its collective bargaining contracts, and a clause protecting probationary employees against arbitrary dismissal.[104] Investigating Commissioners have recommended or required the improvement of job referral procedures,[105] the formalization of grievance procedures,[106] and the inclusion therein of opportunity to present grievances alleging discriminatory refusal of employment.

The Commission has required respondents to assist in the publication of Commission literature of a general nature. It is customary, in conciliation agreements and Hearing Commissioners' orders, to require that the respondent display the Commission's poster relating the substantive provisions of the Law. The Commission has, by regulation, imposed this requirement upon all employers, employment agencies, labor organizations and joint labor-management committees, whether or not they are respondents in verified complaint proceedings.[107] Its power to make this requirement has been upheld by the Courts.[108] The Commission has required a respondent agency of the state government to display, also, the Governor's Code of Fair Practices.[109]

The Commission has required respondents to distribute Commission lit-

---

100. Martinez v. Lido Toy Co., 1956 Report 89.
101. Feuer v. United Press Associations, 1955 Report 32.
102. Miller v. Checkers & Clerks Union, 1959 Report 106, enforced *sub nom.* Matter of State Commission Against Discrimination v. Gleason, N.Y.L.J. Oct. 8, 1962, p. 13, col. 2.
103. Martinez v. Lido Toy Co., 1956 Report 89.
104. Waiters & Waitresses Union, Local 2, 1950 Report 58.
105. See notes 84-86, *supra*, and accompanying text.
106. Martinez v. Lido Toy Co., 1956 Report 89.
107. General Regulations No. 1, June 1, 1962, 9 State of NY Compilation of Codes, Rules & Regulations, § 466.1 [This work will be cited as NYCRR.]
108. Ross v. Arbury, 206 Misc. 74, 133 N.Y.S.2d 62 (Sup. Ct. N.Y. County 1954), *aff'd mem.*, 285 App. Div. 886, 139 N.Y.S.2d 245 (1st Dep't 1955). The Court cited LAD § 295.5, which empowers the Commission "To adopt, promulgate, amend and rescind suitable rules and regulations to carry out the provisions of this article, and the policies and practice of the commission in connection therewith."
109. 9 NYCRR 1.5.

erature to their employees.[110] Sometimes it has required the showing of Commission films to employees. In one case a respondent union was required to make Commission literature available to its members.[111] In another case, a respondent was required to distribute Commission literature to customers as well as to employees.[112] And a respondent movie theatre chain agreed to show a Commission film to its patrons.[113] These measures assist the Commission in carrying out its educational mission "to promote good-will and minimize or eliminate discrimination."[114]

The education of young people in the purposes of the law is promoted by distributing Commission literature in schools.[115] Once, a complaint was made charging a public school system with requiring an applicant for a teaching position to submit a photograph, and with refusing to employ the applicant because of her race. The Investigating Comissioner found probable cause only with respect to the charge about the photograph. He required the respondent to arrange a planned educational program, including the exhibition of Commission films to faculty and student body and the distribution of Commission literature.[116]

Respondents have been required to issue statements of their intent to obey the law to the complainant, to interracial organizations, such as the NAACP, to guidance counsellors,[117] to public officials and the New York State Employment Service,[118] and to schools where respondents recruit workers.[119] Employment agencies have been directed to send such announcements to their employer clients.

Respondents have also been required to instruct their employees to observe the Law Against Discrimination; to ascertain, by personal interviews, the attitude of their hiring personnel towards the aims of the Law and to report the results of these interviews to the Commission. This is done to assure the Commission that the respondent's declared policy of nondiscrimination will be respected and effectuated.[120] Often statements have been required signed by such employees attesting their understanding of the Law and the individual liability to which they are subject in the event of breach.[121] The action to be taken against offending employers has sometimes been spelled out. The possibility of dismissal is sometimes mentioned. Respondents have agreed to refrain

---

110. Woorm v. Lucas, 1950 Report 53.
111. Carey v. Hall, 1951 Report 63.
112. Magaziners Bakery, 1949 Report 34.
113. Van Dyke Amusement Corp., 1951 Report 68.
114. LAD § 295.9.
115. 1959 Report 55-56.
116. Spratt v. Freeport Board of Education, 1953 Report 30.
117. Van Alstyne v. A & P., 1957 Report 51.
118. Westchester Refreshments, Inc., 1956 Report 37.
119. Campbell v. American Express Co., 1949 Report 33.
120. Ridley v. Montgomery Ward & Co., 1948 Report 27.
121. Franklin v. W. T. Grant Co., 1957 Report 52.

from hiring persons who gave discriminatory advice and to relieve employees who refuse to obey the Law from hiring responsibilities.

Respondents have been required to advise unions which refer job applicants to do so without discrimination. Nondiscrimination clauses in collective bargaining contracts have been recommended[122] or required. As part of the terms of conciliation, a respondent agreed to direct the officers of an employees' social and beneficial organization to admit complainant to the organization's social functions.[123] Often, respondents have been required to direct private employment agencies used by them, to refer job applicants without discrimination. Respondents have also been required to issue such directives to schools, stevedores' hiring agents[124] and subcontractors.[125]

Once the Commission received a complaint that job applicants were being given a personality test with items on religious attitudes. The test is intended for use in diagnosis and counseling, but the publisher of the test admitted that it is subject to misuse. The Commission got the publisher to include in the test an announcement calling attention to the fair employment practice laws. The announcement cautioned that personality tests which include inquiries into religious beliefs should not be used, for scientific as well as legal grounds, in the hiring process as a pre-employment screener.[126]

COMPLIANCE PROVISIONS, REVIEW PROCEDURES AND COOPERATION AGREEMENTS

Once the Commission issues its order, the problem of securing compliance arises. The Law recognizes this problem and authorizes the inclusion in the order of "a requirement for report of the manner of compliance."[127] Thus, the Commission has included, in its terms of conciliation and orders, provisions for making available to the Commission information which it can use in checking on and securing compliance.

Terms of conciliation have required respondents to furnish information about their operations. An employer was asked to furnish the name of the union representing its employees. Another was asked to report the results of a survey to determine whether employees were hired on a nondiscriminatory basis. An employer was required to report the results of a re-interview with a complainant and another was asked to report its experience with a broadened recruitment policy.

Terms of conciliation have required employers to report the reactions of their customers to the Commissions' pamphlets,[128] or to ascertain the reaction

---

122. McNair v. Barricini Co., 1949 Report 34.
123. Lightbourne v. Allied Chemical Corp., 1962 Report (Mimeo ed.) 57.
124. Applegate v. Universal Terminal & Stevedoring Co., 1959 Report 76.
125. Saunders v. Knickerbocker Construction Corp., 1950 Report 38.
126. Minnesota Multiphastic Personality Test, 1951 Report 66.
127. LAD § 297.2.
128. Magaziners Bakery, 1949 Report 34.

of their employees to the Law.[129] An employment agency was required to report the results of a referral of complainant. Some employment agencies have been required to report to the Commission the names of employers placing discriminatory job orders and the New York State Employment Service has agreed to do likewise.

Respondents have been required, by terms of conciliation, to make available applications and rosters which the Commission may use to ascertain if the discriminatory practice has been eliminated. A union was required to furnish its membership rules and a list of membership applicants.[130] Some unions have been required to notify the Commission of action taken on transfer requests.[131] Another was required to submit the names of persons referred to work. A university placement service was required to keep on file the reasons for rejecting students for referral. An employment agency was required to make books and records available to the Commission.[132] Some employers have been required to furnish lists of rosters of furloughed employees. Others have been required to keep records of job applications and the reasons for rejection of the applicants.

Some terms of conciliation have required the compiling or reporting of information by ethnic categories. Employers have been required to record the color of job applicants,[133] to retain the applications of rejected Negro applicants[134] and to report upon the employment status of Negroes,[135] or of female Negro employees, or the number of Negroes and Jews in each job classification. An employment agency was required to record and to report the color of applicants referred.

Although a requirement of reports compiled by ethnic categories furnishes a direct means for determining whether an exclusionary policy has been eliminated, the compilation of such information may arouse suspicions of discrimination. Emphasis on ethnic records and statistics may engender the erroneous[136] notion that the laws against discrimination may be satisfied by accepting a token number of the previously excluded group or by giving it a quota or by proportional representation. For example, a federal contracting agency once claimed that it was implementing a Presidential order requiring nondiscrimination clauses[137] when it prescribed, in addition, a provision that the payment of a specified proportion of the payroll to Negroes would "be considered as prima facie evidence that the contractor has not discriminated against Negro labor."

---

129. Campbell v. American Express Co., 1949 Report 33.
130. Miller v. Checkers and Clerks Union, Local No. 1, 1959 Report 106.
131. Carey v. Hall, 1951 Report 61.
132. Westreich v. Wall Street Employment Bureau, 1952 Report 53.
133. Ridley v. Montgomery Ward & Co., 1948 Report 27.
134. Willis v. Long Island R.R., 1955 Report 88.
135. Patterson v. Grace Line, 1960 Report 110.
136. See note 94 *supra*.
137. Executive Order No. 8802, June 25, 1941.

The Commission has formulated guide lines to be used when there are legitimate circumstances in which it is necessary to conduct research involving the collection of information by ethnic categories. The guide lines provide that such information should be obtained in an inoffensive manner, that it should not be recorded in conjunction with the names of individuals, and that records pertaining to specific individuals should not be made available to operating personnel and should be destroyed when they have served the purpose of research. By the use of these guide lines and the compliance review procedure,[138] the Investigating Commissioner may guard against the misuse of a technique designed to verify the elimination of discrimination.

Terms of conciliation have required respondents to submit certain forms and documents to the Commission for review. A union agreed to submit its admission tests for evaluation, and an advertising agency agreed to submit its ads soliciting business for itself. Employment agencies have been required to submit job orders raising questions of *bona fide* occupational qualifications[139] and to submit their application forms.[140] This technique of reviewing job application forms can prevent the use of discriminatory questions, and once was applied not only to respondents, but also to all employers of 100 or more persons.

In addition to requiring the respondents to report about their compliance with its orders, the Commission sends its own representatives to check on compliance. The Commission described this long-standing practice in its 1949 Report:

> Each complaint is reconsidered by the investigating commissioner approximately six months after closing to determine whether a case review by field investigation or otherwise is necessary . . . The Commission maintains this continuing interest in each case for the purpose of measuring the extent and effectiveness of compliance with the terms of the adjustment agreement. The review procedure also enables the Commission to evaluate the different types of conciliation agreements thereby assisting the investigating commissioners to perfect the conciliation process."[141]

One of the Commission's functions is to "obtain upon request and utilize the services of all governmental departments and agencies."[142] The Commission has worked out cooperation agreements with many such agencies to further the enforcement of the Law in various fields. In the employment field, it has made agreements with contracting agencies and with licensing agencies. Employment agencies in the City of New York are licensed by that city's De-

---

138. See note 141 *infra* and accompanying text.

139. Woorm v. Lucas, 1950 Report 53; Westreich v. Wall Street Employment Bureau, 1952 Report 53.

140. Holland v. Edwards, 116 N.Y.S.2d 264 (Sup. Ct. N.Y. County 1952), *aff'd*, 282 App. Div. 353, 112 N.Y.S.2d 721 (1st Dep't 1953), *aff'd*, 307 N.Y. 38, 119 N.E.2d 581 (1954).

141. 1949 Report 17.

142. LAD § 295.4.

partment of Licenses. As early as 1949, the Commission worked out an arrangement with that Department under which the Department would consider disciplinary action against employment agencies violating the Law.[143] The agreement was strengthened in 1957.[144] The Commission has authorized negotiation of a similar agreement with the New York State Department of Labor, which recently has been given authority to license employment agencies outside of New York City. The Governor has directed all state licensing and regulatory agencies to take appropriate action against respondents found to have engaged in unlawful discriminatory practices.[145]

Labor Law Section 220-e requires nondiscrimination clauses in public works contracts. Recently, improved procedures have been established for the Commission to notify the contracting agencies of findings of discrimination. In this way, the contracting agencies will be able to lend their weight to the enforcement of the Commission's orders.

CONCLUSION

Through the years, the Commission has adjusted the majority of its complaints by conciliation agreements designed to eliminate and to prevent unlawful discriminatory practices. It has tried to administer the law in an atmosphere of cooperation, not conflict. It has tried to obviate the need of a police operation so extensive as to make enforcement impossible. It has tried through education and persuasion to change the thinking and mores of our people. The fact that the Commission has the power to order cases to public hearing helps to persuade respondents to enter into conciliation agreements. In these agreements, the Commission has sought action to reassure the groups discriminated against, to sensitize and educate the respondent's personnel to the requirements of the Law, to redress the grievances of the particular complainants, and to promote better human relations in the industrial community. The Commission has sought to prevent future discrimination by encouraging respondents to use more open and objective procedures, and it has made use of its power to require "report of the manner of compliance."[146] The terms of relief here discussed are not ends in themselves, but devices for the elimination and prevention of unlawful discriminatory practices. "They are not fixed and rigid but subject always to modification and change in the light of accumulating experience."[147]

The Commission has always attempted to tailor its techniques to the facts of the specific case. It maintains an awareness of the underlying problems. It realizes the importance of obtaining complete information concerning the specific employment situation. The Law can not be satisfied by mere lip-

---

143. 1949 Report 26.
144. 1957 Report 78.
145. Governor's 1960 Code of Fair Practices, 9 NYCRR 1.5.
146. LAD § 297.2.
147. 1948 Report 83-84.

service or token compliance. What was said by the court in a housing case is equally applicable in the employment field:

> A partial or limited compliance with the statute does not, and cannot, constitute a substantial compliance therewith. A contrary decision would confer upon the petitioner an exemption from substantial compliance. His position, if sustained, would, in effect, amend the law to provide that an occupancy by a Negro of one apartment out of a total of eight apartments, permits the petitioner "to refuse to sell, rent, lease or otherwise to deny to or withhold from any person or group of persons such housing accommodation because of the race, creed, color or national origin of such person or persons", contrary to the express mandate of the statute. The statute does not permit a gradual, partial or progressive application of the law. Obviously, the court may not change or amend the law by judicial construction. It must apply the statute as it is written.[148]

Employment discrimination against minority groups has often resulted in the use of counter measures to combat it. Among these measures have been the use of economic pressures to compel operators of retail stores to "give employment to [N]egroes as clerks, particularly in stores patronized largely by colored people."[149] In one case, the Commission received a report that it was respondent's policy, allegedly dictated by the Harlem Labor Union, Inc., to employ only Negroes. The Commission advised that it could not condone this.

> The Commission pointed out that it is not desirable to countenance discrimination in any particular area in favor of the inhabitants preponderant in such area, despite the fact that they had for many years endured great hardships and handicaps because of their race and color, for the reason that the exertion by Negroes of a right to preemption over the employment in one area will ultimately tend to segregate them in that area and exclude them from employment elsewhere, to their over-all disadvantage."[150]

The Commission has consistently held that "quota employment based on neighborhood population is no exception."[151] With respect to an agreement to promote the integration of Negroes in the brewing industry, the Commission wrote:

> The Commission does not look with favor on any agreement designed to promote integration in employment of minority groups which is instinct with the concept of quota employment. In fulfillment of its statutory mandate, the Commission must process verified complaint cases on the merits. Agreements entered into by employer and em-

---

148. Cooney v. Katzen, 41 Misc.2d 236, 238, 245 N.Y.S.2d 548, 550 (Sup. Ct. Onondaga County 1963).

149. New Negro Alliance v. Sanitary Grocery Co., 303 U.S. 552, 556 (1938). (Such pressures are a "labor dispute" within the meaning of Norris-LaGuardia Act—29 U.S.C. § 113 (1958)—restricting use of labor injunctions.)

150. Teddy's Shanty, 1951 Report 39.

151. Moe v. H.R.H. Construction Co., 1950 Report 38.

ployee groups based on considerations of race, creed, color or national origin, regardless of their well intended motives, cannot be deemed a defense to a charge of unlawful discrimination in employment.[152]

The continuance of minority group counter measures is an indication that much work remains to be done to wipe out all vestiges of employment discrimination.

---

152. 1953 Report 73.

ENFORCEMENT OF LAWS AGAINST DISCRIMINATION IN EMPLOYMENT

Sol Rabkin*

L AWS against discrimination in employment are now a well-established aspect of our American legal scene. They have been in effect and in operation for a large part of the 20th century. Were it not for some of the discussions now going on, on and off the floor of the United States Senate, concerning the fair employment practice provision of the pending civil rights bill, one could safely have assumed that the principles upon which such legislation are based are now beyond question.

A reasonable man might well doubt the validity of any claims that the adoption of a federal fair employment practices law by Congress calls for the imposition of any pattern of "due deliberate speed" aimed at cushioning the impact of such a law on established customs. One would never think, from reading about these discussions, that fair employment practice laws have been in operation in New York and a few other states for almost nineteen years with none of the horrendous effects which were cited as imminent dangers which must be guarded against.

But we are not here to convince the doubting Thomases or, should I say, Senators. Rather, we are here to discuss the experience accumulated under those laws—and there are now twenty-five such state laws in operation—to see how their effectiveness can be improved. This paper will deal with one aspect of that problem, techniques of possible improvement of enforcement of such laws. It will not undertake to deal with even all aspects of that subdivision of the problem. Rather, it shall be confined to a consideration of methods of reducing delays in the handling of complaints, methods of insuring compliance with the law and methods of strengthening existing sanctions for use against violators of laws against discrimination in employment.

Discussion of easing the initiation of complaints of violation of the laws, of liberalizing formal requirements for such complaints, altering and lowering the established standards for finding of probable cause are all to be dealt with in another paper to be presented to this conference. That other paper will also deal with the wisdom of separating the enforcement and adjudication functions of executive agencies enforcing such laws. We shall endeavor in this paper to observe the limitations described above. Occasionally, however, it may be necessary in connection with the subject matter of this paper to make mention of some of the proposals which are outside the scope of this paper. If that happens, we beg your forgiveness and the forgiveness of the author of the paper dealing primarily with those aspects of the problem.

Even though this paper deals with a limited aspect of possible changes in

---

* National Law Director, Anti-Defamation League of B'nai B'rith.

enforcement of laws against discrimination in employment, it is impossible to deal with even such a limited phase of the problem without some consideration of the background of FEPC statutes and their purposes. The first such law was the statute adopted here in New York in 1945. This pioneering law really embodied a recognition that the government of the state has a special interest in vindication of the right to equality of employment opportunity; that the state's countenancing of existing patterns of racial and religious discrimination in employment resulted in the imposition of economic disabilities on the groups thus discriminated against which created hazards to the health, welfare and peace of the entire community.

Implicit in the adoption of this law were several things. First, there was an abandonment of the patterns used in prior laws against discrimination, the state's civil rights law, which barred racial and religious discrimination in places of public accommodation, depending for its effectiveness on the imposition of criminal or civil remedies. It was recognized that such remedies had been of little effect. Another assumption implicit in the New York state fair employment practices act[1] was a recognition of the inequality of resources available to an employer, union or employment agency engaging in racial or religious discrimination and the applicant for work who was the victim of such discrimination.

It was the recognition of these facts that led to the use of a pattern originally established in the first National Labor Relations Act. That Act sought to avoid the delays implicit in any court proceeding. In addition, it was, on its face, a one-sided act intended to lend the aid of the government to one of the parties in an unequal struggle, the struggle between laborers seeking to organize into unions for the purpose of collective bargaining and employers opposing such efforts in order to maintain their existing superiority of bargaining power.

The Act was adopted in 1935 as our country was struggling to recover from the deep economic depression in which it had been. One aspect of that recovery was aimed at increasing the income of the ordinary American consumer, employees in factories, fields and offices. This could be done only if the economic bargaining power of these employees was strengthened by means of collective bargaining between employers and labor organizations created by the employees. In the depression, the workers' organizations for collective bargaining—the trade unions—had suffered severely. Some employers used labor spy agencies to undermine the trade unions and to gain greater economic advantage over their employees.

Hence, the Wagner Act set up an administrative agency which was empowered to help unorganized employees, who sought to organize themselves into trade unions, to achieve recognition by their employers and to engage in collective bargaining with their employers through those trade unions. The administrative agency permitted the processing of complaints of employer interference with trade union organization and other processes of collective bargaining with

---

1. Law Against Discrimination, N.Y. Executive Law, art. 15.

speed and with the insight which was the result of the specialized function of the agency. The agency could dispense with the delays attendant on court procedures and could also speed up the processes of certification of majority unions for collective bargaining. It could put a speedy end to unfair employment practices by issuing a cease and desist order which was enforceable not in the district federal courts but in the federal courts of appeal if the record before the administrative agency contained evidence to sustain its findings.

The administrative agency, even though it had quasi-judicial functions arising from its responsibility to make findings as to the existence of unfair labor practices and as to which of several competing trade unions represented a majority of the workers, was still essentially an agency enforcing the right of workers to engage in collective bargaining. It was primarily an agency which was enforcing a law aimed at insuring that all workers engaged in interstate commerce would have the right to collective bargaining.

The administrative agency established under the New York state fair employment practices act was set up in 'order to insure vindication of the right established by the statute of an applicant for employment or a person already working to be free from discrimination based on race or creed in obtaining a job or in obtaining promotions or other benefits attached to the job. The primary purpose of the agency is to eliminate discrimination based on race or creed in employment. Even though the New York statute requires as a condition of a formal complaint the filing of a verified complaint, we would respectfully submit that the commission, as a law enforcement agency, has a duty not to close its eyes to obvious violations, even in the absence of the receipt of a verified complaint.

Similarly, even though the commission does have an adjudicatory function in connection with its hearings and in connection with its findings of probable cause to credit the allegations of the complaint, we would respectfully submit that this element of adjudication should not be permitted to obscure the basic fact, which is that the primary responsibility of a commission enforcing a state law against discrimination is to bring about the cessation of discrimination in employment wherever it finds it.

When state fair employment practices laws were in their infancy, commissions charged with enforcement of such laws tended to operate on the theory that there was a need to demonstrate to those regulated by the law, employers, employment agencies and unions, that the law would not unduly interfere with their operations nor subject them to the expense and trouble of having to defend complaints by all applicants for employment who were members of minority groups and whom the employer refused to hire. When the laws were originally being considered by the state legislatures which enacted them, there was much talk on the part of employer groups and employment agencies that the result would be witch hunts directed against innocent employers and employment agencies and unions by disgruntled rejected applicants for employment. Most of the agencies charged with enforcement of fair employment laws took cognizance of such talk and tended to insist on airtight complaints and cases before they were willing to press ahead to public hearings in cases where the process of conciliation and persuasion proved unsatisfactory. Furthermore, the agencies sometimes were unwilling to insist on speedy answers by respondents during the process of adjustment by conciliation and persuasion.

The fact is that the experience up to this point, primarily with the labor act, has demonstrated that lawmakers are quick to alter such one-sided laws if it develops that the aid given by government to the victims of discrimination or of interference with the right to organize for purposes of collective bargaining has tipped the scales so as to give such people undue advantage over the employers. The Taft-Hartley law was a reflection of the lawmakers' readiness to adjust any such imbalances which developed.

The technique of administrative agency enforcement of such laws has demonstrated its usefulness. The sanctions available to such agencies, consisting essentially of the right to apply to a court for an order to compel compliance with their determinations, violation of which is punishable by a contempt procedure, have proved more than effective. It is a rare employer or employment agency or labor union officer who is willing to risk imprisonment for even a day in order to give free rein to his racial or religious prejudices. Hence, the sanctions devised in such laws may well have effect far beyond what one would expect. In addition, the virtue of the type of law discussed herein is that almost every such law has a declaration that the policy of the state is opposed to discrimination in employment based on race or creed.

The final virtue of the administrative device for enforcement of laws against discrimination in employment is that these laws are completely consistent with the established customs and mores of the community. Despite the fears of witch hunts expressed by employers and others policed by such laws, there is no danger of popular defiance of such laws such as developed in connection with the prohibition amendment to the federal constitution. Clearly, the vast majority of the people are benefited by such laws and support them. Clearly, defiance of such a law would result in popular disapproval, unlike prohibition.

ENFORCEMENT—REDUCING DELAY

As has been indicated, a most important novel aspect of most of the fair employment practice laws adopted by states, beginning in 1945, was the device of enforcement by an administrative agency set up specifically for that purpose, to which the person believing himself the victim of a violation of the law, of discrimination in employment, could apply for redress. Thus, the complainant could find in one agency an investigator, a conciliator, and finally, if needed, an adjudicator and enforcer.[2]

After a verified complaint had been filed charging a violation of the law— in the preparation of which the complainant could obtain aid from the same

---

2. See for example New York State Law Against Discrimination § 297.

agency—the task of moving ahead with the process of investigation and further steps shifted from the complainant to the enforcing commission. No longer need the complainant obtain his own attorney and undertake at his own expense the onerous and often costly and slow task of accumulating evidence to sustain his charge. Instead, ". . . the chairman of the commission [designates] one of the commissioners to make, with the assistance of the commission's staff, prompt investigation in connection therewith. . . ."[3] It is axiomatic that justice delayed is justice denied.

When the first FEPC statute specifies that the investigation shall be "prompt," it is in recognition not only of this axiom but also of the fact that the person believing himself the victim of racial or religious discrimination is also highly likely to be one whose prior dealings with state officialdom have been such as to cause him, out of ignorance or feelings of inferiority or a distrust of the organs of law enforcement, to view the machinery of the state with suspicion and skepticism.

Viewed against this background, it is surprising that inspection of the annual reports of the various agencies charged with enforcement of the existing twenty-one state enforcement laws, which provide for an administrative enforcement agency, fails to disclose any which includes a report on the length of time consumed in investigation of complaints, or devoted to any conciliation and persuasion which may ensue. No indication is given of how soon after receiving a verified complaint the investigation is begun, how much time is allowed for completion of the investigation, whether the staff member or members assigned to the investigation is pressed to move with all possible speed, whether time limits are applied to the various steps in the investigation.

Manuals of investigation which may have been developed in agencies enforcing laws against employment discrimination are not available to outsiders. Hence, it is impossible to determine whether the established investigatory procedures include an acknowledgment of the statutory injunction of promptness in the investigation. Although, as has been noted by one of the best studies of the administrative enforcement of such laws, "Investigation is not normally governed by rigid procedures, and may serve a variety of formal and informal functions,"[4] it would appear that at the very least, such investigations must be policed to insure speed and avoidance of unnecessary delay. And the annual reports on the activities of enforcing agencies should reflect the machinery set up to insure the required promptness of investigation and information to allow some determination of the effectiveness of such machinery.

Establishment of employment discrimination is often a complex problem. The employment pattern of the respondent is often a major aspect of the investigation. Hence, the investigator may have to look into the racial or religious composition of the respondent's personnel. He must also examine the qualifica-

3. *Ibid.*
4. Note, 74 Harv. L. Rev. 526, 533 (1961).

tions of the complainant as contrasted with those of other applicants for the same position or incumbents of similar positions. This would require him to examine the respondent's records and to meet respondent's employees and other applicants to respondent for employment so he can obtain data on their race, religion or ancestry and on their qualifications. Obviously, the respondent is in a position to impose delay, if he so wishes. Equally obviously, there is no basis in the reports of most commissions to enable a member of the public to evaluate the diligence shown in pressing forward with such an investigation.[5]

RELATION OF INVESTIGATION TO CONCILIATION

Section 297 of the New York Law Against Discrimination provides that if the investigating commissioner determines after investigation that probable cause exists for crediting the allegations of the complaint, ". . . he shall immediately endeavor to eliminate the unlawful discriminatory practice complained of by conference, conciliation and persuasion." The word "immediately" calls for comment, for it, like the word "prompt," which qualifies the direction to investigate in the preceding portion of this sentence of the statute, reflects the legislative recognition of the need for speed in ending any discrimination found to exist.

Of course, the statutory direction to confer, conciliate and persuade necessarily places the power to impose some delay in the hands of the respondent. Conference, conciliation and persuasion, with their implications of palaver and talk and appeal to reason, bar any possibility of "prompt" or "immediate" progress to a public hearing. This process offers to respondents in complaints of employment discrimination the opportunity to extend unduly processing under the statute. If there is to be conciliation and persuasion, it is absolutely necessary for the agency negotiator to avoid any appearance of arbitrariness or impatience. These attitudes are hardly consistent with the attitude of reasonableness and willingness to negotiate which is an essential prerequisite of successful conciliation.

Other sources of delay may arise at this stage of the handling of the complaint from the fact that the greater resources of the respondent can here be involved. He may bring into the conciliation discussions his legal counsel, his personnel specialists and all the other resources which his economic reserves make available to him. Furthermore, by indicating a willingness to go to public hearings and to resort to court action, if necessary, the respondent may inject an additional element of delay by causing the enforcing agency to lean over backwards to establish a record of reasonableness in conciliation intended to strengthen its hand with possibly unfriendly courts. This might well occur even though the statute provides that what goes on in the process of conciliation may not be disclosed by members of the commission and its staff.[6] While no

---

5. *Id.* at 534.
6. New York State Law Against Discrimination § 297.

disclosure may be made as to what transpired in the course of such endeavors, the time between the date of the complaint and the noticing of the matter for public hearing is easily calculable from the bare dates shown in the administrative record of the case.

The language of most state fair employment practice laws clearly distinguishes between the process of investigation which leads to a determination as to whether probable cause exists to credit the allegations of the complaint, and the ensuing process of conference, conciliation and persuasion called for if there is a finding of probable cause. Yet, there is no indication in the reports of the various enforcing agencies that the investigation does not often, in fact, merge into the efforts of the enforcing agency to resolve the matter by conciliation.

Such a development is hardly unexpected, since what is more normal than for the respondent to ask the investigator as to the reason for his inquiry and, on being told, to protest his innocence and his eagerness to do the right thing, if it be shown that he, the respondent, has erred. But an equally inevitable concomitant of such a development is the merging of the process of investigation and the process of conciliation, the delaying and possible frustration of a finding of probable cause, and the creation of a possibility of substantial delay.

It may well be that the procedures followed by agencies enforcing laws against discrimination in employment are framed to avoid this danger. But since this issue is not discussed in reports of such agencies, and what occurs in the conciliation process must be kept secret by them, it cannot be known whether this potential source of delay is avoided or minimized. It would seem desirable to formally separate the process of investigation aimed at establishing whether probable cause exists to credit the allegations of the complaint from the ensuing process of conciliation. Such a separation would also allow the maintenance of a time check to make it clear even to the most skeptical complainant that his charge of discrimination is receiving the prompt investigation required by statute, whether or not this has resulted in a finding of probable cause, and, finally, whether it is being moved immediately thereafter to conciliation.

Mention has been made of the danger of delay inherent in the process of conference, conciliation and persuasion. While this cannot be wholly avoided, its effect as a source of distrust for members of those racial and religious groups which may be more subject to discrimination than others may be minimized if agency procedures set time limits on this process as well as on the process of investigation. If such limits are set—and, of course, they may be varied where the chairman of the enforcing agency makes a finding that such a variance is proper—the annual reports of the agency should include sections on the time needed for successful handling of complaints, with indications of cases in which the time limits were waived and those in which the handling was even faster than the established limits. In establishing good faith and dedication to those whose rights the statute is intended to protect, such time reports would be most helpful.

And that this is important is clear from the unwillingness of members of many civil rights groups to accept the delays in dealing with employment discrimination which are all too often characteristic of agencies enforcing such laws. While such delays are by no means the sole cause of such reluctance, it may safely be assumed that they are a contributing factor to the picketing and chain-ins, which have occurred at many construction sites, aimed at alleged job discrimination in the building trades in a number of FEPC states.

Where sufficient progress is being made in the process of conference, conciliation and persuasion to justify its further extension, it is suggested that the person carrying through the process for the enforcing agency seek to condition such extension on a commitment by the respondent to keep open the job vacancy in question pending the completion of the conciliation and to make up for the complainant any loss in pay he may suffer as a result of the delay. Such requirement would serve to demonstrate to the complainant the zeal and good faith of the enforcing agency in carrying out its responsibility to prevent discrimination in employment. It would make clear to the complainant, and others in like situation, that the enforcing agency is committed to protection of members of his group against employment discrimination, to make his right to equality of employment opportunity a present and immediate right, not a distant goal.

Finally, it is suggested that consideration be given to amending the statute to make it follow more completely the pattern established by the Wagner Act. The enforcing agency should be allowed to seek court enforcement of its cease and desist orders issued after hearing, not in the trial courts of its state but rather in the appellate courts thereof, with the appellate court's review of the findings of fact being limited to determining whether such findings are based on evidence. Similarly, if a respondent resorts to the courts to estop the enforcing agency from proceeding with a complaint against it, such action should be removable to the appellate courts, if the suit is brought after hearing.[7]

What is essential is that the enforcing agency adopt a philosophy consistent with the major role assigned to it by the statute it is enforcing. Such statutes are enacted under the police power of the state. Many of the statutes specifically provide that they are to be interpreted liberally to effectuate thier purpose, which is to eliminate discrimination in employment based on race or creed.[8] They are remedial statutes enacted to meet a danger to the public peace and welfare found to exist by the legislature. Hence, even though the enforcing agency may be given quasi-judicial powers in connection with its authority to hold hearings and its responsibility to determine if probable cause exists to credit the allegations of the complaint, it does not follow that the agency should

7. N.Y. Civ. Prac. Law & Rules § 7804.
8. See for example New York State Law Against Discrimination §§ 290, 300.

conduct itself like a court of law seeking merely to adjudicate disputes between complainants and respondents. Rather, the enforcing agency should, it is submitted, regard itself as a means set up by the state to combat discrimination whenever and wherever it has reason to believe it exists and is amenable to its powers.

Thus, where there are rumors that in a certain area of employment a policy exists of excluding members of one racial group, the enforcing agency should look into the matter on its own, informally if necessary. If it finds reason to believe that the rumors are well based, it should seek to invoke whatever power the state may have to bring the matter to public light in order to remedy the situation. For example, in New York, where the statute requires a verified complaint as a basis for a formal investigation, such problems might well have brought into use paragraph 9 of Section 63 of the Executive law which authorizes the state's enforcing commission to request the Attorney General to bring any civil action necessary for effective enforcement of the state's laws against discrimination. The State Commission For Human Rights is to be commended for its recent ruling against the Sheet Metal Workers Union in such a situation, but one might wonder why it took so many years for it to move into the matter when the pattern of exclusion was one well known to anyone acquainted with the employment pattern in this field.

Insuring Compliance

Examination of the statistics contained in the reports of the various agencies enforcing laws against discrimination shows that very nearly all of the cases which involve findings of probable cause are ultimately settled by means of conciliation agreements. As has been indicated, the process of conciliation is required by statute to be shrouded in secrecy. Of course, the conciliation agreement itself need not be kept secret though, possibly in an excess of zeal, some agencies enforcing laws against discrimination in employment maintained a policy of secrecy with respect to conciliation agreements for a while. It is suggested that any consent order entered into through conciliation proceedings should be made a matter of public record.

Many of the statutes give the investigating commissioner free rein in seeking to adjust a complaint by conciliation. Of course, if the commissioner views his job as being primarily one of eliminating discrimination and only secondly one involving exercise of quasi-judicial powers, he will insist on conciliation agreements which advance the goal of the law, the elimination of discrimination in employment. On the other hand, it is understandable that the investigating commissioner, when entering into the process of conciliation, may well seek to achieve the speediest possible compromise by splitting the case down the middle. This may result in the denial to the victim of discrimination of complete redress of his grievances. It is suggested that every conciliation agreement, before being finally accepted and approved by the commissioner, should be submitted to an automatic review by the entire commission. In other words, every enforcing agency should set up a procedure for auditing proposed conciliation agreements to make sure that the agreement does the maximum job for advancing the goal of the law, the elimination of discrimination in employment.

Within the past few years, some enforcing agencies have sought to embody in conciliation agreements consent orders under which the respondent not only agrees to take such action as is necessary to implement the law, but also consents to the issuance of a court order against him if he should fail to carry out his responsibilities under the conciliation agreement. It is suggested that this means of proceeding be expanded by administrative means and, where necessary, by statutory means.

A number of the agencies enforcing such laws include in most conciliation agreements a provision calling for reinspection of the respondent's working staff and hiring practices at specified periods after the completion of the conciliation agreement. It is suggested that one aspect of such reinspection should be an examination of the sources and techniques of staff recruitment employed by the respondent. This would insure that respondents could not adversely affect a proposed pattern of nondiscriminatory hiring by stressing sources of recruitment which are in themselves selective in terms of race or religion. Where such reinspections leave the commission in doubt as to whether the conciliation agreement is being implemented with the best possible speed, the commission might well refer the question of this implementation to the Attorney General so that the resources of his office can be brought to bear on the complex fact problem involved.

In such reinspections, the enforcing agency might properly undertake, through its research division, to make an independent survey of the respondent's working staff if the respondent is an employer, of its employment seeking clients if the respondent is an employment agency, or of its membership if the respondent is a union, in order to determine whether the groups examined are reflecting in terms of their racial or religious composition progress in manifesting a pattern of nondiscrimination. Such research surveys might also look into the matter of promotions within a respondent-employer's working staff. Naturally, the data on race or creed accumulated by the enforcing agency's research division would be obtained on the basis of a promise of confidence and would under no circumstances be made available to the respondent in such terms as to enable him to identify particular employees in terms of their race or creed.

The enforcing agency should also establish a policy of speedy publicity in cases where it finds that respondents have breached conciliation agreements. In addition, they should establish procedures under which, where such breaches are found to have occurred, the enforcing agency should be able to revive the original complaint and proceed with the greatest possible speed to public hearings on it. In this connection, the enforcing agency should explore means of setting up close lines of contact with minority group agencies concerned with problems of equality of opportunity. Through these contacts, it should call to the attention of such agencies the breach of previous conciliation agreements and the fact that certain respondents, under such a conciliation agreement, are now more likely to welcome applicants from the minority groups which might formerly have been the objects of discriminatory treatment.

Finally, in this regard, it is suggested that the enforcing agencies adopt a policy of allowing only one conciliation to a respondent. Where, if a conciliation agreement has been reached and supposedly implemented, the enforcing agency receives a complaint on which it finds probable cause, it should then advise the respondent that unless he immediately settles the complaint satisfactorily to the enforcing agency, or produces strong proof to rebut the finding of probable cause, it will notice the case for public hearing and bypass the conciliation process as demonstratively an unnecessary waste of time.

POSSIBLE ADDITIONAL SANCTIONS

It has been noted above that the technique of enforcement by exercise of the contempt power of the courts is generally a most effective technique. The threat of imprisonment to a respondent, even brief imprisonment, serves to make most people eager to comply with orders enforceable by the courts. Unfortunately, however, this ultimate power of enforcement by court order, violation of which is punishable by exercise of the contempt power, cannot be invoked until far too many hurdles have been crossed and far too much time has passed. Furthermore, the enforcing agency charged with administration of laws against discrimination in employment has often tended to avoid resorting to the courts for fear that courts will react with hostility to new-fangled administrative agencies whose quasi-judicial activities necessarily diminish the court's jurisdiction. Hence, enforcing agencies have generally shown an unwillingness to proceed with cases where the preponderance of truth was not so strong as to greatly minimize the likelihood of court reversal.

In the early days of FEPC laws, this attitude may well have served a purpose. It may have tended to make otherwise reluctant courts more willing to exercise their powers to enforce cease and desist orders aimed at employment discrimination. Those enforcing agencies which have had to resort to the courts or which have been brought into the courts by respondents have maintained an excellent record. The proportion of victories is overwhelming. It is submitted that most courts in states with laws against discrimination in employment are long past the attitude of distrusting administrative agencies charged with combating discrimination in employment.

It is not surprising that Mr. Justice Hofstadter of the New York Supreme Court, in *Bachrach v. 1001 Tenants Corporation*, 245 N.Y.S.2d 912 (1963), has said, "Public policy in this direction has continued to date as is evidenced by the recent report of the New York County Lawyers Association Civil Rights

Committee which called for 'a shift in emphasis from persuasion and conciliation to vigorous law enforcement.' "

Mention has been made of the fact that the technique of enforcing by administrative agencies in discrimination complaints was developed because of severe defects in the techniques of enforcement by penal provisions or by private civil suits. The defects of use of the ordinary procedures of criminal law enforcement still make it unwise to authorize penal sanctions, except in the limited cases where a person interferes wilfully with the employees of the enforcement agency carrying out their duty, or deliberately and wilfully prevents the carrying out of a conciliation agreement or a cease and desist order. An example of such limited use of penal sanctions appears in Section 299 of the New York State Law Against Discrimination.

Mention has also been made of the difficulties normally faced in using the device of enforcement by civil suit. However, since the climate of public opinion has changed substantially with respect to such laws and since there has been an increasing general concern with the existence of racial or religious discrimination in such fundamentally important fields of community life as employment, it may well be that juries faced with civil suits in such issues would be less reluctant to find for the complainant. Furthermore, it may well be that complainants in such matters, because of a possible distrust of the dedication of the enforcing agency, might prefer to seek redress in the courts by means of their own civil suit. Such procedures should certainly be allowed and, if the statute bars such alternative remedies, the statute should be amended.

Another reason for permitting such an election of remedies is that it may well be that complainants in some instances may have sufficient financial and legal resources to make them prefer to deal with the respondent in the neutral forum of the courts. After all, as has been pointed out above, state laws against discrimination in employment setting up administrative agencies were enacted on the assumption that most victims of employment discrimination are not able to deal on a basis of equality with those responsible for such discrimination. If, in fact, they are so able, there is no reason why they should not be allowed to elect to handle the case themselves with their own counsel in the courts as a neutral forum.

THE SANCTION OF PUBLICITY

Throughout the discussion of the development of statutes against discrimination in employment, notice has been taken of the fact that publicity with respect to complaints of such discrimination might well entail substantial dangers. Premature publicity based on a complaint which is founded on probable cause might severely damage the innocent respondent. The result might be rumors of hostility toward the group of which the claimed victim is a member, and this, in turn, might result in baseless boycotts. Furthermore, the complainant in such matters is often a victim. First, he may become in the eyes of members

111

of the public a troublemaker and someone who has been branded as undesirable and, therefore, subjected to discrimination. Secondly, other employers may be unwilling to hire him because he has acquired a reputation as a troublemaker. Finally, premature publicity might well tend to harden the position of the respondent and make him less amenable to speedy adjustment of the complaint by conciliation. It was some of these considerations which may have impelled the legislature to impose a gag on the enforcing agency with respect to what occurs in the conciliation process. At the same time, the limitations of publicity have made more difficult the job of the enforcing agency because it imposed clogs on the agency program of educating the general public to the existence of a statutory right against discrimination in employment. Of course, here in New York, as long ago as 1951, the enforcing agency has followed a policy of releasing selected conciliation agreements without first obtaining the consent of the respondent.[9]

It is suggested that an important aid in implementing the findings of the enforcing agency and its decisions would be a substantial expansion in its efforts to obtain publicity for its reported successes. Furthermore, the agency should develop a pattern of making awards for cooperation to employers, unions and employment agencies which demonstrate their dedication to the principles of the laws against discrimination in employment.

The terms of conciliation agreements should be made public. Such a practice will serve to demonstrate to respondents that their fears of adverse repercussions are baseless. Furthermore, it would serve to prevent rumors of discriminatory policies from circulating among the groups which are generally the victims of employment discrimination and thus would serve to prevent improper boycott developments.

Such publicity would make known to the public the existence of a statutory right to be free from discrimination in employment. It would encourage members of minorities which have in the past been the subjects of discrimination to make application to employers who, by conciliation agreements, have demonstrated their desire to comply with the ban on employment discrimination. Such publicity would also alert the recruitment sources of respondents to the fact that their major client is committed to fair employment practices.

Consideration should also be given to giving publicity to complaints where the investigating commissioner has found probable cause to credit the allegations of the complaints. Such publicity might well prove helpful in speeding up the process of conciliation. Furthermore, there is nothing in existing statutes which bars such publicity since the imposition of a secrecy requirement is applicable only to endeavors to eliminate the unlawful discriminatory practice complained of by conference, conciliation and persuasion. Such early publicity on the filing of complaints would also serve to demonstrate to the skeptics

---

9. Spitz, *Patterns of Conciliation under the New York State Law Against Discrimination*, 125 N.Y.L.J. 1246 (April 6, 1951).

among the groups which are normally victims of discrimination that the enforcing agency is fully committed to carrying out the law and to seeking the elimination of discrimination in employment wherever it can be found.

Finally, it would be helpful if enforcing agencies announce programs of research in fields where it is rumored that discrimination exists. For example, much furor has developed leading to picket lines and chain-ins and lie-downs on the major building projects because it is charged that there is widespread racial discrimination in the building trades. Before the situation reached its present heat, rumors had long been rife of the existence of such discrimination. It is suggested that an aggressive program of research by enforcing agencies might have headed off such demonstrations leading to violence both by showing to the claimed victims that the enforcing agency is concerned with and seeking to deal with the problem and by demonstrating to the employers and unions in the field that unless they could show compliance with the ban on discrimination, they would soon be the subjects of complaints of employment discrimination.

So, too, programs of research into the population mix of the executive suites in major companies operating in states with fair employment practice laws would do much to insure equality of opportunity at this higher employment level. There is no reason why such research projects should have to be initiated by private defense agencies such as that from which I come, the Anti-Defamation League of B'nai B'rith.

CONCLUSION

What has been said above, while critical in tone, is in no way intended as destructive. It is our hope that those of us who are concerned with this problem will be able to work constructively with the enforcing agencies to achieve the speediest possible elimination of discrimination in employment everywhere in this country. Certainly, the problem of such discrimination should have been substantially solved at all levels in states such as New York where we are in our 19th year of living under such a law. Let us work together to make equal opportunity in employment a present and immediate right.

SOME GENERAL OBSERVATIONS ON ADMINISTRATION OF STATE FAIR EMPLOYMENT PRACTICE LAWS

ROBERT A. GIRARD*
LOUIS L. JAFFE**

WE think it is time for major changes in the administration of commission enforced fair employment laws. These laws were born in an atmosphere charged with uncertainty, fear and hostility. Many thought they were doomed to ineffectuality, that they were likely to aggravate racial problems, indeed that their constitutionality was doubtful. Therefore, it was natural for the commissions established to enforce the laws to proceed cautiously and discreetly, and, for the most part, to take the position that their principal role, apart from general educational efforts, was to resolve specific complaints formally presented to them by persuasion and conciliation, causing as little antagonism on the part of respondents as possible. In large measure these attitudes continue to dominate the commissions.

Now, however, we think there is a substantial consensus in jurisdictions which have adopted fair employment laws that discrimination in employment because of race or religion is wrong, and that it is proper for government to condemn such discrimination and to take moderately strong measures towards its elimination. The fair employment laws in these jurisdictions seem well-established; the opposition, the concern, the scepticism that surrounded them has substantially dissolved. For this, we owe much to the restrained, responsible performance of the commissions. At the same time, by their educational programs, their enforcement activities, their existence generally, they have produced important gains in economic opportunities for minorities. These substantial commission accomplishments should neither be overlooked nor belittled. Nevertheless, it seems clear that much employment discrimination remains and that in many areas the commissions and the law have hardly scratched the surface. This, at a time when it is important that we progress rapidly in improving the economic situation of Negroes and other minority groups.

We believe that the commissions should assume a much more active and significant part in this effort—that they should diligently seek out important discrimination and make well-planned, imaginative, forceful efforts to eliminate or ameliorate it on a plant-wide, organization-wide, even industry-wide basis. It is no longer adequate for them to proceed wholly, or even principally, on the basis of complaints filed by private parties. Within the framework of flexible, general plans designed to make most effective use of their resources, the commissions should systematically initiate their own inquiries, negotiations and complaints where they have reason to believe significant discrimination

---

* Associate Professor of Law, Stanford University School of Law.
** Byrne Professor of Administrative Law, Harvard Law School.

is being practiced. In jurisdictions where commissions lack power to initiate these various proceedings, legislatures should not only give them authority, but, in view of past experience, direct them to exercise it. We realize, of course, that there are dangers and disadvantages in these proposals but are convinced they would be greatly outweighed by the benefits which would result.

From the beginning the number and quality of complaints received by the commissions has been disappointingly low. Failures by commissions, as well as by civil rights organizations, are responsible in substantial measure. For the most part, however, this dearth seems inherent in the plight of minority groups, the law's inevitable delays and burdens, and the inability of the commissions fully to protect complainants. True, the number of complaints has increased recently. Nevertheless, the impression remains that the number is small compared with unlawful discrimination and, more important, that the complaints continue to come before the commissions in haphazard and fragmentary patterns. The number of complaints undoubtedly could be increased (*e.g.*, by faster, more adequate relief for aggrieved parties, by more extensive and forceful publicity about commission action, by dispersal and relocation of commission offices), but even if the number could be multiplied several fold, this does not seem the best approach. Complaints would still not present any systematic, comprehensive pattern, let alone fit a thoughtful, well-integrated, prearranged program for commission action, which we regard as a vital reform. They would still frequently involve dissipation of commission resources on unrelated, relatively insignificant, less tractable aspects of discrimination.

Even under an approach based on private complaints, of course, commissions frequently should attempt to eliminate all discriminatory practices of respondents, although the discrimination charged has no relation to the discrimination found. Existing statutes apparently confer this power despite its seeming inconsistency with lack of power to initiate complaints. Some commissions appear to do little more, however, than adjust the well-founded grievances of particular complainants, and then only if they persist to the end in their demand for relief. Action on this basis seems plainly inadequate—an indefensible frittering away of the commissions' resources and potentialities, like trying to drain a swamp with a teaspoon.

In undertaking a much more spontaneous and affirmative role against discriminatory practices it appears that commissions can rely, to a large degree, on informal, noncomplaint inquiries and persuasion, taking advantage of the greater flexibility this involves. The pressures and influence which the commissions can exert in this fashion frequently will secure substantial compliance with the law. (Here we have in mind unfavorable publicity, difficulties with other government agencies, problems with civil rights groups, possible commission resort to complaint and enforcement procedure, as well as appeals to the conscience, the sense of social responsibility, the publicly proclaimed principles of those who control economic opportunities.) Today, much of the vital discrimination in connection with *employment opportunities* seems not to be rooted deeply in powerful psychological or emotional needs or in vital economic self-interests, but rather is primarily a matter of ignorance, of habit, of vague concern about the reaction of employees or customers, which can be overcome with a skillful blend of education, persuasion and subtle pressure. Even the mere presentation of relevant facts about minority persons can have potent effect. Of course there may be some resistance by lower echelon management people, by employees and others, particularly as discrimination shrinks toward the hard core, which can only be countered by more severe means.

In handling investigations and complaints which disclose unlawful discriminatory practices, commissions generally should seek comprehensive and definite commitments from violators, including formulation of detailed personnel programs which are effectively communicated to responsible officials throughout their organizations. Furthermore, perceptive compliance reviews should be made until the commission is fully satisfied that the respondent observes and will continue to observe both the letter and spirit of its requirements. To this end violators should be directed generally to submit compliance reports and to keep adequate records available to commission inspection. Apparently a number of commissions, at present, do not make any substantial effort to check on compliance with conciliation agreements. This is thoroughly unsatisfactory and undoubtedly deprives the commission's efforts of much of their possible effect.

In addition to these basic measures, we believe commissions now can properly be expected to go beyond discrimination in attempting to make economic opportunities available to minorities, to accept broader responsibility for better racial balance in the labor force. In large part the absence of minorities in certain employment classifications cannot be attributed to present discrimination, but to narrow recruitment policies and to minority ignorance or lack of qualification. Commissions should strive to induce those controlling job opportunities to broaden their sources of recruitment, to abandon frequent unnecessary tests and requirements (*e.g.*, high school diplomas, which many Negroes do not have, for every employee), to provide special training programs to increase the number of qualified minority applicants. Furthermore, we think commissions should cooperate with public and private employment services, guidance counselors, civil rights organizations and others by seeing that they receive information about openings gained by commission efforts, and by encouraging and assisting them in whatever way practical to induce minority persons to prepare themselves and to seek these opportunities.

Frequently there are accounts of desirable jobs available to Negroes which go begging because qualified and interested Negroes do not present themselves. In addition to lack of knowledge, a significant barrier here is the Negro attitude that it is pointless to try for many jobs traditionally closed to their race, often accompanied by ignorance of antidiscrimination laws or belief that enforcement

116

bodies are ineffectual and perhaps indifferent to protection of Negro interests. To inform possible minority applicants, to encourage them to prepare and to apply, commission activities ought to be publicized more extensively and forcefully, particularly through popular media likely to reach substantial numbers of minority persons. This is particularly true with respect to the nature and significance of conciliation agreements and the products of informal negotiations, since virtually all of the commissions' impact has been and will continue to be at these levels. This publicity should stimulate complaints, particularly in the areas involved, and these complaints in turn should facilitate commission programs. On the other hand, much of the general educational work which commissions have long emphasized now seems relatively unproductive and should be given low priority so far as commission resources are concerned.

The changes suggested in commission administration of the fair employment practice laws call for large increases in present inadequate commission appropriations and in the size of their staffs. However, an increase of three or four hundred per cent would still leave the cost below ten cents per capita in most jurisdictions—a small price for the unique and vital, even though limited, functions the commissions can perform in dealing with what has been aptly described as our "Negro economic crisis." Of course legislatures may refuse to appropriate such amounts—though their resistance might be less than anticipated if presented with effective and comprehensive commission plans. To the degree that commissions must proceed with less than optimum appropriations, thoughtful advance planning to obtain maximum effect from commission resources rather than *ad hoc* reaction to whatever results from private complaints becomes more vital. Related here is our concern whether commissions have been spread too thin by being assigned responsibility for discrimination in public accommodations and private education, as well as discrimination on such diverse grounds as age, sex and military status, thus contributing to the fragmentary and superficial aspects of their performance.

Finally, with respect to commission personnel there seems to be great need for a substantial infusion of new blood, of new outlook, to accomplish what we regard as more constructive administration of the laws. Every effort should be made to appoint dedicated, imaginative, first-rate persons to commission positions, particularly as the responsibility and discretion of the commissions increase, if the laws are to have maximum beneficial effect.

We turn now to several special problems as to formal commission powers and organization. We believe the determining consideration in the solution of these problems will be the point that we have made above; namely, that the basic commission tool will be persuasion and negotiation rather than adjudication. Accordingly, the precise forms of adjudication are not highly significant. What is significant is that the commissions do have some effective enforcing powers or that there be such powers they can invoke.

Probable Cause

There is considerable controversy concerning the requirement that commissions find probable cause of unlawful discrimination as a condition for exercise of their enforcement powers. Civil rights organizations, for example, have demanded more elaborate and precise definitions as to this requirement, arguing that their activities in support of the law and their appraisal of commission determinations are handicapped by present uncertainty. Putting to one side the great difficulty in formulating more precise standards, we do not believe, however, that implementation of the laws, by civil rights organizations or otherwise, has been retarded materially by indefiniteness in the probable cause concept. As a matter of fact, indefiniteness has a positive aspect to the extent that it gives commissions more flexibility and control over their activities. What critics really want seems not so much greater definiteness or elaboration as relaxation of the requirement as it has been applied by commissions. There appears to be considerable justification for this demand. From commission dismissal of about one-half of the complaints filed with them for lack of probable cause and from other evidence, one gets the strong impression that commissions have required too rigorous a showing of discrimination. Standards for applying the law here certainly should not be as strict, for example, as those used in the criminal law. This is particularly true when the focus of agency action is shifted from specific instances of discrimination to improvement of industry or area hiring and job practices generally.

Combination of Investigating, Initiating, Conciliating and Judging Functions

The combination of initiating and/or conciliating and judging functions and the combination of conciliation and judging functions are in certain situations highly controversial. Generally speaking, our tradition is against combining the functions of prosecution and adjudication in the same officers or organization. One who prosecutes a claim is apt to look at evidence with an eye to confirm his prosecutory intention. A somewhat different question is raised by the combination of conciliation and arbitral or adjudicatory functions; and there is a great deal of dispute, especially in the world of labor arbitration, whether the two functions should be combined. An arbitrator who has attempted to conciliate may learn certain things or may acquire certain attitudes toward one or the other party which, when he becomes a judge, distort his application of the law to the facts. Nevertheless, the values of combining prosecutory and adjudicatory functions have sometimes (as, for instance, with the National Labor Relations Board and Federal Trade Commission) been thought to outweigh its disadvantages, though even here the law has in recent times been modified significantly. The Labor Board now has a prosecuting arm distinct from the members of the Board, and the Administrative Procedure Act has provisions which attempt to mitigate the disadvantages of combination. Thus there must be an independent trial examiner who is required to conduct a hearing and make a report, and the Board itself in making its decision must not consult with the prosecutory staff.

However, the problem is much less significant in our situation. We base this statement once more on our basic premise that conciliation rather than adjudication will be at least for some time the chief reliance. Obviously this consideration cuts both ways. It makes it of less significance than in Labor Board cases (for example) that functions are combined. But also it makes it less important from the point of view of enforcement that the agency have the power both to prosecute and judge. Insofar as experience were to show that the combination of functions creates resistance or provides a basis for criticism, probably not much would be lost by providing some form of independent adjudication. It might be as in the case in Minnesota, a panel of hearing officers from which choice may be made. Such hearing officers might have the power of final decision or might, as under the Administrative Procedure Act, be limited to intermediate decision with ultimate authority in the agency. One question concerning the use of *ad hoc* hearing officers is whether they will be sufficiently aware of developments and concepts in the field. That depends on whether the questions are of a technical character and whether the ideas are those of the society at large and as such known to the intelligent layman. Because it is hoped that these laws rest on an enlightened public opinion and an acceptance of the basic premises of our society, there may be certain advantage in using *ad hoc* lay hearing officers.

Rights of Aggrieved Persons

There is a question whether aggrieved persons should have the right to compel the agency to investigate, conciliate and adjudicate and whether such a right should be reinforced by judicial review. In systems in which adjudication proceeds on the basis of a formal complaint filed by an aggrieved person, the assumption may be that the agency must adjudicate the case and that its duty to do so can be enforced by judicial procedure. Under the procedure of the Labor Board and Trade Commission the issuance of a complaint is in control of the agency, and the refusal to investigate or issue a complaint cannot be questioned in the courts, though there may be an exception if the refusal is based on the premise that the agency does not have jurisdiction. This procedure is justified on the ground that the agency should have the power to control the deployment of its limited resources of men and energy. It does place an enormous power in the hands of an agency, and where there are no alternatives opened to an aggrieved person, it is a questionable policy. One alternative is to allow the aggrieved person to bring an action in court either at his option or if the agency refuses to act.

The solution that we would tentatively suggest is that the agency's refusal to proceed should not be subject to judicial control but that the aggrieved person should have a right to proceed on his own in court if the agency refuses to act. In our opinion, the agencies are presently confronted with an enormous potential workload. We have emphasized the great importance of agency initiative, of industry-wide investigations, of concentration on significant employer situations in terms of employer's entire hiring policy. Proceedings of this sort consume enormous time and energy, and for this reason the agency should have the power to refuse to investigate or to proceed in cases which it regards as marginal or of minor significance, or based on unfounded claims or distorted conceptions. For these reasons we suggest that aggrieved persons do not have a right to compel an agency to proceed.

We recognize, of course, that as the statutes presently read agency discretion is not that broad. At least if the agency is driven to the conclusion that there is probable cause, it may well be that it is required to process a complaint even though in terms of the whole program its significance may not be thought to warrant the expenditure of time. But it would still be within the agency's power to treat the case in more summary fashion and to limit its objective to removing the specific discrimination. In any case, to the degree that the agency can be master of its agenda, it should concentrate its resources on the broader objectives.

A different question is raised where the agency has proceeded and after formal hearing decides against the complainant for assertedly insufficient or incorrect reasons of law. It is customary for such determinations to be reviewed, and there is no reason for not applying the customary policy in these cases.

COMMENT

Joseph B. Robison*

I AM not quite sure just what the difference is between a commentator and a speaker. Whichever you are, you tend to express your own point of view.

Let me say first that I reject the view that the fair employment laws have failed or that the commissions have failed. While more might have been done, there have been substantial gains.

The test of effectiveness is not to be found in the statistics concerning commission operations but in actual changes in employment practices. I believe that changes have taken place. This, of course, is not a documented conclusion. It is peculiarly difficult to measure quantitatively how many minority group workers have obtained jobs they would not have held twenty years ago. It is even more difficult to determine whether the changes that have occurred are due, directly or indirectly, to anti-bias legislation. Hence, we must rely on observation and guess. My own observations and guesses lead me to believe that the laws have had favorable results.

There are at least two reasons why there is, nevertheless, a feeling of failure. First, more progress could have been made. Second, there are factors at work in our economy, which were reviewed last night, which are rapidly making things worse for minority groups. Apparently, the gains that have been made in the last two decades under the various statutes have not kept up with the losses. That is why we face such an urgent situation today.

Previous speakers have referred to the National Labor Relations Act and noted that the procedural provisions of the various fair employment laws used that act as a model. The procedural similarity between the federal and state labor relations acts on the one hand and the state fair employment laws on the other naturally prompts speculation as to why they operate so differently in practice. Why, for example, is there a tradition of prompt action under the labor relations acts, while proceedings under the anti-bias laws tend to be leisurely? Why do some 10 per cent of the Labor Board cases go to formal hearing and generate a large body of litigation while only a handful of anti-bias cases get beyond the stage of informal investigation?

One reason for this difference is the existence of an organized group that has a direct economic stake in getting action out of the labor boards. The unions, of course, have an ideological sympathy with the objectives of the labor relations statutes, as the civil rights organizations have with the anti-bias laws. However, there is also the simple fact that, if a union wins a Labor Board case, it is in business in the plant. If it loses, it is out. It is that fact that gives the proceedings under the labor laws a sense of urgency from the time the charge or complaint is filed. That sense of urgency is seriously lacking in the work of the anti-bias commissions.

---

* Assistant Director, Commission on Law and Social Action, American Jewish Congress.

The week following the day on which a complaint is filed is a critical period. The complainant should have the feeling that, if he goes to the commission office and files a complaint on Monday, by Thursday or Friday at the latest he will know from the commission that it has been in touch with the employer and has received some indication of what the employer's defense is.

When I file a complaint with an anti-bias commission, neither I nor the complainant knows what the employer's response is going to be. It may be a general denial or a frank admission. It may be something totally unexpected, an explanation that we did not in any way anticipate. Thus, one goes down to the commission office with a very real sense of curiosity—"What is going to happen now?" Unfortunately, too often the weeks drag by with no indication to the complainant as to how the case is shaping up.

It does not need to be that way. I know in particular that the New York City Commission, which has enforcement jurisdiction only in housing cases, has set up its procedures so that there is contact with the landlord named in the complaint within a matter of two or three days after the complaint is filed.

This approach runs some risks. Haste always increases the possibility of legal boners that can cause trouble if the case turns out to be a long drawn-out test of strength. But the important thing to remember is that most cases do not turn out that way. A high proportion of the cases, probably as high as 80 or 90 per cent of those with merit, are what might be called "soft touches." These are the cases where the employer (or the owner of housing) is obviously in the wrong. If he sees from the start that the commission means business, he is likely to settle quickly. But you do not get quick settlements unless you have a procedure and an organization geared to quick action.

I might make a parallel with the New Jersey courts where, in 1948, the state Supreme Court imposed a set of strict requirements on the lower court judges. Among other things, they were told that, if any case was not decided within a specified time, a written explanation was to be given to the Chief Justice. One result was that, when we had a case before the New Jersey courts involving discrimination at the Levittown housing development, it was decided by the state Supreme Court only a year and a half after the complaint was filed with the state antidiscrimination agency. Those of you who are lawyers know that that is a very short time for getting a case through the highest court of a state.

I do not believe that time limitations should be written into statutes or even into formal rules and regulations. (They were not in New Jersey.) However, benefits would be obtained by internal, housekeeping regulations requiring reports on all pending cases at regular intervals, including explanations of any proceedings that are not in fact proceeding.

Let me make one more point. Professor Girard suggested that the general acceptance of the fair employment laws that we see today may well be the result of the cautious and studied approach that the commissions have followed up to now. I agree—except that I am not so sure about that phrase, "general acceptance."

We have heard a great deal of talk recently about the "white backlash." This phenomenon is primarily due to the fact that the effects of the civil rights movement have been felt for the first time by the man in the street. The great bulk of the white people are now facing changes in their own affairs. Integration is no longer an abstract question to be discussed in legislatures. It is no longer a goal to be fought for in distant states. It is a matter of having a Negro family move in next door, of having Negro children in your child's classroom.

This has provoked resistance in a part of the white population that has been silent up to now. They may have been opposed to fair employment, fair housing and other anti-bias legislation but their opposition has only rarely been expressed. Where it has been expressed (for example, to keep Negro families out of all-white neighborhoods), it has often been successful. We now face the prospect of much more frequent and better organized opposition.

The fair employment laws have not provoked such a backlash up to now. This may be because changes in employment patterns do not arouse deep emotions. It seems more likely, however, that it is because there have not been many changes. And this in turn may be due to the cautious approach of the commissions. We can only speculate as to what will happen if and when the tempo of activity under the fair employment laws is increased. We may discover that the "general acceptance" of the statutes that we have welcomed and praised is in fact illusory.

If there is to be a backlash under the fair employment laws, it will be a matter of regret that we did not get it when they were first enacted. In 1945, when the first fair employment laws were adopted in New York and New Jersey, more vigorous and effective enforcement would have provoked resistance, but there is no reason to believe that the resistance would have been unmanageable. All the evidence indicates that changes in employment patterns do not provoke the kind of emotional response that is aroused by changes in schools or housing. If the employment backlash had been stimulated and met between 1945 and 1950 by more extensive action under the fair employment laws, a different pattern would have been set for the administration of anti-bias legislation generally.

Be that as it may, we have to deal with the situation as it exists now. The principal point I want to make is that we should avoid the tendency to resort to cautious administration in a bid for "acceptance" of fair employment and other antidiscrimination laws, at the cost of failing to do the job that needs to be done.

COMMENT

GEORGE W. BROOKS*

First, I'm struck with the fact that the objectives of the Civil Rights Movement are assumed here to be so limited. Mr. Hill says that the Movement is not a thing in and for itself—rather, it is to be the occasion and the drive for major social change. That may be the case, but there is no evidence of it in these papers. The assumption made throughout is that the Negro has looked at the American establishment, found it good and "wants in." There is no hint of revolution.

This makes the prospect of settlement rather bright. No really sweeping change in society is being asked—we are merely being asked for a different distribution of the existing supply of goods and services. The issues revolve around *how* we do this. Even here, there doesn't seem to be any really significant dispute except around suggestions like Dean Ferguson's that we should somehow unscramble the discriminatory omelet to find those elements which affect Negroes. This suggests certain practical difficulties to the authors but apparently no more than this. The main point is that all the papers assume that Negroes have not been concerned with making this a better world to live in, but only about making it a better world for Negroes to live in. This agreement about goals gives a good deal of unity to the papers.

Henry Spitz' paper cautiously picks its way through a couple of decades of attempting to discover the problems in the enforcement field. Neither in his paper nor any of the others is there a single criticism of what the Commission has done. But there is a great deal of criticism of what it has not done, of the speed which it has not pursued, and of the energy which it has not shown. We are therefore dealing with a very elusive (and partly political) question of what the Commission ought to have been doing in the last fifteen years and what it ought to do now to make up for what it hasn't been doing in the last fifteen years. The least satisfactory aspect of the proceedings thus far is that, within an area of apparent unity, the authors aren't really talking to each other. If we had had the Hill, Jaffe, Girard and Rabkin papers first, we would have been astonished at the extent to which Henry Spitz's paper fails to deal with any of the issues they raise. But the issues they raise—initiation, confidentiality, etc.—are issues which desperately need enlightenment and which get very little of it here. The gap between issues and responses are, in a sense, built directly into the Girard-Jaffe paper. This paper comes charging out of the corner breathing fire. We are told that we must make major changes, must have a Commission animated by a wholly different point of view, which must concern itself with more than discrimination, even with increasing employment opportunity. But their remedies are curiously mild, and in spite of their protestations, they take very little account of political

* Professor, New York State School of Industrial and Labor Relations.

reality. They talk as though it were somehow a responsibility of the Commission to be militant, to go to the Governor and tell him what ought to be done. I suggest to you that if it had been anticipated that the Chairman of the Commission would behave in this way, he would not have been appointed.

I think that the Commission has probably read correctly the political forces in this state, particularly the wishes of the Republican majority in the legislature and in the executive branch of the government, that it has proceeded at the rate, and in the way, which the Republican majority and much of the Democratic minority (particularly that part of it which regards itself as the voice of the labor movement) wants it to proceed. Exhorting the Commission to be braver and more daring is therefore pointless. The Negroes understand this very well. It has been said here that they don't bother with the Commission—which brings me to my last point. In spite of the criticisms of the Commission, the papers all hold to the view (sometimes implicit) that the Commission approach is absolutely indispensable to the solution of problems of discrimination. They are convincing on this point. If so, minority groups make a great mistake in not pressing for more vigorous administration of the Law. It would be much better if Mr. Randolph spent less time pursuing the meagre advantages of an increased minimum wage, and spent a great deal more time pushing the Commission in the ways that Milton Rosenberg suggested he could.

A. *Criticisms of Present Commission Practices*

Much of the Saturday morning discussion focused on the performance and policies of the New York State Commission for Human Rights. As one of the speakers noted, this was the penalty for being the oldest and the best. Much of the criticism appears in the papers presented by Messrs. Hill and Rabkin; Mr. Henry Spitz, General Counsel of the New York State Commission, devoted much of his talk to responding to these criticisms.

As appears from the papers printed herein, the state commissions were criticized for an alleged failure to articulate standards for the finding of probable cause or lack thereof, for the widespread use of conciliation, and for delay. Throughout these criticisms ran a feeling, often made explicit, that these commissions were excessively timid, unwilling to move aggressively, and too reluctant to move at all without very strong legal support. The participants seemed generally agreed that, as put by Mr. Madison S. Jones, Executive Director of the New York City Commission, these commissions must be aggressive. Mr. Jones added that such aggressiveness is necessary regardless of whether there seems to be strong legal support for the position to be taken.

Mr. Rabkin elaborated the criticisms in his paper by stressing that very often members of the minorities who are to be protected under antidiscrimination laws have a basic skepticism about whether authority and the state will, in fact, come to their aid. It is this skepticism toward which the commissions should now address themselves rather than to the predictions of dire results coming from employers, real estate operators, etc., whose rights to discriminate are being curtailed by such a law. He also suggested that the commissions lay bare their method of investigation to the complainant in order to overcome the complainant's basic skepticism. Overall, Mr. Rabkin felt that an FEP commission should consider itself a law enforcement and policing agency, rather than a judicial body whose primary job is to hold hearings and give impartial answers.

Mr. Spitz rejected many of these criticisms as baseless and uninformed. As to zeal and initiative, he pointed out that despite the legislature's failure to grant the New York State Commission power to initiate investigations, the Commission had initiated over 1000 such investigations. Marvin Karpatkin, Esq., representing the American Civil Liberties Union and a volunteer attorney for CORE expressed surprise at the figure, noting that there were many instances in his own experience where an industry-wide investigation utilizing creative techniques, such as the extensive compulsory questionnaires used by the Federal Trade Commission to ferret out illegal anti-trust practices in an entire industry, would have disclosed considerable evidence of discriminatory practices and patterns.

Mr. Spitz also noted Professor Jaffe's comment that courts have been unsuccessfully struggling with definitions of probable cause for over 500 years.

Mr. Rabkin retorted that he was only seeking some clarification of the standards by which the Commission decides to process some cases and not others.

Mr. Spitz added that once probable cause is found and no settlement is achieved, the Commission *must* notice the case for a public hearing. He personally deplored the absence of discretion in cases which perhaps should not have gone to Court. Mr. Rabkin stressed, however, that he was talking about discretion with respect to the finding of probable cause.

Complainants, moreover, continued Mr. Spitz, are always given a written explanation by the investigating commissioner for the findings on probable cause and these decisions can be appealed to both the Commission Chairman and the courts. Mr. Rabkin replied that he found these written explanations uninformative.

As for any alleged delay, Mr. Spitz stated that all cases noticed for public hearing are thoroughly prepared on the law and the facts, and he pointed to several recent setbacks suffered by other commissions and voluntary organizations where an adverse result had followed hasty preparation. He stated that the Commission has not lost a single litigated case in all of its nineteen years of existence. Mr. Rabkin replied that sloppiness was not a necessary incident to speed. Moreover, most respondents will not resist vigorously if the Commission moves quickly to enforce a complaint. He also observed that civil rights groups often looked to the speed with which the action was taken as an index of the agency's zeal.

In support of the need for speed, Mr. Karpatkin noted that complainants often were very discouraged by both the delay in action and the fact that while the complaint is being processed, the complainant is unable to learn anything about its progress. He described one case of a clear-cut housing violation, where delays which were not explained to the complainants—and were perhaps not explainable—resulted in direct action: sit-ins, arrests for trespassing, and heated Criminal Court proceedings, all of which could have been avoided had the Commission proceeded with dispatch; and if for any good reason the Commission could not have proceeded with dispatch, it should have found some way to communicate this to the community civil rights group, together with some reasonable assurance as to when an order would be issued.

Mr. Spitz denied these charges and said that the commissioners and staff are always available to advise complainants of the progress of their cases.

At the afternoon session, New York State Commissioner J. Edward Conway declared that some proceedings simply cannot be speeded up. Thus, in one case involving the Ironworkers Union, the matter was almost settled several times, but each time there was a change in union leadership and it was necessary to begin again. Finally, a public hearing was started.

Mr. Spitz concluded his response with some comments on conciliation standards. He noted that although there were no standards for conciliation agreements in the statute, the Commission tried to have respondents accept all

127

that they might have to accept after a full public hearing. In elaboration of this, Commissioner Conway stressed that conciliation did not mean bargaining. Thus, where investigation shows either probable cause of a violation or a clear violation the Commission informs the respondent of its terms, and as to these there is no bargaining. There could be some leeway with respect to what constitutes affirmative action to comply with the statute, depending on the situation.

B. *Possible Improvements*

Professors Jaffe and Girard, as did several others, discussed more effective use of agency resources, along the lines developed in their paper. They suggested that the present climate might permit much more spontaneous and vigorous action by the commissions and asked whether widespread employer and union resistance to equal employment opportunities still existed. Professor Girard raised the possibility that wilful union discrimination, particularly in the building trades, might not really affect very many jobs in the total picture and that wilful discrimination by employers had declined materially. Professor Jaffe and others noted that antidiscrimination proceedings were unlike proceedings against employers before the National Labor Relations Board where employers had a direct financial interest in fighting the agency's activities; thus, antidiscrimination proceedings might be easier to process quickly and successfully.

Much controversy erupted with respect to both questions. As to employer resistance, Mr. George Culberson thought there was very little overt employer discrimination on the part of top management; tradition is the real problem, for the employers are not eager to change traditional and efficient hiring procedures. On the other hand, lower echelon employees, often with a great deal of hiring power, might discriminate. Mr. Jones commented that because discriminatory attitudes on these lower levels are so widespread, the New York State Commission always tried to work first with top management. Mr. Rabkin, however, thought that the extent of discriminatory attitudes varied greatly from industry to industry. Thus, many top men in small firms might have the same prejudiced attitudes as the lower echelon personnel in the huge aircraft and space enterprises with whom Mr. Culberson dealt.

Professor George Brooks of Cornell argued that resistance to fair employment opportunities was still very strong in certain industries. For example, in the building trades, he emphasized that both employers and unions were adamant. He denied that this situation did not involve very many jobs, stressing that the number of jobs involved in construction and in apprenticeship programs was very significant. In the afternoon session, as well as in the Friday night session, conference participants working in and with the building trades noted that in the Buffalo area, unlike many others, construction work was relatively meager, and many construction workers, union and otherwise, were unemployed.

As to how best to use the commission's resources, Mr. Culberson noted that the filing of numerous complaints really impeded effective work, for each individual complaint took time away from other activities which could open up more jobs. Earlier, Mr. Milton Rosenberg, a representative from the New York State Commission, declared that the individual complaint system was indispensable but inadequate and stressed that the Commission was looking for and experimenting with other ways to use its resources. Commissioner Conway elaborated on this by declaring that complaints "unlocked the door to evidence of discrimination," but case-by-case adversary proceedings alone cannot make even a dent in the problem. The great value of the individual cases method is that it dramatizes the situation and shows that the statute has enforcement powers. Mr. Rabkin, however, denied that there was any real difference between an individual and a broad approach, for an individual case could unlock a whole industry.

A few specific improvements were also discussed. In response to a question, Professor Jaffe stated that if there were in fact no general and hard resistance, it would be dangerous to use punitive measures in the present climate of opinion where so many are concerned about the problem and there are many unused measures short of penal sanctions.

In this connection, it was brought out that few people thought it would be difficult to prove the existence of discrimination if it existed.

Finally Mr. Karpatkin stressed the importance of having an agency office in the heart of the ghetto neighborhood, since many Negroes and Puerto Ricans are afraid or otherwise reluctant to take the trip down to the City Hall area. Similarly, he pointed out the desirability of agencies having evening hours, so that the filing of a complaint would not necessitate losing a day's pay or a half-day's pay.

PART III: SUPPLEMENTS TO DIRECT ENFORCEMENT

STATE AND LOCAL CONTRACTS AND SUBCONTRACTS

J. Edward Conway*

Background and Estimate

The initial question presented for consideration at this session of the Symposium is whether state and local contract powers can be used to further equal employment opportunities. It is my own estimate that such powers can be so used. I reach this estimate on the basis of my experience as a member of the New York State Commission for Human Rights[1] since 1954, and particularly on my experience as the liaison commissioner in charge of the most recent and still developing phase of New York state's contract compliance program.

I should add at least one caveat to my estimate and one note of limitation on the statement of experience to support it. The conception of using state and local contract powers has been proposed and recommended in some instances to fill a need deemed to exist because of the absence of a detailed equal employment opportunity statute under the administration of an adequately staffed and financed operating agency.[2] I have no experience in the use of state and local contract powers standing apart from the kind of statutory and administrative foundation which does exist in the state of New York; nor does it appear from the literature that any clear evaluation can yet be made as to the effectiveness of such contract powers when they stand alone.[3] Thus, my estimate and comments are confined to the situation where the use of state and local contract powers is not an alternative to direct enforcement in the sense of a substitute for it, but to a situation where such a power is supplementary to or coordinate with those possessed by a commission such as my own.

Exercise of Contract Powers as an Expression of Public Policy

Responsible and experienced public officials are not unaware of the administrative and legal questions which may come into being upon the institution of any program based upon the use of government contract powers. It is also clear, however, that the correlation of government contract powers with equal employment opportunities constitutes an underlining of public policy, which is of extreme importance because it is so readily understandable. The

---

* Commissioner, State Commission for Human Rights.
1. Known as the State Commission Against Discrimination from July 1, 1945 to March 20, 1962.
2. The Potomac Institute, State Executive Authority to Promote Civil Rights (1963).
3. See, *e.g.*, Corwin, The President: Office and Powers—1787-1957 (rev. ed. 1957), ch. IV; Speck, *Enforcement of Nondiscrimination Requirements for Government Contract Work*, 63 Colum. L. Rev. 243 (1963).

fact that the government is prepared to give notice of its policy to all affected groups and persons and to the general public by presenting the possibility of such action as contract cancellation, termination or suspension and a declaration of ineligibility for future contracts, makes pointed and real, to at least a certain number of individuals and groups, a set of rights and duties which were formerly largely diffuse and academic.

The Statutory and Contractual Framework

There are advantages and disadvantages to a Symposium in the selection of a person such as myself to lead a discussion of a program with which he is associated. I have no reluctance, as I have already demonstrated, to stating a personal estimate of general values. On the other hand, I would not myself raise nor suggest the answer to any of the particular legal questions which may eventuate as the program develops. I will presumably be involved in the disposition of such questions, and I would certainly await a framework of actual fact and the benefit of argument under it before venturing a conclusion. Perhaps more important, many, if not most, of the questions I would propound may prove to be speculative and largely rhetorical. In this area, I will therefore simply call attention to the fact that there has developed, particularly on the basis of federal experience, a fairly substantial literature which raises and discusses a variety of problems and calls attention to the direction for further inquiry.[4]

It would, at the same time, seem useful to provide some analysis and history of the principal statutory provisions and standard contract clauses which come into play in the state of New York in connection with the exercise of state and local contract powers to further equal employment opportunities.

Section 220-e of the New York Labor Law

Article 8 of the New York Labor Law deals with the general subject of public work. Among its provisions are a number which go back as far as the Laws of 1909; and some appear to have even earlier antecedents.[5] Certainly, the idea that public work contracts may be the subject of special

---

4. Speck, *Enforcement of Nondiscrimination Requirements for Government Contract Work*, 63 Colum. L. Rev. 243 (1963); Birnbaum, *Equal Employment Opportunity and Executive Order 10925*, 11 Kan. Law Rev. 17 (1962); Birnbaum and Burch, *Executive Order 10925 on Equal Employment Opportunity*, 8 Fed. Bar News 159 (1961), *and President Issues New Executive Order Extending Non-Discrimination Principles*, 10 Fed. Bar News 299 (1963); Pollitt, *Racial Discrimination in Employment: Proposals for Corrective Action*, 13 Buffalo L. Rev. 59, 66 (1963); Hannah, *Government by Procurement*, 18 Bus. Law 997 (1963); Note, 74 Harv. L. Rev. 526, 575 (1961); Van Cleve, *Use of Federal Procurement to Achieve National Goals*, 1961 Wis. L. Rev. 566; Miller, *Administration by Contract: A New Concern for the Administrative Lawyer*, 36 N.Y.U.L. Rev. 957 (1961); Heyman, *Government by Contract: Boon or Boner?* 21 Pub. Admin. Rev. 59 (1961); *Employment Discrimination*, 5 Race Rel. L. Rep. 569, 578 (1960); Pasley, *The Nondiscrimination Clause in Government Contracts*, 43 Va. L. Rev. 837 (1957).

5. *E.g.*, the provisions covering hours and wages such as the so-called eight hour law. *Cf.* State v. Metz, 193 N.Y. 148 (1908); Yerry v. Goodsell, 4 A.D.2d 395, 166 N.Y.S.2d 224 (3rd Dep't 1957), *aff'd*, 4 N.Y.2d 999, 152 N.E.2d 535, 177 N.Y.S.2d 514 (1958).

treatment, under the legislative and the executive power, is not novel nor is it peculiar to the state of New York.[6] The legislative conclusion that there is a particular antithesis between public work and discrimination because of race, creed, or color was brought into Article 8 of the New York Labor Law by the addition of section 220-e in 1935.[7]

Section 220-e, as originally enacted, applied to contracts for the state or municipalities for the construction, alteration or repair of any public building or public work. The bill was introduced by Assemblyman J. E. Stephens[8] and became Chapter 158 of the Laws of 1935. So far as appears from a study of the official papers of that period, the 1935 bill was not a formal part of any executive program for that year, and no public document has been found which indicates that it was the bill of any particular state department.[9]

There were no changes in section 220-e until 1945 when the Temporary Commission Against Discrimination, as part of its report concerning the proposed Law Against Discrimination, suggested a number of amendments to existing statutes for the purpose of achieving "uniform phraseology." Section 220-e prior to the enactment of this bill for uniform phraseology used only the terms *race, creed* or *color*. The amending law in 1945 (Chapter 292) added the term *national origin*.

The second amendment to section 220-e of the Labor Law was adopted in 1950.[10] The change made by this amendment was to expand the scope of the section to include contracts for the manufacture, sale or distribution of materials, equipment or supplies.[11] This additional coverage applied to operations performed within the territorial limits of the state of New York.

Thus, in its present form Section 220-e of the Labor Law provides that every contract on behalf of the state or a municipality for the construction, operation or repair of any public building or public work or for the manufacture, sale or distribution of materials, equipment or supplies shall contain pro-

---

6. See Cohen, Public Construction Contracts and the Law (1961); Perkins v. Lukens Steel Co., 310 U.S. 113, 127-8, (1940).

7. L. 1935, ch. 138, amended by L. 1945, ch. 292. Library of Congress, Legislative Reference Service, has compiled a list of states having laws particularly providing for nondiscrimination by public contractors. See its *State Laws Dealing with Non-Discrimination in Employment* (1962) 48-9. As amplified by information from the U.S. Civil Rights Commission and data in the Race Relations Law Reporter, the following states would seem to warrant inclusion, although they present varying degrees of coverage:

Arizona, California, Colorado, Illinois, Indiana, Kansas, Maryland, Michigan, Minnesota, Nebraska, Nevada, New Jersey, New Mexico, New York, Ohio, Pennsylvania, Vermont, Wisconsin.

8. Assembly Intro. No. 1223, PR 1308.

9. In the same year (1935) an amendment was made to section 4 of the Tax Law with reference to nondiscriminatory use of the facilities of non-profit educational organizations exempt from the real property tax, L. 1935, ch. 852. This provision was transferred to the Law Against Discrimination in 1958 to form, with adapted language, subdivision 4 of section 296. This amendment to the Tax Law, however, was introduced by a different Assemblyman (Mr. Hefland) and there is nothing to indicate that this provision and section 220-e of the Labor Law were associated or formed part of any special program.

10. L. 1950, ch. 424.

11. The 1950 amendment was suggested by the State Commission Against Discrimination (Assembly Intro. No. 1396, PR 1427).

visions by which the contractor agrees (1) that in the hiring of employees for the performance of work under the contract or subcontract, no contractor or subcontractor shall, by reason of race, creed, color or national origin, discriminate against any citizen of the state of New York who is qualified and available to perform the work to which the employment relates; (2) that no contractor or subcontractor shall discriminate against or intimidate any such employee on account of race, creed, color or national origin; (3) that there may be deducted from the amounts payable to the contractor by the state or municipality a penalty of five dollars for each person for each calendar day during which such person was discriminated against or intimidated; and (4) that the contract may be cancelled by the state or municipality and all money due or to become due may be forfeited for a second or any subsequent violation.

The exact language of the existing provisions is as follows.[12]

220-e. Provisions in contracts prohibiting discrimination on account of race, creed, color or national origin in employment of citizens upon public works

Every contract for or on behalf of the state or a municipality for the construction, alteration or repair of any public building or public work or for the manufacture, sale or distribution of materials, equipment or supplies shall contain provisions by which the contractor with the state or municipality agrees:

(a) That in the hiring of employees for the performance of work under this contract or any subcontract hereunder, no contractor, subcontractor, nor any person acting on behalf of such contractor or subcontractor, shall by reason of race, creed, color or national origin discriminate against any citizen of the state of New York who is qualified and available to perform the work to which the employment relates;

(b) That no contractor, subcontractor, nor any person on his behalf shall, in any manner, discriminate against or intimidate any employee hired for the performance of work under this contract on account of race, creed, color or national origin;

(c) That there may be deducted from the amount payable to the contractor by the state or municipality under this contract a penalty of five dollars for each person for each calendar day during which such person was discriminated against or intimidated in violation of the provisions of the contract;

(d) That this contract may be cancelled or terminated by the state or municipality, and all moneys due or to become due hereunder may be forfeited, for a second or any subsequent violation of the terms or conditions of this section of the contract; and

(e) The aforesaid provisions of this section covering every contract for or on behalf of the state or a municipality for the manufac-

---

12. During the 1964 Legislative Session a number of amendments to section 220-e were proposed, and one such bill was sent to the Governor. Its principal effect would be in connection with contracts for the manufacture, sale or distribution of materials, equipment or supplies in that it would delete from section 220-e the limitation of coverage to operations performed within the territorial limits of the state of New York.

ture, sale or distribution of materials, equipment or supplies shall be limited to operations performed within the territorial limits of the state of New York.

Section 343-8.0 of the New York City Administrative Code

The instant discussion, as defined by the title of the topic, includes local contracts as well as state contracts. It is accordingly appropriate to note that there is an increasing body of local legislation and to present for consideration by the Symposium the effect of such legislation.[13] Perhaps the best known of such local legislative enactments in New York is section 343-8.0 of the New York City Administrative Code. This section, relating to discrimination in public contracts of the City of New York, was added to the City Administrative Code in 1942.[14] The provision prohibits discrimination because of race, color or creed. (Like the first version of section 220-e of the New York State Labor Law, it does not include national origin.) It covers "any person engaged in the construction, alteration or repair of buildings or engaged in the construction or repair of streets or highways pursuant to a contract with the City, or engaged in the manufacture, sale or distribution of materials, equipment or supplies pursuant to a contract with the City." The wording in section 343-8.0 has not been altered since its enactment in 1942, and declares as follows:

> 343-8.0 Discrimination in employment. —a. It shall be unlawful for any person engaged in the construction, alteration or repair of buildings or engaged in the construction or repair of streets or highways pursuant to a contract with the city, or engaged in the manufacture, sale or distribution of materials, equipment or supplies pursuant to a contract with the city to refuse to employ or to refuse to continue in any employment any person on account of race, color or creed of such person.
>
> b. It shall be unlawful for any person or any servant, agent or employee of any person, described in subdivision a to ask, indicate

13. The existence of local laws in addition to state laws extends to jurisdictions other than New York. For example, instances of each coverage as reported by various sources (see note 7, *supra*) are found in the following jurisdictions:
Arizona—Phoenix.
California—Bakersfield, San Francisco.
Illinois—Chicago.
Indiana—East Chicago, Gary.
Maryland—Baltimore.
Michigan—Ecorse, Hamtramck, Jackson, Lansing, Pontiac, River Rouge.
Minnesota—Duluth, Minneapolis, St. Paul.
Ohio—Cleveland, Toledo, Youngstown.
Pennsylvania—Braddock, Pittsburgh.
Wisconsin—Beloit, Milwaukee.
There are also instances where a local law exists in a state in which there is no comparable state law, *e.g.*, Des Moines, Iowa.
14. L.L. 1942, No. 44. The bill was introduced in the City Council in 1942 as Intro. No. 13, PR 13, and after committee amendment was PR 78. It represented a number of changes in language from a bill introduced by the same sponsor (Councilman Diogiovanna) in 1941.

or transmit, orally or in writing, directly or indirectly, the race, color or creed or religious affiliation of any person employed or seeking employment from such person, firm or corporation.

c. The wording of section 343-8.0, subdivisions a and b, shall appear on all contracts entered into by the city, and disobedience thereto shall be deemed a violation of a material provision of the contract.

d. Any person, or the employee, manager or owner of or officer of such firm or corporation who shall violate any of the provisions of this section shall, upon conviction thereof, be punished by a fine of not more than one hundred dollars or by imprisonment for not more than thirty days, or both.

Although, as noted, there has been no change in the wording of section 343-8.0 of the Administrative Code, it has been implemented by an executive order dated February 7, 1962, issued to all city departments and agencies, by Mayor Wagner. This order includes use of the term "national origin." With a supplement, entitled "Supplement 1," the order sets forth the jurisdiction and supervision of the City Commission on Intergroup Relations (now the City Commission on Human Rights) with respect to the Code provision, and provides a compliance hearing and complaint procedure.[15]

Action by Local Subdivisions of Government

In 1963 the New York Legislature added Article 12-D to the General Municipal Law to provide for the creation of local human relations commissions. More than a score of such commissions have already come into existence and it appears that there will be a substantially greater number. Action in connection with contract compliance by the state and federal government has obviously engaged the interest of these commissions and it appears that their programs have begun to include recommendations to local units of government to adopt resolutions or local laws dealing with equal employment opportunities in public contracts. For example, the Rockland County Human Relations Commission has proposed the following resolution for the County of Rockland:

---

15. The "Purpose" and "Policy" paragraphs of the Mayor's executive order (Executive Order No. 4, February 7, 1962) declare:

" I. *Purpose.* This order and its supplement implement section 343-8.0 of the Administrative Code of the City of New York which provides for equal employment opportunity in the policies and practices of contractors for goods and services paid for by the City, and set forth the jurisdiction and supervision of the Commission on Intergroup Relations with respect thereto.

"II. *Policy.*—A. Qualified persons employed by or seeking employment with contractors of departments or agencies of the City of New York shall have equal employment, promotion and training opportunities regardless of race, creed, color or national origin.

"B. Positive and affirmative steps shall be taken by officials of city departments and by contractors to promote and assure equal employment opportunities.

"C. Compliance, hearing and complaint procedures are set forth in Supplement 1.

PROPOSED RESOLUTION COVERING DISCRIMINATION ON THE PART
OF SUPPLIERS OF THE COUNTY OF ROCKLAND

WHEREAS, Article 15 of the Executive Law of the State of
New York finds and declares that practices of discrimination because
of race, creed, color or national origin are not in the best interest of
the public welfare, and

WHEREAS, the United States and the State of New York and
other government agencies decreed that all contracts shall contain a
clause prohibiting discrimination because of race, creed, color or
national origin in matters of employment, now therefore be it,

RESOLVED, the County of Rockland restate and reiterate the
principles set forth in Article 15 of Executive Law of the State of
New York, and be it further

RESOLVED, that all contracts with the County of Rockland
contain an appropriate clause against discrimination as set forth in
Article 15 of Executive Law of the State of New York.

Standard Contract Form for Use by New York State Contracting Agencies

On September 12, 1963, Governor Rockefeller announced the promulga-
tion of a new standard contract form for use by state contracting agencies,
including public authorities. The form describes its seven clauses, lettered (a)
through (g) as "non-discrimination clauses."

The contractor's fundamental agreement is that set forth in clause (a),
namely: "The contractor will not discriminate against any employee or applicant for employment because of race, creed, color or national origin, and
will take affirmative action to insure that they are afforded equal employment
opportunities without discrimination because of race, creed, color or national
origin. Such action shall be taken with reference, but not be limited, to: recruitment, employment, job assignment, promotion, upgrading, demotion,
transfer, layoff or termination, rates of pay or other forms of compensation,
and selection for training or retraining, including apprenticeship and on-the-
job training."

Clause (b) is directed to the giving of notice to labor unions or representatives of workers with whom the contractor has agreements or understandings
and it provides for a number of contingencies.

Clauses (c) and (d) are directed to the giving of general public notice
of the contractor's agreement. Clause (c) covers the posting of notices by the
contractor; and clause (d) covers the inclusion of an equal employment opportunity statement in solicitations or advertisements for employees by the
contractor.

Under clause (e) there is a reiteration of the contractor's existing duty
to comply with the Law Against Discrimination and the Civil Rights Law
and an agreement to furnish all information and reports necessary to ascertain
compliance with the nondiscrimination clauses and with the Law Against Discrimination and the Civil Rights Law.

Clause (f) is the heart of the enforcement procedure and clause (g) provides for inclusion by the contractor of the nondiscrimination clauses and requirements in subcontracts and purchase orders.

The full text of the standard contract form is attached as an appendix.

The Enforcement Clause of the New York Standard Contract Form

It would appear useful to draw particular attention to some of the features of clause (f) of the New York nondiscrimination contract clauses. The powers stated in clause (f) are the powers to cancel, to terminate or to suspend, in whole or in part. The authority to take such action is given to the contracting agency. The clause also states that the contractor may be declared ineligible for future contracts made by or on behalf of the state or a public authority or agency of the state.[16] Such sanctions may be imposed and remedies invoked independently of or in addition to sanctions and remedies otherwise provided by law.

Action by the contracting agency is authorized "upon the basis of a finding made by the State Commission for Human Rights that the contractor has not complied with [the] non-discrimination clauses."

A number of steps are required before any such finding is made by the Commission. Thus, clause (f) contains the statement that, "Such finding shall be made by the State Commission for Human Rights after conciliation efforts by the Commission have failed to achieve compliance with these non-discrimination clauses and after a verified complaint has been filed with the Commission, notice thereof has been given to the contractor and an opportunity has been afforded him to be heard publicly before three members of the Commission."

In summary, then, the authority to exercise the sanction is the authority of the contracting agency; and the responsibility for making the finding upon which such authority may be based is the responsibility of the State Commission for Human Rights.

The On-Going Question

It has been my intention in presenting for discussion the topic assigned to me at this Symposium, to give some detail concerning the complex of legislative and executive directives which bear upon the general question of how state and local contracting power can be used to further equal employment opportunity. It is submitted that it is not particularly profitable to deal with the subject in terms of isolating contract compliance clauses and viewing them as if there were no correlative or coordinate legislation in existence. It would appear to be more helpful to the public which is directly affected, to the

---

16. The ineligibility, once declared, continues until the contractor "satisfies the State Commission for Human Rights that he has established and is carrying out a program in conformity with the provisions of [the] non-discrimination clauses."

segments of industry and labor involved and to the public administrators who are charged with enforcement, if an effort were made, by the kind of expert commentators and analysts gathered here today, to explore and define the most viable framework for action in jurisdictions such as New York where contract compliance powers do not stand alone.[17]

Accordingly, it is to be hoped that this kind of discussion will eventuate under the impact of the ever-increasing importance of public contracts upon the general economy and with specific relationship to the type of question which has brought this Symposium into being. Such analysis, discussion and recommendation, I assure you, is vital to give direction and cohesion to the efforts of those who, like myself, must assume the responsibilities of day-to-day administration.

APPENDIX

EQUAL EMPLOYMENT OPPORTUNITY

NON-DISCRIMINATION CLAUSES IN NEW YORK PUBLIC CONTRACTS

During the performance of this contract, the contractor agrees as follows:

(a) The contractor will not discriminate against any employee or applicant for employment because of race, creed, color or national origin, and will take affirmative action to insure that they are afforded equal employment opportunities without discrimination because of race, creed, color or national origin. Such action shall be taken with reference, but not be limited, to: recruitment, employment, job assignment, promotion, upgrading, demotion, transfer, layoff or termination, rates of pay or other forms of compensation, and selection for training or retraining, including apprenticeship and on-the-job training.

(b) The contractor will send to each labor union or representative of workers with which he has or is bound by a collective bargaining or other agreement or understanding, a notice, to be provided by the State Commission for Human Rights, advising such labor union or representative of the contractor's agreement under clauses (a) through (g) (hereinafter called "non-discrimination clauses"). If the contractor was directed to do so by the contracting agency as part of the bid or negotiation of this contract, the contractor shall request such labor union or representative to furnish him with a written statement that such labor union or representative will not discriminate because of race, creed, color or national origin and that such labor union or representative either will affirmatively cooperate, within the limits of its legal and contractual authority, in the implementation of the policy and provisions of these non-discrimination clauses or that it consents and agrees that recruitment, employment and the terms and conditions of employment under this contract shall be in accordance with the purposes and provisions of these non-discrimination clauses. If such labor union or representative fails or refuses to comply with such a request that it furnish such a statement, the contractor shall promptly notify the State Commission for Human Rights of such failure or refusal.

(c) The contractor will post and keep posted in conspicuous places, available to employees and applicants for employment, notices to be provided by the State Commission for Human Rights setting forth the substance of the provisions of clauses

---

17. See also, *e.g.*, California, Illinois, Indiana, Minnesota, Ohio, and notes 7 and 13 *supra*.

138

(a) and (b) and such provisions of the State's laws against discrimination as the State Commission for Human Rights shall determine.

(d) The contractor will state, in all solicitations or advertisements for employees placed by or on behalf of the contractor, that all qualified applicants will be afforded equal employment opportunities without discrimination because of race, creed, color or national origin.

(e) The contractor will comply with the provisions of Sections 291-299 of the Executive Law and the Civil Rights Law, will furnish all information and reports deemed necessary by the State Commission for Human Rights under these non-discrimination clauses and such sections of the Executive Law, and will permit access to his books, records and accounts by the State Commission for Human Rights, the Attorney General and the Industrial Commissioner for the purposes of investigation to ascertain compliance with these non-discrimination clauses and such sections of the Executive Law and Civil Rights Law.

(f) This contract may be forthwith canceled, terminated or suspended, in whole or in part, by the contracting agency upon the basis of a finding made by the State Commission for Human Rights that the contractor has not complied with these non-discrimination clauses, and the contractor may be declared ineligible for future contracts made by or on behalf of the State or a public authority or agency of the State, until he satisfies the State Commission for Human Rights that he has established and is carrying out a program in conformity with the provisions of these non-discrimination clauses. Such finding shall be made by the State Commission for Human Rights after conciliation efforts by the Commission have failed to achieve compliance with these non-discrimination clauses and after a verified complaint has been filed with the Commission, notice thereof has been given to the contractor and an opportunity has been afforded him to be heard publicly before three members of the Commission. Such sanctions may be imposed and remedies invoked independently of or in addition to sanctions and remedies otherwise provided by law.

(g) The contractor will include the provisions of clauses (a) through (f) in every subcontract or purchase order in such a manner that such provisions will be binding upon each subcontractor or vendor as to operations to be performed within the State of New York. The contractor will take such action in enforcing such provisions of such subcontract or purchase order as the contracting agency may direct, including sanctions or remedies for non-compliance. If the contractor becomes involved in or is threatened with litigation with a subcontractor or vendor as a result of such direction by the contracting agency, the contractor shall promptly so notify the Attorney General, requesting him to intervene and protect the interests of the State of New York.

LOCAL CONTRACTS AND SUB-CONTRACTS: THE ROLES OF CITY GOVERNMENT AND PRIVATE CITIZEN GROUPS

Madison S. Jones*

The Role of Government

MOST American Negroes consider equality of opportunity in employment without regard to race or color the core of America's civil rights problem. While there have been many efforts for several generations to outlaw lynching and the poll tax, it was the emergence of the concept of fair employment practices that high lighted current civil rights legislative objectives of today. This would indicate, therefore, that the paramount civil rights objective of the federal government and numerous similar state and municipal bodies is the elimination of bias in employment and job opportunities.

In 1941 we witnessed the first modern-day mass protest effort on the part of the American Negro in the creation of the March on Washington movement. Negro leaders, lead by A. Philip Randolph, realized a sense of urgency for a vigorous effort on the part of all Negroes for greater participation in the wage-earning class of America's economic life. This effort was followed in 1943 by launching one of the most consistent efforts on the part of approximately three score national organizations to achieve the enactment of the federal fair employment practices legislation. The very nature of the interstate complexion of American industry and commerce causes an intensification among civil rights advocates in their efforts for the enactment of federal legislation in this field.

We notice the emergence of state action in this field by the creation in 1945 of the New York State Commission Against Discrimination (now called State Commission for Human Rights). The New York State Commission created by legislative action was followed by the emergence in twenty-one other states of the creation of commissions or committees. This is not to say that each state has recognized equally with all other states the magnitude of the problem and expressed determination to deal with it forthrightly by effective legislation. Indeed, unfortunately, many states have almost insulted the problem as far as its magnitude and seriousness is concerned with almost ineffective legislative or executive action.

However, the important point at this time is an official recognition of the existence of the problem. The future will tell whether people of good will can relate a concern and demand for action commensurate with the magnitude and seriousness of the civil rights objective. To achieve equality of opportunity in employment without regard to race or color demands vigorous and forthright federal legislative action. For federal law would hasten the city's objectives in this field.

Municipal authorities witness today, especially in the large industrial cities,

---

* Executive Director, New York City Commission on Human Rights.

an increasing concern for their own specialized human rights commission. There is a limitation of the jurisdiction of the city agencies in this field, although they have an important function either by direct or concurrent jurisdiction and/or by supplementing and complementing state and federal agencies in this field.

In the larger cities, especially New York for example, the concern and determination by responsible city officials including municipal legislators can do much to achieve results in this field. This is especially true where City funds are involved and also where the principal executive offices of national private corporations are located.

The New York City Commission on Human Rights is a case in point. This commission has major functions which, pursued successfully, can do much to guarantee that all the people of the City of New York shall live and prosper in what we regard as an "Open City": an "Open City where all the facilities for job opportunities, housing and education shall be on an equal basis without regard to race, color, religion, national origin or ancestry."

It is essential that the construction and maintenance projects for which City funds are appropriated—public schools, public markets, police buildings, laying of sewers and streets—be accomplished with a contractual obligation guaranteeing that employment is available to all people without regard to any consideration of the applicant's ethnic background. This guarantee must include with equal emphasis the right to apprenticeship training.

New York City, with a budget exceeded only by the federal and its state government, has great opportunities in this field, through its contract compliance program. The City having in effect at any one time awarded over 1,000 contracts can do much through its contract compliance program to eliminate racial bias both in trade unions and employment.

But our cities can do even more. They are the locale of large industries which in many cases offer attractive job career opportunities. In the minds of many of those who believe that they are excluded for racial reasons there is an element of glamour and attractiveness. These industries provide new areas of concentration by human rights agencies seeking to expand the frontiers of employment opportunities for ethnic minorities.

This does not always mean that overt acts of race discrimination are the current reasons for the nonappearance of a Negro or some other racial minority in a particular company's work force. But it does mean that a long history has developed in a particular company which indicates a persistent practice of bypassing certain racial groups in the company's recruiting and employment programs.

It was in this light that the New York City Commission recently convened a meeting of the leaders of the City's giant advertising industry. A similar gathering of leaders of the brokerage and investment industry was also convened. In both cases a challenge was hurled to these leaders to recognize their responsibilities in seeking out Negroes and Spanish-speaking Americans for job opportunities in their employment. A responsibility born by the very nature of the respectability and prestige which such industries maintain in the community poses a real challenge. A forceful and vigorous city commission has the responsibility, which it must always assume, for vigorously challenging and inspiring leaders of these industries to play their role in the City's human rights objectives.

What is the role then, especially of a City Commission in the field of human rights in a significant-sized industrial metropolis? Is such a commission to pursue its official responsibilities with an objectivity usually and rightfully found in courts of law? By the very nature of the problem can such a commission's policies and programs be in the hands of appointed officials and staff representatives who lack a sympathy for the very existence of these problems of racial bias? Can the very damaging effects that these problems create in many ways be ignored and their harmful psychological reactions upon the individual personality be passed over?

It would seem that the very nature of the problem and the responsibility of human rights specialists require always a warm sympathy and concern not only for the problem, but also for the individual who looks to such commissions for help and guidance.

Further, it would seem that such a commission must recognize by aggressive action a definite responsibility for provoking thought and through such provocation help create a better informed public on the real issues which underline a current civil rights issue or crisis. For it is at these times that the cry for bold, imaginative, moral and visionary leadership must be answered. It is not enough for such a commission to be in step; it must rather to be out in front providing leadership.

This leadership often must be provocative and controversial. It must not be expected that this leadership will always, in the initial stages, be popular. In the beginning it may find itself supported or rejected by the majority of the City's population. At other times it can find itself supported only by those ethnic groups around which the conflict stirs. Such a commission can find itself frustrated by public and private groups in its efforts. But what such a commission, including state and federal bodies in this area can never permit itself is a lack of conviction. For its own positions once taken must be pursued, in light of the established facts, with vigor and determination.

For in the final analysis, the very fact that racial bias has existed with great damaging economic, political, social and moral consequences for a period predating the life of the nation assures success in this field only by remaining consistently on the offensive. It is an aggressive position of leadership, a recognition of the historic human rights goals to which our nation is dedicated, that compels the City Commission on Human Rights of the City of New York, as it does many other bodies similarly concerned, to justify its existence.

Currently there are vigorous efforts by many local Civil Rights groups to crack a virtual "iron fence" against the employment of qualified Negro journeymen and Negro apprentices in the construction trades industry of our large industrial cities.

In New York City last summer we experienced numerous demonstrations which resulted in work stoppages on vital projects being erected with public funds. Recognizing a threat to the public welfare, Mayor Robert Wagner requested his Commission on Human Rights to conduct public hearings. It would seem to me appropriate to set forth here the results of those hearings as an illustration and also as a means for helping other cities to deal with the problem which may currently be of some concern to them.

Perhaps you would be interested in first knowing what were the charges leveled by civil rights spokesmen. I would like to enumerate them:

1. That unions control employment by restricting union entry through sponsorship requirements, by hiring hall agreements with contractors and by a system of issuing work permits.
2. That unions with the tightest control of jobs discriminate the most.
3. That "no union jobs—and this includes all public construction and all major private construction—can be performed without members of these unions being involved."
4. That Negro and Puerto Rican vocational school graduates are unable to enter unions and apprenticeship programs of the crafts for which they have been trained.
5. That apprenticeship and on-the-job training is denied minority group members. In this connection the civil rights spokesman cited a New York State Commission Against Discrimination (SCAD), now State Commission for Human Rights, 1960 study, which said that "the nature of the internal union political structure and process" is a major factor responsible for this denial. He also referred to a 1948 SCAD order to the sheet metal workers to desist "from executing and/or maintaining constitutional or by-law provisions which exclude Negroes" and pointed out that the 1960 SCAD analysis reported little, if any, progress in that area since 1948.
6. That conscious discrimination is practiced in the construction craft unions, the reference in this connection is a United States Civil Rights Commission report.
7. That the foregoing pattern of exclusion helps perpetuate disparity of income, adds to the burden of Negro and Puerto Rican unemployment, and discourages Negro and Puerto Rican youth from completing their high school education, especially those in vocational schools.
8. That unions have offered nothing of substance for solving the problem.
9. That state and city officials have failed to enforce existing anti-bias laws.

As a result of these charges and after appropriate conclusions based on the testimony of more than a score of witnesses, our commission, in the interest of the general welfare of the City of New York, made the following recommendations. These recommendations, we believe, can help other cities through similar difficult problems.

A. *City Policy for Integration*

In order to encourage full integration in the construction industry and promote equal employment opportunity, by encouraging the recruitment of qualified nonwhite craftsmen, it is recommended:

That the city require, as a prerequisite for obtaining a contract, that an employer secure and maintain an integrated work force, just as he must show financial stability, administrative competence and wholesome industrial relations;

That each city official responsible for the awarding of such contracts be accountable for proper enforcement of nondiscrimination clauses contained in each City contract;

That city officials include in every contract a stipulation by the contractor that the work force will be fully integrated, and that the contract include a provision that the City Commission on Human Rights shall have the power to determine whether discrimination exists before, during or after awarding the contract;

That failure to fulfill contract provisions on integration to the satisfaction of the City Commission on Human Rights result in appropriate action by the City to cancel the contract;

That the Mayor, by Executive Order, require that all contractors with the City in the initial stages of implementing the personnel requirements of a contract insure that all employees and all applicants for employment receive fair and equitable treatment including opportunities for promotion without regard to race, creed, color, ancestry or national origin and that this policy apply to unskilled, semi-skilled and all work categories in the clerical, technical, professional and administrative jobs and positions of the contractor.

That contractors be required by such Executive Order to:

1. Include nonwhite workers on every level of their work forces.
2. Institute aggressive and affirmative programs to assure the inclusion of minority workers in every job category.
3. Assure that a policy of inclusion and emphasis upon equal employment opportunity of minorities not only be recognized and stated publicly, but also effectuated through all administrative and supervisory forces as a major policy and administrative objective of the contractor.
4. Assure that in implementing an aggressive and affirmative action program that recruitment sources be considered and used which complement and re-enforce the City's programs to accomplish equal employment opportunity for all workers.

5. Establish procedures assuring that hiring and placement be administered with emphasis on aggressive and affirmative action to achieve equal employment opportunity for all of the City's minority workers.

6. Make certain that promotion procedures are consistent with the aforementioned objectives.

7. Take cognizance of the neighborhood residential concentrations of ethnic minority residents and the implications such concentrations have for the locale and direction of their recruitment programs.

8. Assess the available skills and manpower resources in these neighborhoods and, in recognition of such circumstances, establish recruitment offices or maintain representatives of these offices in close proximity to these residential concentrations.

B. *Freedom of Entry into Union Membership and Apprenticeship Programs*

The City has no authority to enact legislation to outlaw race discrimination by trade unions. However, Section 43 of the State Civil Rights Code and the State Law Against Discrimination in employment provide a legal basis for correcting the abuses herein described. It is therefore incumbent on the appropriate state agencies to fully enforce these laws.

Specifically, all apprenticeship training programs sponsored by New York labor unions, jointly or independently administered, should be required to meet the following standards.

1. The selection of apprentices on the basis of merit alone, in accordance with objective standards which permit review, after full and fair opportunity for application, unless the selections otherwise made would themselves demonstrate that there is equality of opportunity.

2. The taking of whatever steps are necessary, in acting upon application lists developed prior to this time, to offset the effects of previous practices under which discriminatory patterns of employment have resulted.

3. Nondiscrimination in all phases of apprenticeship and employment during apprenticeship after selections are made.

C. *Priority for Nonwhites Over Out-of-Towners*

To promote maximum utilization of the City's nonwhite manpower and nondiscrimination in the construction industry, by encouraging the recruitment of nonwhite craftsmen, it is recommended:

That contractors be required to give priority to nonwhite qualified journeymen, when faced with a shortage of workers in a particular craft, before employing journeymen residing outside the New York Metropolitan area;

That in order to insure an integrated work force where none or a token few nonwhite workers are employed, local trade unions—prior to issuing work permits to out-of-town white union members—be required to refer qualified nonwhites, whether union members or not, whenever these unions are unable to supply workers from their New York City membership.

D. *An Apprenticeship Training Program for the City*

To afford youth entering the labor market full opportunity to develop their full skill potential, it is recommended that city agencies responsible for maximum utilization of available manpower, in cooperation with local vocational schools and city contracting agencies, take immediate steps to:

1. Broaden the training courses offered in local schools so as to provide students with training in the full gamut of construction trades;
2. Develop cooperative work programs whereby graduates from local vocational schools will be enabled to make an orderly transition from school to work, at the craft of their choice, in City operated agencies;
3. Insist that unions and contractors currently sponsoring apprentice programs in the construction industry:
   (a) Review present apprentice-to-journeymen ratios and revise entry quotas to meet fully estimated manpower requirements of the future;
   (b) Insure that skilled-craft training opportunities be afforded the City's nonwhite youth either through expansion of existing apprentice programs (as recommended above) or by alloting a portion of the existing openings to nonwhite high school graduates.

These are specific proposals that illustrate the present and future course of this problem in the nation's largest City. To those who are similarly situated and have similar responsibility in this difficult field, I hope the proposals will succeed in pointing a positive and vigorous course.

THE ROLE OF PRIVATE CITIZEN GROUPS**

How have private groups—citizen and trade groups and organizations receiving no public funds—operated to achieve progress toward the goal of equal employment opportunities by persuasion rather than by formal enforcement procedures? Since I am unable to indicate specifics, it all depends on how you interpret the word "persuasion." Some private groups have been able to persuade through picketing and demonstrations and have therefore, made many changes in the industrial life in some areas of the country.

First: I have seen some private and community groups, not through picketing or boycott or demonstration, negotiate directly across the table with management in an effort to employ Negroes and Puerto Ricans. I think you have seen this most effectively in some neighborhood operations. In Brooklyn, for example, a group negotiated with one of the chain stores. I do not believe there was any

---

** Mr. Jones agreed to comment on this topic in place of an absent speaker.

demonstration or picketing in that case, but the group was able to get Negroes and Puerto Ricans employed.

Second: Last summer the CORE group in the Bronx picketed White Castle and through subsequent negotiation were able to get people employed. This situation was interesting because the Commission became the mediator in the dispute. White Castle sent its chief attorney from Columbus, Ohio to join its local staff in the negotiations with CORE and the Commission's representatives. In the beginning there was no confrontation. White Castle would meet with the Commission's representatives and then the CORE group would sit down with us. Two or three days elapsed before everyone sat around the table together. I think a great deal was learned on all sides. All of the demands were not met but people did get jobs. Not only did we mediate this dispute but a procedure was set up with the company wherein Commission representatives would survey and give some guidance to their employment operations over the months. We are still active in the case, finding out who is employed and apprising the CORE group of what is going on.

This also happened in the dispute between CORE and the Waldorf Astoria Hotel. There again, not only did we settle the dispute, but management took upon itself, as a result of negotiations, to take affirmative steps to go out and seek nonwhite workers. This is very important.

Someone said this morning, "How do you know there is discrimination?" "If there are no Negroes or Puerto Ricans employed, industry should try to find them." Local groups can help whether it be through overt action by demonstration or other action by negotiation with company representatives.

Many of these industries and companies have had no contact with minority groups. They know nothing about the community. They know nothing about resources that are available in a community. I think community groups have a great responsibility to be of assistance, not only in helping with dissident organizations, but educating the dominant groups in what their responsibilities are and how they can find the answers.

I think this has been evidenced a great deal in New York.

Third: I would like to point out what may be a unique approach; the interest of a Commission in practices which discriminate against the consumer. We find that in minority neighborhoods higher prices are being charged, that shoddy goods are being foisted on the public and that quality goods are not sold in all neighborhoods. For instance, in one section of Harlem, we found a chain store that was selling black pepper, I believe, for about thirty-five cents over what had been advertised. We did not just go in and find that. A community group shopped the area. The group sat down with management and not only was the question of goods and prices discussed but also the question of jobs. Now, these community groups have to be stimulated; I use that word advisedly. But such local groups can prod the community to realize and resolve its problems.

SUPPLEMENTARY ACTIVITIES FOR STATE GOVERNMENTS SEEKING TO ELIMINATE DISCRIMINATION

FREDERICK B. ROUTH*

THERE is no adequate substitute for the administrative enforcement of legislation in state governmental activities aimed at the elimination, prevention, or lessening of discrimination. Most public administrators, who head state FEPCs, acknowledge the validity of the old saw "A dog with good teeth will have his bark heard." Law, with teeth—while no end in itself—is the necessary tool for those who would work at the task of ending discrimination. Persuasion and conciliation *are and should be* the first steps to be taken in dealing with a respondent. But a state agency which administers an *enforceable* statute is more persuasive and the respondents which come before it are more conciliatory than in those situations in which the agency lacks enforcement powers.

While it is true that there is no adequate substitute for enforcement powers, there are certain supplementary actions which a state government may undertake to strengthen and expand its role in combating discrimination. In certain cases where state legislatures have failed to enact enforceable—or, for that matter, any—legislation, the suggested activities which follow may serve as stop-gaps (not substitutes) until such time as effective statutes have been passed.

The Governor, as chief executive officer of the state, can play a determining role in setting state policy in the area of antidiscrimination as well as in other areas in which governors have historically exerted leadership. The Governors of New York and Michigan have led the way in promulgating a GOVERNOR'S CODE OF FAIR PRACTICES. Other state chief executives have followed suit. A Governor's Code of Fair Practices does several important things:

1. It formally declares the public policy of the state to be for equality of opportunity and against discrimination;

2. It invokes the wide range of state administrative power to carry out this public policy;

3. It calls for affirmative action more so than do the corrective activities of processing complaints;

4. It directs itself to internal and external governmental activities and functions;

5. It places responsibility for follow-through on each department and agency head;

6. It calls for regular reports, making possible evaluation of progress (or lack of it) in each department and agency.

---

* Executive Director, National Association of Inter-Group Relations Officials.

It is not enough for the Governor to quietly issue a Code of Fair Practices—he must make it known to the heads of all state departments and agencies and, through prominent posting in all state buildings, offices, and facilities, to all state employees and to the public at large. Governor John B. Swainson of Michigan called a special meeting of all state department and agency heads to announce and explain his Code, to stress that he "meant business," and to ask each executive to study ways of furthering the purposes of the Code, under existing legislation. The success of this meeting and one subsequently held suggest the advisability of regular meetings between the Governor and the leaders of the executive department of government focused on civil rights.

In addition to the Governor's Code of Fair Practices, which declares over-all state policy and sets over-all state practice, each department and agency of the executive branch may strengthen the state's war on discrimination by promulgating a clear, definitive, written policy of equal employment opportunity. The state should put its own house in order as an equal opportunity employer.

State agencies and departments which contract with outside, private corporations for supplies, services, material, or work should negotiate contracts containing nondiscrimination clauses covering contractors and subcontractors; breach of such contractual provisions, it should be specified, will be regarded as a material breach of the contract.

State licensing authority may be utilized in carrying forth the public policy against discrimination. No one argues that it is unconstitutional, illegal, or even improper for state licensing agencies to set certain standards of safety, cleanliness, or usage; indeed, most licensing agencies have a list of rules with which applicants-for-license and licensees must comply. While guarding against arbitrary and capricious acts, licensing agencies may, in many cases, add an antidiscrimination article to the rules. When licensees then violate this rule the licensing agency should take such disciplinary action as may be provided in the statute or the administrative code for rules violation. A broad or liberal construction of the statutory authority of licensing agencies should reveal a goodly number of legal ways to utilize that authority in effectuating a state public policy of equal opportunity.

State governments, in the middle to latter part of the twentieth century, offer many services and facilities which were unheard of in earlier times. They are engaged, directly and indirectly, in such wide ranging activities as: higher and public education; health services; apprenticeship and on-the-job training; vocational guidance and counseling; employee recruitment, classification and referral; research, both pure and applied; agricultural experimentation; raising fish, fowl, and wildlife; exploring for natural resources; to name but a few. In many of these activities, government itself does not actually engage; rather, it makes grants to institutions, agencies, companies, and even individuals who specialize in such activities. The axiom that "Public policy follows the public purse" should be applied to all who receive, or seek to receive grants from state governments. As the Michigan Governor's Code of Fair Practices puts it, "All state agencies engaged in granting financial assistance shall deny it to any applicant and withdraw it from any recipient engaged in discriminatory practices, consistent with the statute under which they operate." Such a policy should not be limited to financial assistance but should equally apply to other forms of aid, assistance, or grants. The leasing of a research facility for a dollar-a-year, the free provision of seedlings, the free or reduced rate of providing testing facilities are also important "gratuities" received by many companies, unions, and institutions. Those who receive such benefits should be required to pursue a nondiscriminatory policy and practice.

The most important asset any state possesses is its human resources—its citizenry. Human resources, like natural resources, must be safeguarded. It is the proper role of state government to use its authority in further developing all its resources. The elimination of discrimination, the creation of equality of opportunity greatly enhance the worth of human resources. Obviously, then, it is proper for any state government to utilize all legal means at its disposal, to bend the efforts of every department and agency to the accomplishment of easing, ending, and preventing discrimination.

VOCATIONAL TRAINING TO IMPROVE JOB OPPORTUNITIES FOR MINORITY GROUPS

JOHN PATRICK WALSH*

THIS paper presents some reflections on vocational training for improving job opportunities of disadvantaged minority groups. In keeping with the theme of the symposium, emphasis is given to the role of state and local agencies. However, the background of new federal government programs and resources for strengthening local action in the job training field will also be touched upon.

Job training is but one of many approaches for achieving equal employment opportunity considered in this symposium. This fact helps to set the role of training into proper perspective. It is not a cure-all for unemployment problems. Training programs do not in themselves create jobs. Nor do they automatically eliminate discriminatory employment barriers. Job training is simply one of a number of essential tools which can profitably be used to help open up employment for disadvantaged groups.

JOB AND TRAINING NEEDS

The importance of vocational training for minority group members stems from their unfavorable position in today's labor market. Four basic facts need only be mentioned to illustrate this point. First, minority group workers are concentrated in jobs at the lowest end of the skill ladder. A far higher proportion of nonwhites than of whites are employed as farm hands, non-farm laborers, low-skill service workers, semi-skilled operatives, and at related jobs. In the average month of 1963, for example, one-fifth of all nonwhite male workers were nonfarm laborers and 8 per cent were hired farm hands. The corresponding figures for white workingmen were only 6 and 3 per cent, respectively. At the other extreme, nonwhites are grossly underrepresented in the professional, technical, managerial, clerical, sales, and skilled craftsman fields.

Second, the lowest skilled occupations are not only the lowest paid, but they have the highest rates of unemployment. Laborers had the highest average unemployment rate last year—12 per cent—and semi-skilled operatives, low-skill service workers, and related occupations were also well above the national average for joblessness. In contrast, the unemployment rate for professional and technical workers was only 2 per cent, and other white collar and skilled workers experienced less than average joblessness. Overall, the unemployment rate of nonwhites averaged 11 per cent in 1963, compared to only 5 per cent for whites. Unemployment rates for predominantly white minority groups, such as Puerto Ricans, are also excessive. Moreover, even when members of minority groups do have work, they experience involuntary part-time

* Deputy Director, Office of Manpower, Automation and Training, U.S. Department of Labor.

joblessness and other forms of underemployment to a much greater extent than other workers.

Third, employment for unskilled and low-skill workers in future years will be increasingly scarce and sporadic. It is this segment of the labor force which will be most affected by automation and other technological change. The occupations which will have the highest growth rates in coming years are those requiring relatively advanced education and technical skills.

Fourth, a very high proportion of minority workers lack the educational attainment and vocational skills needed to move into the technical, skilled, or white collar occupations which offer the best future job oportunities. In 1960, 16 per cent of all nonwhites in the labor force had less than 5 years of schooling; 4 of every 10 had less than 8 years of school. Only one-fourth of the total had a full high school education. Although the level of schooling attained has been rising generation after generation, the complexity of job requirements has also been increasing. There remains a wide gap between the qualifications of minroity workers and the kinds of jobs that they must look to in the modern labor market.

The combination of these four adverse conditions highlights the role that training can play in improving job opportunities for minorities. Youngsters need to be equipped with appropriate academic and technical skills to qualify for the expanding technical, white collar, or craftsman occupations. Employed workers need assistance to retrain for steadier, higher-paying jobs and to upgrade their skill levels. And unemployed workers need help in obtaining both training and some means of subsistence while preparing for new jobs.

The Hereditary Nature of Unemployment and Poverty

Evidence has now been clearly marshalled to show the critical importance of intergenerational mobility in this country. Witness these facts—in a nation which prides itself with considerable justification—that social and economic status is not a matter of heredity:

> In this country one out of every three unemployed persons never went beyond grade school.

> Two out of three unemployed persons in this country are high school dropouts.

> Incredible as it may seem, one out of every three persons being examined for service in the Armed Forces fails—and one-half of the failures are persons who cannot pass the Armed Forces Qualification Test, a test designed to measure an individual's ability to serve in the Armed Forces—equivalent to the attainment of something less than an elementary school education.

> Currently, about one-quarter million people fail the AFQT and the number is expected to go up to about one-third of a million annually in the years ahead.

In a recent survey of these mental rejectees we found that:

Almost one-half came from families which have 6 or more children.

One-fifth have fathers who are not working.

One-fifth are from families which have been on relief in the last five years.

Seventy per cent of them never went beyond grade school.

Over half of the fathers of the rejectees had never finished the eighth grade. Only 16 per cent of their fathers had finished high school.

And so the picture develops—with minority groups making a sizable contribution to the rejectee group.

The following table highlights the relationship between educational attainment of young people and their parents' economic positions.

Father's Occupation	Per cent of persons 14-24 whose educational attainment is below the national average for their age (1959)[1]
Professional	4%
Managerial	7
Sales	7
Clerical	11
Skilled	14
Semi-skilled	21
Unskilled	37
Service	21
Farmers	28
Farm Laborers	52

The range is enormous (4 to 52 per cent). Among manual workers the proportion of young people, who are educationally disadvantaged and whose fathers are unskilled (37 per cent), is 2 ½ times the corresponding proportion (14 per cent) for those whose fathers are skilled.

Similarly, family income clearly has a critical role in affecting the relationship between father's educational attainment and college attendance thus underscoring the "social heredity" concept. This is how the data look for October 1960.

PER CENT OF PERSONS 16-24 WITH COLLEGE ATTENDANCE[2]

	Family Income			
	Under $5000	$5000-7499	$7500-9999	$10,000+
Father did not graduate from high school	13%	23%	33%	41%
Father graduated from high school	45%	55%	71%	74%

1. Census Bureau, Series P-20 No. 112 (Dec. 29, 1961).
2. Census Bureau, Series P-20, No. 110 (July 24, 1961).

The pathway out of the circle of poverty and unemployment is through programs of education and training geared to the needs of the future—programs that break the bonds of "social heredity" and lead individuals to new ways of life. To do this certain barriers must be broken.

VARIED APPROACHES

Granting that job training has a major role in helping minority groups move into the mainstream of productive life, we may next ask which specific approaches are most likely to achieve the best results. Much remains to be learned about the provision of job training for disadvantaged people. We are learning every day that special techniques and adaptation of programs are essential for successful training projects.

To begin with, there is increasing awareness that the kind of skills which many minority workers must acquire are much more complex than superficial occupational techniques. For a large proportion of minority group workers, a program of vocational training must take into account and attempt to influence unfavorable character and behavior patterns resulting from cultural influences and conflicts, physical and cultural deprivation, and adverse family and neighborhood pressures. Attitudes, motivation, and self confidence become a part of preparing for better jobs.

Second, experience under the Manpower Development and Training Act has called attention to the necessity for providing elementary literacy and related academic education to many minority group members before or simultaneous with specialized vocational training. Without such basic education, many workers could not even qualify for regular vocational training courses, which require specified levels of reading and arithmetic for admission. Some groups are handicapped by language problems; for them, language courses are an essential part of vocational training. Obviously, too, teaching methods, curricula, and textbooks require adaptation to meet the job training needs of individuals lacking language, reading, or similar skills.

Third, mention should be made of the host of non-educational needs that must be met to help disadvantaged workers enter and stay in training. The provision of baby-sitters, transportation, counseling on family or health problems—all are a part of vocational training for problem groups. So, often, is training in hygiene, conventional courtesy, and how to dress properly. Such problems offer a challenge to the creativity and ingenuity of local and state vocational training, employment, welfare, and other agencies concerned with this matter. They offer a wide field for forward-looking and varied experimentation to seek out unique procedures tailored to the employment needs of particular components of different minority groups.

With this introduction, I would like now to offer some more detailed thoughts on the kinds of approaches that require consideration in job training for disadvantaged minorities. Because of the wide differences between the training needs of different components of minority groups, it may be helpful to consider three categories of people separately: in-school youth, the "dropouts," and adult workers.

In-School Youth

Most of the responsibility for preparing the individual for effective participation in the labor market falls upon the regular system of public elementary and secondary schools. It is encouraging to note, therefore, that school systems are increasingly aware that for minority groups this responsibility cannot end with the mere establishment of courses to teach specific occupational skills. The schools are stepping in to help overcome the total range of social and psychological problems which handicap the minority worker in search of jobs.

Not only job skills, but appropriate character and personality development are required for a successful adaptation to the labor market. Early school experiences must help, for example, in the development of good work habits, patterns of cooperation, amenability to supervision, orientation to the routines of steady job-holding, responsiveness to economic incentives and penalties, and career-orientated "ambition." As part of this general orientation, the youth must learn proper speech, dress, and interpersonal relationships. As he advances in high school, the student must somehow learn how to seek and hold a job.

For some groups who have special problems of adjusting to the expectations of employers and other workers in the labor market, this kind of school preparation may be extended even further afield. For example, many youths in rural farm areas must migrate to the city in search of a job. For them, the regular educational program may well include special counseling on such items as how to adjust to city life, how to find a place to live, how to manage wisely on cash incomes, where to get medical and other kinds of help, etc. Teaching the children of migratory farm workers how to use modern plumbing and electrical appliances is as important a part of their vocational training as teaching specific job content. Teaching the use of public transportation systems and city maps may be essential for equipping Indians and Puerto Ricans for industrial jobs.

A second point with respect to in-school youth is the increasing recognition of the need for adequate vocational counseling. This includes early identification of the aptitudes and interests of students, often by measures custom tailored to the cultural backgrounds of the youths involved. For minority groups, counseling also requires active efforts to develop career aspirations and to expose young members of poor, isolated minorities to the widest possible range of job experiences. We cannot expect Negro slum children to strive to become economists or chemists unless they first learn about the content and utility of such distant occupations. Cooperative efforts of school systems and the public employment service have been useful in this aspect of vocational preparation.

Third, it must be accepted that a high school education is almost essential for any youth who is entering the labor market in the near future. Although a reasonable case can be made to the effect that a high school diploma is not really necessary for many of the beginner jobs for which it is currently required, the fact remains that persons who have not completed high school will face increasing difficulty in the job market. This has many important implications for the educator of disadvantaged youths. He is being called upon to make extra efforts to keep problem youths in school who previously dropped out and became society's problem. Some local authorities have responded to this challenge by new approaches: the adjustment of school curricula to the special aptitudes and interests of the students, incentives to attract exceptionally well qualified teachers to schools in which minority group members are heavily concentrated, special counseling and individual tutoring, and various forms of financial assistance. Significantly, the "War on Poverty" program, recently outlined by the President, includes the provision of part-time jobs to help keep needy students in school.

Discussion of ways to supplement and support occupational training for disadvantaged persons should not, of course, cause us to lose sight of occupational training, itself. It is in this area that the most experience and the most definite answers are available. Here the problems are more tangible—the need for the latest shop equipment, the need for better school books, and so on. Of particular importance to this conference is the well-documented fact that schools for nonwhites are substandard in some parts of the country. Another problem in this area has been the failure of some vocational training to keep up with the rapid pace of technological change, or with changes in manpower requirements. Industrial processes may change faster than school equipment and school teachers. Some rural schools are still focusing heavily on training for agricultural occupations, even though a high proportion of their students must seek nonfarm jobs. Also, some schools accommodating mainly minority groups are said to be giving inadequate emphasis to training for more skilled, technical occupations which the erosion of job discrimination has recently brought within the reach of Negroes and other sub-groups. The solution of such problems is essential to enhance equal employment opportunities.

One should note that the recently enacted Vocational Education Act of 1963 expands federal assistance for updating vocational education and relating it more closely to manpower needs and trends. However, it should be emphasized that responsibilities for preparing youths for the labor market in the regular school system are overwhelmingly of a local or state character. Although the federal government seeks to encourage the improvement of the school systems and provides some financial assistance for vocational education meeting appropriate standards, it is the state and local educational and allied authorities who are faced with the challenge of devising and applying the most effective on-the-spot programs.

Young "Dropouts"

What about youths who do not complete high school or who otherwise enter the labor market without adequate occupational skills? How can state and local agencies meet their responsibilities to such young people? This question is of particular importance for minority groups, for disadvantaged youths have the highest "dropout" rate of all.

If the "dropouts" do not acquire an adequate vocational education, they can look forward to persistent joblessness and under-employment. Unemployment rates vary directly with the education of workers, rising from 1.5 per cent for college graduates to 10 per cent for individuals with only a few years of school. The unemployment rate of 16- to 24-year-old youths who never completed high school is almost double the rate for high school graduates—14 and 8 per cent, respectively. A recent study of nonwhite youths who left high school in 1962 found that fully one-third of those who left before completing their studies had no jobs 4 months later. Moreover, a disproportionately large number of the "dropouts" were holding unskilled or temporary jobs making for a life of sporadic unemployment and chronic underemployment. Unless effective means are found to prepare the "dropouts" for productive employment, society will be shouldered with more serious burdens and adjustments—unemployment and underemployment, the vicious cycle of poverty, the climbing crime rate, mounting "relief" rosters, and a host of related welfare problems.

The point that I would like to underscore is that the job training needs of the "dropouts" cannot be met in the same way as the needs of in-school youth. It is becoming increasingly clear that programs which merely establish ordinary vocational training classes and invite the "dropouts" to return to a formal school setting cannot meet their special needs. New approaches are required, designed to solve the varied social, psychological, and economic problems that led to discontinuing formal schooling in the first place. This involves developing ways to offset adverse attitudes and motivations to create aspirations for further schooling and better jobs, and to gear training to the level of ability and interest of the "dropouts." It involves attention to introducing new environments and social settings in which training can be accepted and supported. Often, youths who entered the labor force without adequate vocational preparation are unable to take training unless they are assisted to meet special financial needs; e.g., they may have family obligations rarely found among in-school youths.

Work in this challenging field has demonstrated the usefulness of intensive vocational and personal counseling to help disadvantaged youths avail themselves of vocational training and employment opportunities; enlistment of family and neighborhood support; individual tutoring; financial assistance; and training in basic literacy and related academic skills as a prelude to occupational training. Since the "dropouts" are unreceptive to institutional train-

157

ing, the development of on-the-job training programs in cooperation with employers and other organizations in the community is of particular value. Wages paid to on-the-job trainees, the encouragement of co-workers, and the direct relationship between the training and future employment, help to motivate the student in this type of occupational program.

Recently, recognition of the importance of the total environment and outlook of disadvantaged youths in the training process was shown in the President's proposal for a "Job Corps." If this proposal is accepted, young volunteers with employment or training needs will receive work experience and vocational training away from home, in a camp setting where wholesome attitudes can be developed and facilities conducive to vocational training will be available. The theory here is, in part, that youngsters with special learning or motivation problems cannot be expected to show good performance in unfavorable social and physical environments—in poorly lighted and heated rural shacks or crowded slum apartments amid persons unlikely to encourage work or study. The human and physical environment of the camps would be structured to foster character development and good citizenship as well as skill training. A similar approach is found in the Vocational Education Act of 1963, which authorizes and finances projects to test the feasibility of providing vocational training on a residential basis.

Unemployed and Underemployed Adult Workers

The third category of minority group workers requiring consideration in vocational training programs are the adults who lack adequate ocupational skills to obtain steady work. These include jobless workers, those employed intermittently or at very low wages, and workers who must retrain because demand for their occupations is declining. In the latter group are the pick and shovel laborers, the seasonal farm hands, and other occupational groups in which minority workers tend to be concentrated. Sometimes, the problems of the adult workers are complicated by old age or bad health. As previously noted, they are often complicated by very low educational attainment—inability to read the labels, instructions, and manuals, or to write the bills and requisitions which are an essential part of today's jobs. In the case of Americans of Mexican descent, Puerto Ricans, Indians, and others, there may be language problems which tend to disqualify workers from training and jobs.

The adult group presents perhaps the greatest challenge of all. It is truly a "hard-core" group, lacking the potential adaptability of younger members of minority groups, often bordering on illiteracy, and often hampered by inability to adjust to the dominant American culture. State and local authorities are faced with this key question: Is it too late to equip unemployed or underemployed disadvantaged adult workers with marketable occupational skills? Within this key question there are more specific ones. For example, how can vocational training be supported by measures to retread interpersonal skills, to inculcate behavior patterns acceptable to future co-workers and potential supervisors, to shift orientation from outdoor to indoor work, from active to sedentary work, and from manipulation of large tools to handling of small and delicate work instruments? Also, how can reading and writing be taught quickly to persons of advanced years to prepare them for the unfamiliar routines of formal training? It is at the grass roots level that ways must be found to teach the unemployed middle-aged Negro laborer how to hold a pencil properly, how to speak clearly and dress appropriately, to develop the self-confidence required to ask questions and give answers in class, and to develop the habits of regularity required for coming to classes and keeping job appointments.

Also a knotty problem in providing new job training opportunities for disadvantaged adults is the need to finance the cost of training and to provide some means of earning a livelihood for the trainees and their families. Programs which do not meet this basic need cannot, of course, hope to reach the minority group members who need the most help. It is worthy of note that a number of states had taken steps to pay for training and to provide living allowances for unemployed workers even before the federal government moved into this field in the last several years. Some states also permitted workers to enter vocational training courses without losing their unemployment compensation benefits. There has been experimentation with vocational training for public welfare recipients. As usual, the 50 states and the local governments served as laboratories for the development and testing of pioneering programs which were later accepted and enacted by the national government.

FEDERAL ACTION—
THE MANPOWER DEVELOPMENT AND TRAINING ACT

No discussion of job training to improve employment opportunities for minority groups can omit mention of some of the new tools made available in this field by federal action. Just recently, for example, the Secretary of Labor issued new rules for apprenticeship programs supervised by the Department of Labor which are expected significantly to reduce discriminatory practices and to create new opportunities in craft occupations. In this paper, however, I will limit discussion to the law which has so dramatically opened new horizons in job training—the Manpower Development and Training Act of 1962 (MDTA).

The MDTA establishes a program for training unemployed and under-employed workers in occupations in which there is a reasonable expectation of finding a job. Weekly living allowances are authorized for unemployed heads of families with at least two years of work experience, and for jobless members of families in which the head is unemployed. Allowances may be received for as many as 52 weeks, with an additional 20 weeks for workers who require literacy and other preliminary education to qualify for admission to occupational training courses. The amount of the weekly allowances equals the average unemployment compensation benefit paid in the trainee's state of residence (the national average is about $35) but may be increased by up to $10 a week under special conditions.

Provision is made for special training programs for youth in need of further schooling or vocational preparation. Reduced living allowances of not more than $20 a week may be paid to youths in the 17 through 21 age group enrolled in such programs.

The MDTA is administered jointly by the Secretary of Labor and the Secretary of Health, Education, and Welfare. The Secretary of Labor is responsible for determining the areas and occupations for training, testing and counseling workers, and selecting eligible workers for training. He also has the task of helping to place individuals who complete their training in suitable employment and of evaluating their progress after completion of their courses. The Secretary of Health, Education, and Welfare is responsible for the actual provision of training when it is handled by schools on a classroom-type basis.

The Act also requires the Secretary of Labor to encourage on-the-job training (OJT) programs for training jobless workers or for upgrading the skills of underemployed individuals. Such programs may be proposed by employers, employer organizations, labor unions, community groups and other qualified bodies.

The relevance of the MDTA to the problems of training minority group members is quite clear. I would like to call attention, however, to the flexibility which was written into the law so as to provide adequate services to the "hard-core" unemployed or underemployed. For example, provision has been made not only for actual training, but for intensive counseling, testing, and related services to support the training process. The establishment of separate youth training programs permits the identification of disadvantaged young workers who need special handling, the preparation of curricula and teaching methods tailored to their special needs, and the provision of a variety of supportive services to encourage successful completion of training and successful job experience. Availability of weekly allowances for both adults and young trainees has made it possible for many low income people to take training who could otherwise not afford to do so. Training in basic literacy, arithmetic, and other fundamental educational skills has been provided to supplement job skill training. Use of the training and related facilities of private agencies with special expertise in solving difficult manpower problems or working with problem groups has been authorized to supplement government resources. In many other ways, a flexible approach has been followed to maximize the contribution of the MDTA in ameliorating the Nation's manpower problems.

Perhaps the best illustration of the open-minded and searching outlook which has been shown in administering the Act is the authorization of a wide variety of experimental and demonstration projects. The purpose of these projects is to test, develop and demonstrate pioneering approaches and procedures for trainihg, counseling, or otherwise assisting unemployed and under-employed workers with especially difficult training or employment problems. These programs have often involved the participation of private agencies and a variety of local and state government bodies in order to bring the best available resources to bear on difficult situations.

As one would expect, most of the experimental and demonstration projects undertaken to date have dealt with the needs of disadvantaged workers, primarily minority group members. The projects cover experimentation with methods of testing and training illiterate nonwhite workers for semi-skilled job opportunities: using closely supervised workshops to provide on-the-job training to problem youths, developing job opportunities for disadvantaged groups, trying advanced counseling techniques to motivate out-of-school and out-of-work youngsters to adapt to training and employment, retraining displaced factory workers for nonprofessional jobs in the growing health occupations, reducing discriminatory job requirements and a wide variety of other very interesting activties at the frontier of our knowledge in the manpower field.

In many cases, the conduct of experimental and demonstration projects is associated with intensive research programs developed and financed under the MDTA. By means of the broad research program authorized by the Act, answers to a variety of very basic questions about the employment problems of minority groups and other workers will gradually be brought to light.

Let's look at what can happen as exemplified by our experience with experimental and demonstration projects. As I have said, we cannot make jobs; but we can make opportunities. The job crisis confronting the Negro is so grave that I think it worthwhile to tell some success stories focused on the Negro, especially Negro youth. I do not say to you that we have solved the problem or even that we have worked out the way to solve it—but these stories can give us hope that there *will be* a solution—or an array of solutions—if we are constant in our search, bold in our devices and generous in our devotion to the cause of social justice and equal opportunity to reward equal effort.

In Norfolk, Virginia, the branch of Virginia State College, a Negro institution, undertook to train 100 "hard-core" unemployed for a year. The men averaged four children each, they were paid $27 a week training allowance, and they were required to sign weekly certificates that they earned nothing on the side.

When the training was over, although the defense economy drive had closed off many of the usual Norfolk job opportunities, the dedicated staff of that college (1) placed the first Negro lineman with the telephone company, a man working in high visibility on the pole in the street, (2) placed the first mechanics with the local bus company, (3) placed the first production-line workers with a major automobile assembly plant, (4) placed sheet metal men in a major shipyard.

Now, many of those jobs were there all along, but no one knew it. The bus company said it had "always" been willing to hire Negro mechanics, but none ever applied—because no Negro had such a job there. Retail stores said they wanted Negro clerks and Negro store guards. There had been none. Only vigorous job development campaigns flowing out of the need to place the trainees uncovered these openings.

There is a particularly tragic kind of American, the minority man who has doggedly pursued his education and then found he could not get the kind of job usually rewarding that effort. This is the Negro college graduate who does not catch on as a teacher in his southern home town—what other white collar job is there for him?—and who drifts north or gives up and settles down in sullen sureness he is rejected by his culture. Our training projects are discovering these men and either helping them acquire new skills or helping them directly to the right kind of job.

The experimental program in New Haven has been especially effective in breaking down the usual but meaningless barriers to entry-jobs set up by employers as mere screening devices—such requirements as a high school diploma, for instance, when that diploma has no bearing on job performance. But the New Haven manpower people have also been adept in opening what they call "real good jobs" for well educated youth and young men and women. Their first training programs for disadvantaged Negro and white youth were for high-status factory jobs—industrial draftsmen, laboratory technicians, industrial X-ray technicians. Young men, many of them Negroes, lacking high school diplomas were successfully trained and placed in heretofore unavailable jobs that had been opened up to them by the removal of the unrealistic diploma barrier. Given the opportunity they dedicated themselves to gaining needed skills and knowledge.

There remains the bottom of the barrel: the hopeless Negro youth marooned in city ghettos, ignorant of the geography of his own city, alienated from the educational system, out of school and out of work. He represents what James Conant calls "social dynamite."

In Chicago, the three major youth-serving agencies are the Y.M.C.A., the Boys Clubs, and the Youth Centers. They have pooled their resources under an experimental contract to prepare 1,000 school "dropouts," most of them Negro, for the world of work.

There is a difference, you see, and a vital one, between being able to do work and being able to get and hold a job.

MDTA ACCOMPLISHMENTS

By the end of 1963, training under the Manpower Development and Training Act was substantially upgrading previous skills or providing for the learning of new skills, for the majority of persons enrolled in training programs. After sixteen months of operation under the Act, a total of 120,000 men and women had been approved for training in 450 different occupations. These various jobs represented just about every rung in the occupational ladder. Significantly, for the great majority of persons being trained, the occupations involved a new and improved skill. Comparing the kinds of occupations being learned by trainees with the occupational groups in which they were last employed before entering the training program, underscores the substantial upward shift in skill level involved in the training effort.

One out of every three trainees was authorized for·training in a skilled occupation; another one-third are preparing for a white collar job, in the clerical, sales, or semi-professional areas. Together, the proportion being trained for the skilled and white collar jobs is double the proportion of the men and women employed in these areas prior to their entry into training.

Also significant is the fact that better than seven out of ten of those completing training in the programs for higher occupational skills are being placed and are finding steady employment. This is the "focus" of the program.

Nowhere is this laddering-up more evident than in the activities of non-white MDTA trainees. In the professional and managerial, clerical and sales, skilled and semi-skilled occupational groups, nonwhites were being trained in 1963 in larger proportions than their representation among all employed workers. Most significant is the training of over half the nonwhite enrollees in skilled and semi-skilled occupations, compared with only 27 per cent employed in these occupational categories. The following table shows this relationship.

OCCUPATIONAL TRAINING OBJECTIVES OF NONWHITES ENROLLED
IN 1963, AND OCCUPATION OF EMPLOYED NONWHITE PERSONS
IN 1963
(Per cent distribution)

Occupational Group	Nonwhite MDTA trainees enrolled in 1963	Nonwhite employed persons, 1963[3]
	100.0	100.0
Professional and managerial	8.9[4]	8.7
Clerical and sales	19.8	9.0
Service	17.3	32.8
Skilled	21.6	6.5
Semiskilled	29.4	20.4
Other	3.1[5]	22.6[6]

Increasing attention is being given to include the "hard-core" unemployed in the program. Almost half of the trainees had been out of work for 15 or more weeks prior to selection for MDTA courses. Over 40 per cent had never completed high school. The proportion of nonwhites in the group was 24 per cent—about the same proportion that nonwhites constitute of all unemployed

3. Bureau of Labor Statistics, Monthly Report of the Labor Force (Jan. 1964).
4. Occupations in this group are all refresher training or at the subprofessional or technical level.
5. Mostly agricultural.
6. Mostly unskilled.

workers. Almost one-third of the trainees were less than 22 years old and 10 per cent were over 45 years of age.

Of special importance is the fact that most nonwhite trainees are being prepared for the kinds of occupations which are expected to provide the best job opportunities in future years and which represent a marked advance over the lower occupational levels at which nonwhites have tended to be employed in the past. Of course, training of severely disadvantaged workers for more modest occupations in which job opportunities exist cannot be overlooked where necessary to help persons with low learning potentials adjust to labor market demands.

It is of special interest to this symposium that the MDTA assigns a key role to local and state agencies. The Congress recognized that use of the existing network of public schools and public employment offices was essential to the rapid and effective implementation of a large scale program to train the unemployed. Mobilization of state and local resources was backed by the financial facts of life; the law requires the states to pay part of the cost of training and training allowances after June 30, 1965.

State employment service agencies have been assigned major responsibilities for testing, counseling and selecting MDTA trainees. They play major roles in surveying local areas to determine occupations in which training needs exist, in placing "graduates" in jobs, and in evaluating their subsequent progress. The state vocational education agencies have been assigned major responsibilities for arranging classroom-type or institutional training in public and private schools. Several state apprenticeship agencies help the Department of Labor to establish and supervise on-the-job training. Development of training programs also involves consultation with local advisory committees which include labor, management and other representatives.

The point of this state and local participation is the wide range of initiative which it permits, the elbowroom for experimentation. No state or local organization need sit back and wait for final answers from Washington; it can start developing and initiating practical and forward-looking projects to help solve training and employment difficulties. This federal-state partnership will help make the manpower development and training program an effective and key part of the total fabric of national policies and programs for improving and conserving our human resources.

COMMENT

MEYER FINE*

FIRST, I should say that it is indeed a privilege and a pleasure for me to be with you, to participate with this distinguished group of educators and leaders in the field of civil rights and human relations.

As the representative of the American Jewish Committee, one of the organizations whose cooperation helped make possible this symposium, I wish to record our deep appreciation that this Conference is convened in tribute to the late Justice Philip Halpern. His inspiring qualities of heart and mind and his many brilliant achievements are well known to all of us. I merely wish to acknowledge the Committee's debt of gratitude to Philip Halpern for his pre-eminent contributions as a member of our National Executive Board and for his many years of distinguished leadership as Chairman of the Executive Committee of the Buffalo-Niagara Frontier Chapter of the American Jewish Committee.

Now, as a commentator, I intend to react briefly to the government contract matters which have been discussed at this and other sessions. First, I would suggest the following procedural changes in government agencies which would strengthen their effectiveness in achieving the fuller establishment of nondiscriminatory policies:

1. *To assure employment integration within state agencies.* The State Commission for Human Rights should be ordered to review the existing employment practices of all state agencies and departments, including the Civil Service Commission, to determine the extent to which established nondiscriminatory policies have been translated into effective recruitment, hiring and promotion practices within the state government. Where reforms seem indicated, the individual agencies and departments involved should be instructed to develop a positive program for the recruitment of qualified minority group members.

2. *To assure integration in private industry.* The State Employment Service should be instructed not merely to refuse to handle discriminatory job orders, but to require fair employment pledges from all employers. The State Commission for Human Rights should be authorized to initiate complaints of employment discrimination on the basis of its own investigations and without waiting for individual complaints.

3. *To assure integration in state contract employment.* State agencies should be instructed to initiate a program of inspection, reporting and compliance for private employers holding contracts with state agencies, along the same lines as the program now in force in the federal government. Similar affidavits should be required of all craft unions involved in such contracts, providing assurances of nondiscrimination both in union membership and in

---

* Area Director, The American Jewish Committee.

apprenticeship training programs. Businesses and unions unable to provide such affidavits should be declared ineligible for state contracts until documented evidence of reform has been presented.

4. *To assure integration in apprenticeship training.* All companies and labor unions involved in apprenticeship training programs should be required to give proof of nondiscrimination in the recruitment of applicants before such programs are approved by any state department or agency and before such programs are deemed eligible for any form of state aid. In addition, all state contracts with private companies should require the mandatory hiring, without regard to race, religion or national origin, of at least one apprentice or trainee for every five journeymen employed on contract work.

Now, I would like to express my concern over the fact that the many important activities of citizen groups have not been discussed at any length here today. Because of this omission, these citizen groups seem to emerge as "the tail on the dog." The dog, in this case, being the many admirable and important functions performed by federal, state and local commissions and other public agencies.

I speak now as a lay advocate for the citizen groups, if you will, and I appreciate this opportunity to tell you that, despite the many problems and shortcomings that we have all been candidly sharing, you will perhaps be somewhat heartened to learn that you have many allies in the community.

The citizen groups, sectarian and nonsectarian, which support the commissions, swell the ranks of those who have tried to get these equal opportunity laws on the books and to get the strengthening amendments through. But this has not been sufficient in their opinion. They've taken other important action on their own to achieve the kind of job opportunities that we talk about here through non-legal, persuasive, educational efforts in the community. They are not entirely limited to picketing and demonstrations as was indicated by one of the earlier speakers.

Fair employment is a high priority item on the agenda of American business and industrial leaders—including many associated with the American Jewish Committee. All over the country, members and friends of AJC—assisted by AJC's professional staff—are zealously working to make equal opportunity in hiring and promotion a reality in their own firms, industries and cities. The experiences they report, taken together, form a cross section of the integration issues facing commerce and industry today. Some of the more affirmative experiences, I would like to share with you at this point.

1. *Obtaining qualified applicants.* The problem of finding qualified applicants has been referred to by some of our speakers at this panel and others. Finding skilled Negro applicants is one of the first and one of the biggest hurdles in job integration. Our members and friends tell us Negroes, understandably, have been discouraged from preparing for full employment opportunities or aspiring to upgraded employment status.

What have we done about it? I'm talking now about citizen groups throughout the country—the American Jewish Committee and others. I want to underscore the fact that leadership has been given by lay people, in many cases by business executives who own their own retail establishments or industrial firms, in concert with other concerned citizens who might or might not be leaders in employment. What these people have done is to go out into the community to seek qualified Negro talent and one of the first things that they have learned, of course, was that there was a shortage. But, being hopefully the kind of creative and imaginative people whom you've urged us to seek, they looked in the "odd places."

They looked in the post offices, they looked in many other places to find people who would have ability but who are being under-utilized. In a number of instances—this is only one—Negro college graduates have been brought out of the post office, to other jobs where they were given managerial posts in industry. They have taken on supervisory posts, personnel functions, policy-making, and have done exceedingly well.

2. *Publicizing opportunities.* I think an example of one of the more exciting recent developments resulting from citizen group activities has been the recent formation of an "Equal Opportunity Employment Plan" in Milwaukee where thirty leading firms got together to establish a guide for the entire community. The participating companies agreed to describe themselves as "equal opportunity employers" in advertising for help, to instruct employment agencies and other recruitment sources that suitable persons of all races were to be referred for interviews, and reached out to potential Negro applicants through such methods as plant tours, summer employment programs and school "career days."

3. *Increasing training facilities. In Dallas,* a striking start toward providing needed facilities was made where business leaders collaborated with a Negro institution, Bishop College, in setting up a new Department of Business Administration as a source of Negro secretarial and management talent.

In the east and midwest, leading retailers have joined together to set up job preparation programs for disadvantaged youth, under the Federal Manpower Development and Training Act.

4. *Securing acceptance by whites.* Many of the experiences recorded had to do with preventing unfavorable reactions by white workers. A quick transition to integrated conditions was generally thought safest, but there was no consensus on whether staff should be informed ahead of time or not. Several firms did well with advance notification. Others, however, successfully followed the opposite course. A large manufacturing company with several plants in the south reported satisfactory results from confronting the staff with a fait accompli.

5. *Negroes in status jobs.* Where Negro staff members give orders to white employees or represent the firm to the white public, special measures

are sometimes taken to ensure acceptance. The proprietor of a midwestern restaurant safeguards the status of his Negro service manager by periodically holding luncheon conferences with him in sight of patrons and personnel. A midwestern retailing organization, about to acquire its first Negro officer went to considerable length to enlist the good will of the banks, insurance companies and other firms with whom it did business.

6. *The crucial role of top management.* One theme runs through nearly all the experiences reported by AJC's members and friends: The start must be made in the Executive Suite. Both in the small community of the plant and the larger community of the city or the industry, it is the high-level managers who must frame affirmative integration policies and see that they are understood and carried out. As the head of one of the nation's leading construction companies put it, pace setting here, as in any policy situation, "must come from the top, so that people right down the line know the feeling of the boss. . . . If those at the top do not express their feelings definitely, those in a lower echelon may be reluctant to make decisions that are not in complete accord with past practices."

7. *Collaboration with intergroup agencies and Negro groups.* Information and advice available from government agencies, human relations organizations and civil rights groups can be an additional help in minimizing the hazards of desegregation measures. For example, a large company in the business equipment field relies strongly on the American Jewish Committee's field staff for information about racial conditions in cities where it operates plants slated for integration. A number of companies state that they use the Urban League's Skills Banks to recruit qualified Negro help.

Other businesses, north and south, report that they plan desegregation moves in collaboration with their communities' Negro leadership, or periodically review their progress with local branches of national civil rights groups. By thus working with responsible Negro organizations, they are creating a climate of mutual confidence and forestalling unreasonable demands by extremists.

8. *Sparking community action.* I fully agreed with what one of our speakers, Professor Pollak, said last night when he stressed the importance of concerted action in the local community. The biggest forward steps are made when business leaders take the initiative in mobilizing whole communities. For example, in Memphis, business leaders and government officials set up a successful drive for improving Negroes' employment opportunities. The local press was one of the prime movers; local papers vigorously promoted the drive and denied exaggerated publicity to the opposition.

In Dallas, white and Negro leadership groups, with AJC members playing an essential role, devised a plan for employment integration. A policy of step-by-step integration was agreed upon, including preferential procedures designed to help make up for the longstanding handicaps of the Negro group. Because the plan bore the stamp of the city's most respected individuals, little conflict arose.

In Atlanta, a community movement to promote upgrading of Negro workers concentrated, for a start, on government jobs. A biracial Mayor's Committee was formed to hear complaints of discrimination. Municipal departments, including fire and police, moved up qualified Negroes on their staffs, as did the local postmaster; wider drives are foreseen in private employment.

In the east, middle-west and south, chambers of commerce and trade associations have started equal employment opportunity committees—in many cases with the aid of AJC members. These committees undertake surveys of job opportunities for minority group members, to help find people to fill the jobs. They also assist in training programs for insufficiently qualified workers. Finally, they make it their business to help inform employers and employees about the benefits of integration and the ways to achieve it.

We are sending reports of these experiences and comparable success stories to leaders in communities throughout the country. We would hope that your organizations may find similar opportunites to recount these highly effective, creative ventures by citizen organizations.

Equality in employment is no idealistic luxury. Members of the American Jewish Committee and its friends in the business world agree: it is simply good business and the time is right for it. They are fully aware that the goal will not be achieved by half measures or gestures. They understand that they have a job to do and are convinced that there is no longer any alternative to rapid, hard-headed, affirmative action.

COMMENT

GEORGE W. CULBERSON*

I N my letter accepting the invitation to participate in this symposium, I expressed surprise that the subject of a "Contract Nondiscrimination Clause" was considered as a "supplementary or non-enforcement" kind of activity. My experience leads me to the conclusion that proper administration of a nondiscrimination clause is a most effective and efficient method of enforcement. In fact, it is the most effective tool that I have ever used.

Mr. Conway has presented a most careful analysis and performed a real service to all of us in his documentation of the legal authority for and the reasons why states and cities should include a clause in contracts. He has also stated that his only experience had been with a state that had a Commission and staff working on the problem of enforcement. Madison Jones stated that his Commission had not been able to do much about the contract clause because of insufficient resources which prevented them from getting around to it. My ten years' experience in Pittsburgh is precisely that of Madison Jones. My time and that of the staff was taken up with the investigation and processing of complaint cases. That is all we could do with the manpower and budgetary resources available to us. My first point, therefore, is that we will have to redirect current resources or find new ones to do what needs to be done in contract compliance.

The clause in the New York State contracts seems to have a contradiction between the first part and the procedural section, F. The first part requires compliance in an affirmative manner and requires the contractor to do more than just refrain from overt discriminatory action. When you get to the procedural clause, it has a sentence which seems to throw the whole thing back into the complaint frame of reference. The disturbing sentence reads, "After conciliation efforts by the Commission have failed to achieve compliance with the nondiscrimination clause and after a verified complaint has been filed with the Commission." I find that in dealing with legal documents that a few words in a sentence can alter the whole tone of the document. To me, and I could be wrong, my interpretation of this sentence says, when you get right down to the enforcement stage, you have to have a verified complaint. The question would be, "is the contract clause enforceable without a verified complaint?" If not, we are right where we started.

My theory of what is required in terms of administering a contract clause is "surveillance." You live with the contractor during the life of the contract; you don't just go in one time and look at the pattern and come out and mark him A, B, C, D or F. You go in as often as you can, certainly not less than once a year for every contractor and more often for those that require it, de-

---

* Chief, Equal Employment Opportunity Office, U.S. Air Force.

pending upon the circumstances. This requires staff and budget or you just cannot do it.

The Air Force has thirty persons on a staff administering a contract clause on equal employment opportunity. Six of them are assigned to complaint investigations, four to top level administration, and the rest are all in contractor surveillance without any complaint. This ratio is not necessarily one that I would approve of, but it is required because of the number of complaints we have to handle. We are spending too much of our time and resources on these complaints.

I wish that Herbert Hill had not left the room. He says that he has 900 complaints with the President's Committee. Of course, the President's Committee gives those complaints to the agencies to investigate and resolve and I've had 200 of these each year since I have been with the Air Force. About three-fourths of the complaints we get have been stimulated by Herbert Hill. I want him to cut it out. It is not profitable. We're wasting our time and money and our resources in the investigation of these complaints. I could take these same staff people and put them into the contractor surveillance program and get results. The Air Force has actually assisted in the employment and upgrading of thousands of minority workers in new categories under the surveillance program whereas it is a mere handful that result from the complaint investigation. I am quite opposed to the idea of going out and beating the bush or in any way encouraging more complaints. You just continue the practice of dissipating the resources of commissions which are already understaffed and underbudgeted for this kind of program.

Mr. Conway's comment about his experience being limited to Commission operated programs, leads me to say that I do not think it would be helpful to have a nondiscrimination clause in a contract unless there were enforcement possibilities. The head of a department entering into a contract is not interested in employment opportunity for minority workers. He is interested solely in obtaining the product or securing the services or getting the construction completed on schedule. I would go along with the thesis that if there is a clause in the contract, one would have to have an administrative agency to do the checking, making appraisals, and otherwise seeing to it that the contractor lived up to the clause requirements.

Madison Jones has presented quite an imposing list of requirements with emphasis upon affirmative action and initiative on the part of the contractor. He has been very detailed and specific in his list of requirements. In general, I would oppose efforts to try to come up with a check list of requirements, especially in the affirmative action field. The factors in any situation vary so greatly that they are not amenable to a standard remedial action. What we are dealing with here is finding ways and means of breaking with traditional customs and practices of long standing. The intensity of feeling about changing patterns varies from one section of the country to another, from community to community, factory to factory, and department to department, and the degree and extent of affirmative action varies with each individual situation. Government, in contract matters, should consider itself a customer instead of an enforcement agency. The "customer is always right" and therefore, any interpretation of the requirements by the customer is the one that should prevail.

The strong actions proposed by Madison Jones are certainly in agreement with the times in which we live today. I think we have all recognized that we have moved from a period of time when as commissions we have been emphasizing color blindness to a period of color consciousness. Contractors, however, have not yet, quite, got used to the idea of our change of thinking. They are worried about the fact that we have become color conscious. The fact is, if you're not really conscious of what the problem is, you can't analyze it and you are not going to resolve it.

Except in the area of "affirmative action," I think the contract clause should be specific in terms of the requirements and expectations. The New York contract clause is very good. The clause should provide for inspection of records. This is important because the records provide the basic source of information and can be secured without subpoena. I see no reason why the clause should be effective only for contracts above a certain amount of money or based upon the number of employees in an establishment. I notice that the New York contract has avoided these limitations.

Now, I have already made the point that the contract clause requires surveillance. It is my opinion, and it is based upon several years of experience, that there is very little overt, willful and deliberate discrimination on the part of contractor management. What we are bucking here is tradition. The way we have always done things is the way we want to continue doing them. To change, means being resourceful and sometimes it means more expense. Change, frequently brings trouble and this is certainly to be avoided. The only way to root out these problems, and therefore resolve them, is to help the contractor to identify them. This means surveillance.

The specialists employed by commissions must be able to analyze the personnel actions and policy implementation programs of the contractor to determine if and where these have resulted in exclusion of qualified workers for reasons of race, creed, color or national origin. After that, these specialists must be qualified to assist the contractor in affirmative action proposals so that changes can be made. I say to the Air Force specialists, it is not enough for you to point out the problems—you must show him how to resolve them.

Finally, repeating something I previously said, a nondiscrimination clause is worth no more than the amount of surveillance you are going to be able to give it and the amount of assistance you are going to be able to render. This means sufficient resources and staff to do it.

The afternoon discussion centered on (1) methods of implementing programs requiring compliance with equal employment opportunity clauses in government contracts, and (2) the role of private groups.

Contract Compliance Programs

In his comment, Mr. Culberson had discussed the contract compliance procedures announced for New York State by Governor Rockefeller in December 1963, and pointed to a possible inconsistency between the requirement in clause (a) that the contractor not only not discriminate but that he take affirmative action, and the requirement in clause (f) of a verified complaint before a contract is cut off for non-compliance with clause (a). The latter requirement he considered appropriate for antidiscriminatory conduct but not for situations where the contractor is required to take affirmative action, for which regular and intense surveillance is necessary.

Commissioner Conway replied that there did seem to be a contradiction on the surface, but the verified complaint procedure, which would probably be initiated by the Attorney General, applies to the contractor who refuses to take even the most minimal affirmative action possible to comply with the contract. In sum, the contract clause sets up a two-pronged attack: (1) action under both the antidiscrimination law and the contract if there is evidence of discrimination; and (2) action under the contract alone if there is no discrimination but the contractor refuses to take any steps whatsoever to comply with the "affirmative action" obligation under clause (a) of the contract.

In response to a question, Commissioner Conway noted that the statutory "low bidder" requirement of many states was not really a problem in preventing discriminatory contractors from getting or keeping state contracts, since the New York requirement at least, was couched in terms of the "lowest *qualified* bidder" and a discriminatory contractor would not be considered "qualified."

Professor Jaffe asked whether a reporting system might be instituted for each specific job when the work force was first assembled, whereby the employer would report immediately on how many minority group members were employed. This would avoid the difficulty of having to go to each employer to learn this information. Although Commissioner Conway raised the possibility of employer resistance to still another form to file, Mr. Culberson thought government contracts should require such reports on a regular basis so that one could screen them to pick out some for surveillance. These reports need not be monthly or even quarterly, so long as they were regular. There had to be some way to start the surveillance proceedings and such reports were one device; the President's Committee on Equal Employment Opportunity used them. Mr. Jones also approved of the suggestion, but pointed out that policing the accuracy and honesty of the reports is itself a monumental task because of the volume.

173

Private Groups

Mr. Karpatkin noted that private and official groups could often cooperate very effectively. In one case he related, a CORE chapter had managed to increase the number of Negroes employed at a restaurant chain by staging a series of demonstrations culminating in a sit-in, but some of the demonstrators were arrested. At the initiative of counsel for the arrested demonstrators, the New York City Commission was motivated to use its good offices with court and prosecutor, thereby resulting in a dismissal of all charges. Thus the sit-in resulted in both the amelioration of the discriminatory situation and the arrest of the demonstrators. Throughout the demonstrations, the New York City Commission played a significant role in attempting to obtain voluntary compliance from the employer. The negotiations resulted in a written agreement satisfactory to the CORE people. But the nine pending criminal cases would have remained as an unhappy residue of the otherwise successful project, had it not been for the intelligent cooperation of private and public agencies.

Mr. Jones added that private business and trade groups could be more effective if high public officials on each level of government were to meet with such groups and to assume leadership in the civil rights struggle. Such meetings should be held annually or biennially.

The discussion of private groups raised the problem of preferences, discussed at the Friday night session. Mr. Robison pointed out that although governmental agencies can do a great deal for Negro job applicants and employees even without preferences, in order to redress past injustices, he felt that sooner or later, such agencies would have to exercise such preferences, even though they would never admit this openly. Mr. Karpatkin pointed out that here the activity of private groups could supplement the work of governmental agencies, for whereas the latter may not be able constitutionally to require such preferences, private groups are under no such inhibition. Although a good argument can be made, he thought, that no government agency may constitutionally compel a preference based on race or color, it is quite another thing for a private group to seek to influence the community and private employers to take realistic steps to redress past discriminatory practices. Any paradox here is more imagined than real. There are many areas of conduct which are quite blameless, and indeed sound public policy, for private persons to support, but which could not be compelled of government.

State University of New York at Buffalo

SCHOOL OF LAW

★

April 24, 25, 1964

★

Toward Equal Opportunity in Employment:
The Role of State and Local Government

★

A CONFERENCE
IN MEMORY OF HONORABLE PHILIP HALPERN 1902-1963

PROGRAM

Friday, April 24, 1964

FIRST SESSION

Chairman: Dean Jacob D. Hyman

I. Basic Questions

    A. Spheres of Governmental Regulation

        1. How far should Federal Regulation go?

        2. How should state and local regulation be apportioned?

    B. Making Regulatory Action Effective

        1. Can enforcement by commission do the whole job?

        2. What supplements and alternatives are practicable?

Speakers: Dean C. Clyde Ferguson, Jr.
Howard University School of Law

John Feild, Director, Community Relations,
U.S. Conference of Mayors

Herbert Hill, Labor Secretary, NAACP

Commentator: Professor Louis H. Pollak, Yale Law School

176

Saturday, April 25, 1964

SECOND SESSION

Chairman: Professor Herman Schwartz

II. Strengthening Enforcement by Commission

    A. Specific Problem Areas

        1. Tailoring the technique to the employment situation

        2. Access to training for jobs

    B. Possible Changes in Enforcement and Administration

        1. Enforcement

        2. Administration

Speakers: Henry Spitz, General Counsel,
N.Y.S. Commission for Human Rights

Sol Rabkin, National Law Director
Anti-Defamation League of B'nai B'rith

Professor Louis L. Jaffe, Harvard Law School

Professor Robert A. Girard, Harvard Law School

Commentators: Joseph B. Robison, Assistant Director,
Commission on Law & Social Action,
American Jewish Congress

Professor George W. Brooks,
N.Y.S. School of Industrial and Labor Relations

Saturday, April 25, 1964

THIRD SESSION

Chairman: Professor Herman Schwartz

III. Supplements to Direct Enforcement

    A. State and Local Contracts and Sub-contracts

    B. State and Local Grants and Benefits

    C. Expansion of Job Training

    D. Persuasion through Citizen and Trade Groups

Speakers: J. Edward Conway,
New York State Commission for Human Rights

Madison S. Jones, Executive Director,
New York City Commission on Human Rights

Frederick B. Routh, Executive Director
National Association of Inter-Group Relations Officials

John P. Walsh, Deputy Director,
Office of Manpower, Automation and Training
U.S. Department of Labor

Commentators: Meyer Fine,
American Jewish Committee

George Culberson,
United States Air Force

178